Queer Bergman

Daniel Humphrey

Queer Bergman
Sexuality, Gender, and
the European Art Cinema

University of Texas Press ⋏ *Austin*

Requests for permission to reproduce material from this
work should be sent to:
Permissions
University of Texas Press
P.O. Box 7819
Austin, TX 78713-7819
http://utpress.utexas.edu/about/book-permissions

⊗ The paper used in this book meets the minimum
requirements of ANSI/NISO Z39.48-1992 (R1997)
(Permanence of Paper).

Library of Congress Cataloging-in-Publication Data
Humphrey, Daniel.
    Queer Bergman : sexuality, gender, and the European
art cinema / by Daniel Humphrey. — 1st ed.
        p.   cm.
    Includes bibliographical references and index.
    ISBN 978-0-292-74376-2 (cloth : alk. paper)
    1. Bergman, Ingmar, 1918–2007—Criticism and
interpretation.   2. Homosexuality and motion pictures.
3. Homosexuality in motion pictures.   I. Title.
    PN1998.3.B47H86   2013
    791.43086'64—dc23   2012029242

doi:10.7560/743762

For Bill, Douglas, and Marlin

Contents

Acknowledgments

This long-gestating project has benefited from the wisdom of many people over the last several years. First and foremost, I have to acknowledge the heroic wisdom and indefatigable support of Douglas Crimp. As a graduate student considering working on what some acquaintances clearly thought to be a faintly absurd idea (looking at Ingmar Bergman queerly), I occasionally became as neurotic and self-doubting as one of the Max von Sydow characters in the films I was studying. Were it not for his unwavering faith in this project, not to mention his helpful insights, this final summation of my work on the topic might not have reached completion. It would also certainly be a poorer, less interesting study without the perspectives, encouragements, collegiality, and, well, just help of Juan J. Alonzo, Harriette Andreadis, Harry M. Benshoff, Nandini Bhattacharya, Kimberly Brown, Patrick Burkart, Lisa Cartwright, Ashley Currier, Lucy Curzon, Mark Denaci, Tasha Dubriwny, David A. Gerstner, Hal Gladfelder, Elizabeth Goodstein, Sean Griffin, Melanie C. Hawthorne, Michael Ann Holly, Joseph O. Jewell, William E. Jones, Claire Katz, Katherine Kelly, Maaret Koskinen, Antonio La Pastina, John H. Lenihan, David McWhirter, Pamela Matthews, Kathi Miner, Akiko Mizoguchi, Anne Morey, Andrés Nader, Claudia Nelson, Mary Ann O'Farrell, Kathleen O'Reilly, Julie Papaioannou, Kristan Poirot, Kirsten Pullen, Matthew Reynolds, Sally Robinson, James Rosenheim, A. Joan Saab, Robert R. Shandley, Jyotsna Vaid, Neha Vora, Sharon Willis, Joe Wlodarz, Joan Wolf, Janet Wolff, and Daniel Ziegert. Steven Gurr and Marian Eide deserve to be singled out for their utterly invaluable assistance at crucial moments in the production of this book, as well as for their friendship.

Most recently, members of the Queer Studies Working Group at Texas A&M University, particularly Krista May, Rebecca Hartkopf Schloss, and Dianne Kraft, have gone over long, rough chapter drafts and offered me a good deal of much-needed insight and perspective. The gutsy students who took my 2010 Sex, Gender, Auteurism course at Texas A&M also offered a number of helpful comments about various Bergman films as I was pulling together my thoughts for this manuscript. From that class, I must especially thank Keller Davis for pointing me toward an online video clip of Dick Cavett interviewing Ingmar Bergman in 1971. I had heard about their richly informative conversation years before, and Keller, finding it while researching his own paper, immediately knew it was something I would want to see and sent me the link. I am also especially thankful to have been able to work with an amazing team at the University of Texas Press—first and foremost, my wonderful editor, Jim Burr, as well as Molly Frisinger, Victoria A. Davis, and the rest of the staff in Austin.

As I researched the art cinema, Ingmar Bergman, and GLBT history, another small army of helpmates selflessly assisted me: Nora Dimmock, Stephanie Frontz, Jeannine Korman, and Alan Unsworth at the University of Rochester's Rush Rhees Library; Rosemary Hanes, Patrick Loughney, Zoran Sinobad, and Josie Walters-Johnston at the Library of Congress in Washington, D.C.; Kim Hendrickson at the Criterion Collection/Janus Films offices in New York; Victor K. Jordan at the Lesbian, Gay, Bisexual and Transgender Community Center in Manhattan; Anthony L'Abbate, Paolo Cherchi Usai, Jared Case, Dan Wagner, and Caroline Yeager in the Motion Picture Department at George Eastman House in Rochester; Ashlie Mildfelt at the ONE National Gay and Lesbian Archives in Los Angeles; Anne Morra and Charles Silver at the Museum of Modern Art in New York; Nancy Sumpter in the Women's and Gender Studies Program at Texas A&M; and the large, friendly staff of the Division of Rare and Manuscript Collections at the Cornell University Library. Furthermore, a number of institutions provided funding for my travels around the eastern half of the United States to visit archives and libraries: the Susan B. Anthony Institute at the University of Rochester, the Melbern G. Glasscock Center for Humanities Research at Texas A&M University, the Women's and Gender Studies Program at Texas A&M, and the Film Studies Program at Texas A&M.

Of course, without a group of supportive friends, it would have been nearly impossible to get through a project that involves so many serious and sobering films. Alex Davis, Ben Drew, Raymon Gottfredson, Rike Hagemann, Mark Harlow, Jim Hunsaker, Robert Korty, Kudakwashe Kupara, Lára Marteinsdóttir, Raul F. Medina, Roger Palamino, Michael Piaseczny, Brian Porter, David Riddle, Pedro Rojas, T'ai Smith, Mark Terry, Tamela Terry, and Norman Vorono were all there for me along the way.

I want to thank the editors of GLQ: A Journal of Lesbian and Gay Studies for allowing me to use a few extended passages from my essay "One Summer of Heterosexuality: Lost and Found Lesbianism in a Forgotten Swedish Film" (GLQ 13, no. 1 [2006]) in appropriate places in the introduction and first chapter of this book; Gerald Duchovnay at Post Script: Essays in Film and the Humanities, for allowing me to revise and reuse the greater part of my essay "'Blame the Swedish Guy':

The Cultural Construction of a Cold War Auteur" (*Post Script* 28, no. 4 [Fall 2008]) in Chapter Two; Janus Films, for allowing me to use its artwork for the American release of *The Magician*; and William E. Jones, for allowing me to use an image from his video *v.o.*

Penultimately, I must say that in the decades since I was introduced to the work of Ingmar Bergman, first by a virtually lifesaving high school teacher, Marcia Miller, who in her own forceful way convinced me that life would "get better," and then much more fully as an undergraduate at the University of Utah by the estimable Bill Siska, I have remained in those teachers' debt. All these years later, I remember what I learned from them about the cinema and about Bergman, and have continually felt their influence throughout the writing of this book. Finally, I would be remiss if I did not acknowledge that being raised by a mother and father, Rowene K. and R. Marlin Humphrey, who instilled in me a love of learning, particularly of history and of the world beyond the borders of the country I happened to be born in, as well as a love of ethics and justice (and not incidentally, of movies), has also been decisive in me being able to envision and complete a project such as this. My mother drove me to downtown Salt Lake City one night to attend a double-feature screening of *The Seventh Seal* and *Wild Strawberries* when I was fifteen years old, an experience that began my near obsession with the films of Bergman. Although she passed away before this book could be published, I feel that, in some way, she is still watching his films with me now.

Queer Bergman

If I were to rewrite my early books now,
the one on Bergman (published in 1969) would
certainly cause me the greatest problems.

Robin Wood,
"Responsibilities of a
Gay Film Critic" (1978)

Introduction
Ingmar Bergman and the Foreign Self

Originally published in a fairly mainstream magazine, *Film Comment*, the late Robin Wood's "Responsibilities of a Gay Film Critic" justly became a cornerstone text of early GLBT (gay, lesbian, bisexual, and transgendered) cinema studies.[1] It continues to merit attention and respect within the field, despite several paradigm shifts that have seen the emerging discipline challenged (some would say eclipsed) by the distinctly different work begun by queer theorists in the late 1980s and early 1990s. Arguing for the value of what scholars contributing to the latter discourse would define as a queer perspective on the cinema while advocating films with little or no overt homosexual content, from *Rules of the Game* (1939) to *Rio Bravo* (1959), Wood's seemingly modest essay anticipated a still-growing body of work that collapses disciplinary distinctions between aesthetic analysis and political criticism. More importantly, it pointed the way, along with more psychoanalytically oriented work by second-wave feminist critics, toward rich and historicized understandings of cinematic spectatorship as mediated by profound (and profoundly complex) perspectives connected with gender and sexuality. Perhaps most importantly for this book, Wood's article stands, more than thirty years after its appearance, as one of film studies' only well-known essays to offer a direct statement connecting the idea of a specifically homosexual perspective with the films of Ingmar Bergman: arguably *the* paradigmatic figure in the history of mid-twentieth-century European art cinema.[2]

Coming after a number of impassioned feminist indictments of Bergman's work, including Constance Penley's essay on *Cries and Whispers* (1972), which characterizes the author's experience of seeing the film as no less than "one of being emotionally and psychically raped," Wood's own postliberation assessment of the Swedish director is far less ferociously condemnatory—understandably so, considering Wood's almost hagiographic earlier writings on the filmmaker.[3] Nevertheless, Wood's newly radicalized reappraisal of the auteur was only slightly less critical than Penley's analysis. Pathologizing aspects of Bergman's work that auteur critics (including Wood) had essentially celebrated a decade earlier—as expressions of selfhood across a body of work—he now considered the "obstinate recurrence of certain narrative and relationship structures in Bergman's work" to be "plainly neurotic": "What the films repeatedly assert, with impressive intensity and conviction, is that life under the conditions in which it is lived is intolerable."[4]

With some justification and, more importantly, some illuminating power, Wood employs the concept of neurosis to highlight a characteristic attribute of the narrative structure that Bergman used in many of his films, particularly those made from the early 1960s onward. Rather than concluding his cinematic visions of nearly intolerable human suffering with a psychologically healthy (and, presumably, politically efficacious) assertion that "'we must strive to change the conditions [behind this suffering],'" Bergman ended his films, according to Wood, with a "shutter com[ing] down," implying that "'the [intolerable] conditions are something called "the human predicament": they can't be changed.'" Offered as an example of "that central principle of neurosis," specifically, a manifestation of "resistance wherein the neurosis defends itself against cure," Wood's metaphor of a "shutter com[ing] down" was, and indeed remains, an apt description of the sudden endings of a number of the most emotionally charged films the Swedish director produced throughout the 1960s and 1970s.[5]

Exemplifying a utopian radical's optimism, Wood can certainly be forgiven for what later readers might consider a form of political naiveté in his implication that hopefully expressed, politically prescriptive epilogues might actually have given middle-period Bergman films such as *Winter Light* (1963), *The Silence* (1963), *Persona* (1966), *Shame* (1968), or *The Passion of Anna* (1969) some kind of revolutionary use-value. Indeed, something close to such a hopeful, prescriptive dénouement can be found at the end of the director's *Through a Glass Darkly* (1961), when—after the young schizophrenic Karin has suffered two days of emotional and (arguably) sexual abuse while in the care of her husband, father, and brother—a redemptive reconciliation between her father and brother appears as little more than a failure of nerve on Bergman's part. Bergman would mention his own embarrassment about that scene in later interviews, and few observers have come to its defense.[6] Of course, *Through a Glass Darkly*'s coda, expressing its own particularly Christian naiveté in asserting the transcendent power of love, was hardly what Wood, in his post-1968, post-Stonewall-rebellion adoration of political modernism, would have wanted. Still, it can be argued that Bergman's ultimate refusal to give his spectator optimistic closure—as he had done previously in a number of his most popular films, including *The Seventh Seal* (1957), *Wild Strawberries* (1957), and *The Virgin Spring* (1960)—served the very same ideologically prescriptive political modernism that Wood clearly favored, at least in its structurally determined final effects. Furthermore, risible as it might seem, Bergman's neatly resolved films of the 1950s and early 1960s actually resemble Jean-Luc Godard's radical post-1968 features, and despite their obvious differences of tone and political explicitness, they can leave spectators with a lethargic sense of self-satisfaction rather than the urge to act for sweeping social change: "Well, there you go. That's it then." This is not, one must concede, how most observers have assessed the situation regarding the work of Bergman or Godard over the last several decades.

Had Bergman fallen dead from a heart attack in 1962 after winning his second Academy Award (for *Through a Glass Darkly*), his reputation as a progressive filmmaker, even if not a radical one, of the 1950s might well have solidified and stood more or less unchallenged in later decades. Only Maria Bergom-Larsson's class-conscious study *Ingmar Bergman and Society* (1978) offered the English-language reader, in the years when Bergman was still an active filmmaker, a compelling book-length argument taking the director to task for what she called the "patriarchal structure" locatable within his films from the very beginning of his career. Its final paragraph, however, exemplifies Bergom-Larsson's ultimately fair-minded critical engagement: "Bergman's understanding of the individual and society has been decisively shaped by the bourgeois authoritarian family. His world-view is based on a class perspective which is characterised by certain typical repressions. But this does not prevent him from using his extreme subjectivity as a sensitive instrument to lay bare the anatomy of the bourgeois consciousness with tremendous perspicacity."[7] As a general critical position, this remains, thirty-five years later, largely valid.

The complaints against Bergman made by GLBTQ critics (those operating through the earlier gay, lesbian, bisexual, or transgendered paradigms as well as those adding or substituting a queer understanding to their criticism) in the years since the appearance of Wood's groundbreaking essay have been far fewer than those from a feminist perspective, and certainly fewer than one might have expected. Often they offer little more than a damning sentence or two about the director in essays focused on another filmmaker (one inevitably compared favorably against a negatively regarded Bergman) or in general surveys of homosexual characters in film.[8]

On the other hand, in an excellent and still too-little-known recent study, *Gender and Representation in the Films of Ingmar Bergman*, Marilyn Johns Blackwell adumbrates and addresses the complaints many feminist critics—and thus, indirectly, similarly progressive GLBTQ critics—have made about the Swedish director's body of work.[9] Although Blackwell hardly celebrates Bergman as an unrecognized feminist (and, by extension, queer) ally, her work shows how, in his films' savage critique of the workings of patriarchy, Bergman has constructed an impressive, if still very problematic, vision, one that ultimately expresses the untenability of Western patriarchal ideology. Additionally, although not writing from a singularly feminist critical position, Maaret Koskinen—the first scholar writing in English able to consult Bergman's notebooks and diaries in her work—validates many of the insights Blackwell has teased out of the director's films. Koskinen posits "that large parts of Bergman's oeuvre are devoted to the constitution and construction of human subjectivity, oscillating between the poles of masculinity and femininity."[10] The importance of this assertion, which I first read as I was putting the finishing touches on this manuscript, cannot be overestimated in my own reading of Bergman's work. Ultimately, I consider my reading of Bergman's texts to be parallel to those of these two sympathetic feminism-inspired scholars.

Put succinctly, this study was written with the conviction that the conventional wisdom regarding the political value or ideological insight of Ingmar Bergman's films for gender and sexuality, as it has developed over the last thirty-five years or so, can be productively challenged through what I venture to call "queer bifocal lenses," lenses that represent both the re-created perspectives of the queer audiences who would have seen them upon their original releases as well as the perspectives of contemporary queer theorists and critics. I certainly agree with second-wave feminist writers, and with Blackwell, that a number of films Bergman produced in the 1970s, none more so than the ever-risible *Cries and Whispers*, are intensely problematic, so problematic that their influence on Bergman criticism generally might be responsible for diminishing the reputation of the director's earlier and later films. I do not think it follows, however, that those films, which, in addition to *Cries and Whispers*, include *Face to Face* (1976), *The Serpent's Egg* (1977), and *Autumn Sonata* (1978), can be used to discredit the value that the rest of the director's work might have had, and, indeed, might continue to have. In this study, I argue that many of the films Bergman directed in the first twenty-five years of his career, as well as a small number of his final, "summing up" films, have had and might continue to have a positive, largely unacknowledged role in the radicalization of our understandings of sexuality and gender roles, one that merits not hagiography but renewed discussion and debate.

The latter point should not be underappreciated. I am no more interested in "saving" the reputation of a "great man" and his work than Tania Modleski was when she wrote her exemplary feminist study of the films of Alfred Hitchcock in 1988, although I would be lying if I did not admit that like most men, straight or gay, I harbor some deeply ingrained (and undoubtedly problematic) ability to sympathetically understand what it means to have been granted both the benefits and challenges of male subjectivity.[11] More importantly for the goals of this book, however, I am interested in crediting pre-Stonewall-rebellion American homosexuals with having manifested more ideological engagement with the various art-film "texts" that they encountered than they have thus far received, something I focus on specifically in the first chapter. Carrying this forward throughout the rest of this study, I offer evidence showing how those specific spectators "read" Bergman's "texts" with particular enthusiasm and intelligence throughout the height of the director's popularity.

Questioning an Origin Myth

One thing that will become clear fairly quickly as this study unfolds is how straightforwardly a Cold War–era queer spectator would have understood many of these films. This claim may seem counterintuitive because, unlike the same spectator's reading of a queerly evocative Hollywood horror film, which, as Harry M. Benshoff persuasively points out, involves both metaphorical engagement (vampires as homosexuals) and against-the-grain readings ("bad" vampires as tragic heroes), a queer spectator's understanding of a sympathetically portrayed lesbian was often precisely that—an understanding of her as a sympathetically portrayed lesbian.[12] Ultimately, in fact, the queer spectators of a Bergman film differ from the queer spectators of classical Hollywood cinema as well as from the dominant (heterosexual, male) spectators of Bergman's films, who were likely to see many of the characters in metaphorical or symbolic terms.[13]

Noting the difference is important for at least two reasons beyond the need for historical accuracy. First, it sheds light on another telling example of the strategies used by filmmakers, critics, audiences, and others to defend or excuse what was otherwise considered unacceptable content for Cold War–era films. Instead of seeing the two women at the center of *Persona* as, simply, two flesh-and-blood women who have become sexually drawn to each other, one can elide a possible controversy by calling the characters' relationship a metaphor for the divided soul of contemporary mankind. Second, it points toward an often-ignored desire, one surely held by the queer spectator of the Cold War era just as it is by many of us today—a desire for simplicity and directness in a culture that more often than not requires highly coded forms of speech and interpretation, especially of its "deviant" members. For me, this simplicity and directness can be defined as nothing more or less than sincerity, and sincerity is one of the paramount values required in any queer engagement with the work of Bergman. The queer Bergman spectator is not pleased with his or her superior knowledge of the films' hidden meanings, or with his or her sly understanding of any possible camp sensibility they may, theoretically, be argued to have. In this regard, *Queer Bergman* offers an argument for a very different understanding of at least one facet of the postwar American homosexual. At the very least, it argues for the existence of other homosexuals or other ways of being homosexual beyond those that have previously been suggested by much of the existing work on queer cinema spectatorship.

As Robert Corber does throughout his important study, *Homosexuality in Cold War America*, I also want to "contest a view of postwar urban gay communities that first gained currency in the early years of gay liberation and that has gone largely unchallenged in gay studies." Summarizing this view, Corber writes:

According to the received narrative of the postwar gay rights movement, in the fifties urban gay communities revolved around the closeted world of gay bars. The men who participated most actively in this world were supposedly unable to accept their homosexuality and saw the bars as places not where they could experience solidarity with other gay men but where they could solicit sex. This narrative has led to the misunderstanding that gay male resistance was limited to camp, an oppositional practice that destabilized the binarisms governing the production of gender.[14]

Corber problematizes this pat understanding of formative GLBT or queer cultures throughout his study and, in doing so, indirectly offers the most compelling explanation for an omission in current GLBTQ film studies, one that this project seeks to remedy.

After adumbrating a simplistic but widely disseminated historiography, in which the gay rights movement is said to have begun virtually out of nowhere in New York City at the Stonewall Inn on June 27, 1969, "when a group of drag queens . . . violently and courageously resisted arrest on charges of disorderly conduct," Corber offers a counterargument that obliges us to rethink the history of the entire Cold War–era U.S. gay rights movement.[15] Skeptical of any historical interpretation that presumes a single series of riots in lower Manhattan could have motivated and sustained the mass movement for gay and lesbian equality that has existed ever since, Corber asserts the importance of heretofore underappreciated cultural discourses that, however bleak, can be said to have inspired a generation of sexual minorities to stand up against the dominant and dominating ideology of the era. By positing a queer consciousness that developed more gradually, at least in part because of the artistic unmasking of an untenable reality, Corber justifiably credits "[Tennessee] Williams, [Gore] Vidal, and [James] Baldwin, in conjunction with other progressive cultural workers" for beginning "the task of challenging the discourses and institutions that naturalized the construction of gender and sexual identity."[16] In this regard, I am convinced that Bergman's brutal vision of patriarchal heteronormativity, and of how forms of homosexuality have both sustained and destabilized it, has also played an important role.

It seems telling to me that Robin Wood's objection to Bergman's work is accompanied by an even more curtly phrased dismissal of the filmmaking project of Rainer Werner Fassbinder. Dismissing the "sour determinism" and "gay stereotypes" of the fully queer (if hardly "gay") German filmmaker[17] in much the same way Thomas Waugh castigated the young Derek Jarman that same year, Wood's utopian fervor can be forgiven as part of a strategically necessary stance taken against a long tradition of homophobia within narrative cinema.[18] Of course, queer film critics and academics now almost universally applaud the legacies of Fassbinder and Jarman, finally realizing (or admitting) that what once seemed like self-hatred on those artists' parts can now (rightly, I would posit) be defended as magisterial forms of uncompromising honesty. On the other hand, the films of Bergman, which remain yoked to the image of a director who always presented himself as far less politically aware than Fassbinder and Jarman, not to mention very problematically heterosexual, have yet to be similarly reconsidered. A statement Fassbinder offered in defense of his own work, however, might well also function as the best possible defense one could mount against the argument Robin Wood originally made regarding Bergman.

Fassbinder's assertion can be appropriated as a nearly perfect answer to Wood's criticism of those Bergman films ending, so suddenly, in moments of bleak despair: "[My films] are founded in the belief that the revolution doesn't belong on the cinema screen, but outside, in the world. . . . Never mind if a film ends pessimistically; if it exposes certain mechanisms clearly enough to show people how exactly they work, then the ultimate effect is not pessimistic. . . . My goal is to reveal such mechanisms in a way that makes people realize the necessity of changing their own reality."[19]

In my view, Fassbinder's hypothesis can hardly be overvalued. Indeed, it has been repeatedly invoked by film scholars and queer intellectuals and artists, including Todd Haynes, in defense of negatively conceived narratives produced more recently, and it points to the concerns of Fassbinder's generation as well as our own.[20] I would argue that it also describes a significant body of work from the decades just before the German filmmaker's emergence, a body of work that has yet to receive the accounting it deserves and that includes, but is ultimately far more extensive than, Bergman's singular output.

Perhaps Corber's explanation for the reasons behind Vidal, Williams, and Baldwin's temporary erasure from American queer historiography also accounts for at least some of the reasons Bergman's work and, by extension, that of other dark film poets of the European art cinema, have likewise been unacknowledged within the same historiographic tradition, since within the field of queer film studies, "Stonewall as origin myth" seems to have been unduly influential. Featuring drag-queen participants supposedly driven to the point of revolution by not just police harassment but also the recent death of Judy Garland,

the explosive events that unfolded June 27–29, 1969 quite naturally encourage an examination of the political value of camp sensibility as it
had been deconstructed within the queer American avant-garde of the
1950s and 1960s by filmmakers including Kenneth Anger, Jack Smith,
and Andy Warhol. Looking back to the films those queer artists appropriated—Hollywood musicals of the 1940s and 1950s and the Jon Hall–
Maria Montez–Sabu adventures of the same era, for instance—a historiography of queer spectatorship has come into focus, one offering
inarguably invaluable insights regarding the connections between popular culture and political consciousness. While the avant-garde's appreciation of those American B movie camp aesthetics (as well as the ideology beneath it) implicitly encouraged fecund examinations of other
"lowbrow" Hollywood genre films, from horror to film noir, queer
scholarly interest in the European art cinema did not follow, perhaps
contrary to expectations.[21] Granted, a quick look through the GLBTQ
archives might well reveal a few Anita Ekberg drag queens out and
about in the 1960s, but there were probably not very many, and this
would have justified the uninterest of GLBTQ film scholars in pursuing associated cultural environs. This lack also forces one to face an
embarrassing, from my perspective, possibility: could it be that the "art
cinema homosexuals" were an entirely different group from those who
manned the proverbial "Stonewall barricades," and that they essentially
"sat out" the revolution? In other words, were the Monica Vitti queers
content to stay in the dark of the art theaters and the connected clos-
ets of high-culture aestheticism while the drag Judy Garlands (and Car-
men Mirandas and Bette Davises) did the cultural heavy lifting?

The criticism that many in current gay culture make about the art
cinema seems to point to such an interpretation, most clearly in the inevitable use of a single adjective routinely used to dismiss the topic:
"pretentious." Art films and the spectators to whom they speak have
been routinely accused, at least implicitly, of pretending to be something they are not. Furthermore, those sympathetic to the art cinema
are not, it seems, thought to be embracing the (supposedly subversive) form of pretence a drag queen embraces when pretending to be a
woman, but of the (supposedly self-hating) pretence a closeted homosexual affects when pretending to be straight. Following this logic, the
art film itself, by seeming to renounce its roots in the fairground's "cinema of attractions" and the proletarian-immigrant culture of the early
twentieth century and attaching itself instead to the discourses of high
modernism, can be seen to yearn for a kind of cultural legitimacy that,
in its decadent, elitist connotations, connects with a form of homosexu-

Ingmar Bergman and the Foreign Self

He was soon to become
the second most powerful
man in Nazi Germany.

LUCHINO VISCONTI'S
THE DAMNED

An ALFRED LEVY—EVER HAGGIAG Production

DIRK · INGRID · HELMUT · HELMUT · RENAUD · UMBERTO
BOGARDE · THULIN · GRIEM · BERGER · VERLEY · ORSINI
ALBRECHT · RENÉ · FLORINDA · CHARLOTTE
SCHOENHALS · KOLDEHOFF and BOLKAN and RAMPLING
DIRECTED BY   MUSIC COMPOSED BY   PRODUCED BY
LUCHINO VISCONTI MAURICE JARRE · NICOLA BADALUCCO · ALFRED LEVY and EVER HAGGIAG
SCREENPLAY BY
NICOLA BADALUCCO · ENRICO MEDIOLI · LUCHINO VISCONTI · TECHNICOLOR® From WARNER BROS.

AMERICAN PREMIERE THURSDAY
THE festival

Figure 0.1. Newspaper advertisement for *The Damned* (Luchino Visconti, Italy 1969). Warner Bros. *New York Times*, December 14, 1969.

ality that, at the very least, seems closeted and counterrevolutionary. At its worst, it seems politically reactionary, tending toward homofascism. Some of the better-known foreign films with queer credentials can seem to support this claim. Exhibit A: Luchino Visconti's *The Damned* (1969; see figure 0.1).

It must be noted, however, that the rioting drag queens spilling out of the Stonewall Inn onto Christopher Street in the summer of 1969 were quickly joined and supported by a much larger segment of the queer populace. Corber has convincingly shown that many of the activists who emerged out of pioneering homosexual rights organizations like the Mattachine Society or the Daughters of Bilitis were inspired and politically motivated by explorations of queerness (defined as socially determined forms of subjectivity) that they encountered in the less-than-lowbrow artistic discourses exemplified by the currently underappreciated work of Vidal, Williams, and Baldwin. The contributions those writers made to queer culture in the formative years of the GLBTQ movement, like the subsequent contributions of Fassbinder and Jarman, were too hastily criticized by a generation of scholars and critics as the products of self-hatred and repressiveness. Indeed, as Corber points out, despite decades of courageous and valuable work throughout the 1950s and 1960s, organizations such as the Mattachine Society were all too often dismissed by GLBTQ historians and activists as having been politically ineffective because of their assimilationist politics.[22] A careful appraisal of the publications those organizations sponsored throughout those years, which included many sharp analyses of European art films, including Bergman's, suggests the need for a more nuanced understanding.

Organization of the Book

Chapter One is offered, in part, as a contribution to what I hope will be a continuing reappraisal of the perspectives and insights of those more circumspect other activists. It is also something of a preview of what I am hoping to do in my next project: read queerly a much wider range of art-cinema texts by a number of filmmakers that have heretofore not been remembered in those terms. Noting the intersections between Cold War era American queer writers and the nation's art-cinema culture illuminates a productive avenue that allows me to explain the connection between pre-Stonewall queer subjectivity and foreign-film spectatorship. For instance, it is often noted that Tennessee Williams worked with Visconti on the English translation of *Senso* (1954). It is James Baldwin's personal experience with Bergman's films, however, that seems particularly illuminating. Writing in 1961, the gay African American drew parallels between Bergman's Lutheran-inspired cinema and his own background in Southern American Protestantism. In doing so, he admitted to a project of self-discovery that took inspiration from what he approvingly described as the art-film maker's practice of "arduous, delicate, and disciplined self-exposure."[23] Baldwin may have hoped to emulate Bergman's own hard-fought, painful form of self-exposure, on display for a generation of queer spectators across hundreds of art-house screens in the United States, but he left it for others to chart the forms of self-exposure that any number of those queers might have undergone when encountering those films. To put this in the terms of contemporary film studies, one can ask: how might Bergman's self-exposure have become, in its turn, the self-exposure (or self-understanding) of his historically situated queer spectators? I hope this study contributes to answering such questions.

Considering that the formal concept of the cinematic spectator would not be articulated until the end of the 1960s, and that acknowledgment of nonnormative forms of spectatorship—queer spectatorship in particular—would require additional years of debate, it is hardly surprising that Baldwin and his contemporaries stayed focused on the narrative content of the films in question. Postponing a discussion of the "fantasmatic realms" of queer spectatorship, I argue that the radical force of the basic narrative and thematic content of Bergman's cinema has not diminished throughout the years and, in fact, remains essential to the total (ultimately spectatorial) effect of these films' queer power.

On a personal, biographical note, I found Bergman's films to be particularly challenging and radical when I first encountered them, more than two decades after Baldwin had, in the early 1980s, and in ways directly connected with an inchoate sense of my own queer subjectivity. In an environment profoundly influenced by the Church of Jesus Christ of Latter-day Saints, in which heterosexual marriage and child rearing was (and remains) the celebrated and centralized norm and expectation, Bergman's films were the first I encountered that offered a profound critique of that ideal and the ideology behind it. I will never forget my first viewing of *Winter Light* at the Utah Film and Video Center in February 1983, particularly the scene in which its minister protagonist, Tomas, begins to verbally abuse his lover, Märta, finally allowing his long-simmering but heretofore impacted rage to emerge. I was astonished by the radical truth contained in the scene, watching Tomas attack his female partner for being exactly what most heterosexual men, in my admittedly limited experience at that time, had always said they wanted a woman to be. "I'm tired of your loving care, your fussing over me, your good advice, your little candlesticks and table runners," Tomas venomously spits out. "I'm fed up with your . . . timid ways when we make love."[24]

Märta, who begins to quietly weep during the tirade and who, it seemed to me, was being as viciously attacked, emotionally, as Marion Crane had been, physically, in the nearly contemporaneous *Psycho*

(1960), eventually composes herself and manages to ask this man (who can only with intense sarcasm be called her "lover") why he never expressed any of these feelings before. "For a simple reason," he responds with the rational confidence of a civilized man. "I'm well brought up. From birth I've been taught to regard women as beings of a higher order." [25] The stunning irony of this dialogue only increases after Tomas grabs Märta's arm at the end of the scene, seemingly on the verge of a physical assault, just after she, in an attempt to do the opposite of what he savagely criticized her for, belatedly pulled herself together and stood up for herself as a human being. This sequence was a revelation to me.

As the leader of a religious congregation, *Winter Light*'s Tomas was a perfect symbol of what I would later learn to call the patriarchy, something to which I had been utterly beholden. Märta, as a small-town schoolteacher, occupied the only respectable job that an unmarried middle-aged woman could hold according to the culture I had been born into. The situation seemed so appalling to me, and yet somehow it made a dark kind of sense: she was doing everything her society expected her to do, and her lover (who, as a minister, was also her culture's central authority figure) hated her for it. The fact that the infernal scene takes place in the schoolhouse where Märta teaches, with keys to a boys' bathroom and a girls' bathroom clearly marked and separately hanging on the wall in the background, only amplified issues that would become more important to me as I came to understand my own complicated sexuality—the violence and pain associated with learned gender differentiation and the largely mythical state of happiness promised as a final result of heterosexual coupling. [26]

Nineteen years later, during a well-attended screening of *Winter Light* that I scheduled in my capacity as assistant film programmer at George Eastman House in Rochester, New York, a distinctly female quality could be heard in the loud, collective gasp emerging at the moment the savagely attacking Tomas rationalized his behavior as a result of having been "well brought up." But it did not strike me as a gasp of disbelief. Indeed, it sounded like the kind of gasp one emits when being faced with a profoundly painful truth, in this case the appalling truth that contemptuous misogyny, felt but unspoken, was fully compatible with, perhaps even necessary *to*, being "well brought up" in Western patriarchal societies. Certainly, when I had seen the film in Utah two decades earlier, my gasps had been due more to a confrontation with something that seemed to be all too true than to something that seemed to be impossible or wrong.

Ingmar Bergman and the Foreign Self

A few years after my initial encounter with Bergman's films, I read Tania Modleski's feminist analysis of Hitchcock's *Rear Window* (1954) and noted how the author aptly characterized the tendency of James Stewart's character to criticize Grace Kelly's character for her feminine self-expression: it was an example of a "familiar double bind" in which women "are first assigned a restricted place in patriarchy and then condemned for occupying it," and I readily concurred with her analysis.[27] Still, Hitchcock's subversive irony notwithstanding, it seemed to me that, as dramatized in *Rear Window*, this vexing double bind could be laughed off pretty easily. The sense of uneasiness one feels at the end of that Hitchcock film tends to evaporate quickly. No one, however, can easily shrug off the psychic violence occasioned by gender difference and sex roles as dramatized in *Winter Light*.

Insights such as these arguably encourage continued feminist reappraisals of Bergman's work, not necessarily queer ones, and indeed, like some of his fellow art-cinema exemplars—Luis Buñuel, François Truffaut, Michelangelo Antonioni—Bergman always has seemed a decidedly heterosexual filmmaker, one whose interest in homosexuality can appear to be, at first glance at any rate, limited to the arguably pathologized and eroticized forms of lesbianism found in *Thirst* [aka *Three Strange Loves*] (1949), *The Silence*, and *Persona*. Unlike those filmmakers, however, Bergman was crucially seen as Swedish, and Sweden represented, to many in the United States and the United Kingdom throughout much of the Cold War period, particular forms of queerness that, above and beyond Bergman's own consciously queer endeavors as an artist, accrued to the image of the director in those Anglophone nations, whether he was aware of it or not.

Chapter Two will focus more tightly on this single cultural figure, discussing the ways in which Bergman's queer male spectator was encouraged to read the director's films queerly; this was due in part to the filmmaker's culturally constructed, Cold War–era national identity, one that gave what otherwise might have seemed to be homophobic content a productive sense of intriguing ambivalence. Of course, where there is discursive smoke, there is often discursive fire, and the nation of Sweden was demonstrably more queer friendly, and certainly more likely to release films that took homosexual characters seriously and "showed them" in frankly forthright ways, than the rest of Europe—a part of the world whose cinema was still far more open to queer content than was Hollywood. Furthermore, although it could hardly have factored into a spectator's interpretation of his films in the pre-Stonewall era, Bergman would, in subsequent years, out himself, and be outed by others, as something more than a stalwartly heterosexual artist.

Bergman's English-language biographer Peter Cowie may have been the first observer to claim the director had homosexual or bisexual feelings—feelings that emerged in his work, even if only briefly—but statements made by the director himself are the most compelling in this regard.[28] In a particularly revealing passage referring to his 1968 film *Hour of the Wolf*, a darkly comic, gothic tale largely concerned with homosexual repression, Bergman acknowledged this:

> When I see *Hour of the Wolf* today, I understand that it is about a deep-seated division within me, both hidden and carefully monitored, visible in both my earlier and later work: Aman [a heterosexual woman who passes herself off as a man in public], in *The Magician* (*The Face*) [1958]; Ester [a lesbian incestuously drawn to her sister], in *The Silence*; Tomas [a positively presented gay—or perhaps bisexual—man], in *Face to Face*; Elisabeth [a married mother who arguably develops lesbian longings for her nurse], in *Persona*; Ismael [a hermaphrodite], in *Fanny and Alexander* [1982]. To me, *Hour of the Wolf* is important since it is an attempt to encircle a hard-to-locate set of problems and get inside of them.[29]

Looked at in isolation, with its demonically queer phantoms pursuing a repressed, presumably hallucinating protagonist, *Hour of the Wolf* might seem to offer little more than a vulgar gloss on Freudian theories about the relationship between homosexuality and paranoia, and queer viewers at the time, particularly those not connecting it with Bergman's larger body of work, may well have dismissed it as homophobic. But as a single film—albeit one that Bergman himself felt "fails"—in a series of "attempts" to "encircle" "hard-to-locate" problems (read: disparate forms of queer male subjectivity), *Hour of the Wolf* becomes a more interesting chapter in the director's larger examination of subjective sexual fluctuation.

Ultimately, approaching the concept of "Bergman as auteur" as an organizing principle around which spectators are encouraged to read his body of work allows us to consider other ways in which Bergman himself, retrospectively in a series of interviews, seems to have wanted his films to be viewed queerly. Describing formative childhood experiences that Bergman felt contributed to *The Silence*, one of his most erotically troubled films, he offered another queer insight, not only about a single motion picture, but about his investment in cinema as a whole: "At the age of ten I began my life as a vagabond. Often the goal of my wanderings was Birger Jarl's arcade, which to me was a magical place with its peep shows and its little movie theater, the Maxim. For seventy-five öre [about 15 cents], one could sneak into that time's R-rated movies or, better yet, climb up into the projection room manned by the aging homosexual."[30] Previously, in an interview given upon the release of *Hour of the Wolf*, Bergman had put what seems to have been the same experience somewhat differently: "How envious I was of [the projectionist]! . . . I thought of him as someone who went up to heaven every evening. We struck up a friendship and . . . the chap . . . used to cuddle me a bit, I remember, but circumspectly: so I don't think anything untoward happened."[31]

Interestingly, in the earlier account, Bergman referred to the theater as "the Castle Cinema" and remarked that the films shown were not "R-rated," but "suitable for schoolchildren."[32] Among other things, one must, of course, wonder why Bergman offered a seemingly gratuitous assessment of the sexuality of projectionist, and furthermore, why it was "better" for young Ingmar to watch the films in the booth beside the (arguably, gratuitously defined) queer older gentleman rather than downstairs in the auditorium with the general spectators. Whether this was a basically accurate account of real events or what Sigmund Freud would have called a "screen memory" on Bergman's part, constructed to cover and make acceptable sense out of another very different memory or constellation of formative experiences, the filmmaker's statements suggest a connection between homosexuality and the presentation of the cinematic image, or at least the cinematic image as he situated himself in relation to it. Put simply, it was, and maybe still is, far "better," even "heavenly," for Bergman, maybe for everyone, to experience the cinema from a homosexual's, or from a queer, vantage point.

Janet Staiger has recently assessed a number of statements Bergman made over the years that she feels represent more or less conscious efforts on the filmmaker's part to build and secure his reputation as an artist, what she calls his "self-fashioning in authoring and reception." Paraphrasing Michel Foucault's concept of "technologies of the self," Staiger argues that "our repetition creates our subjectivities in relation to others, positioning us within a social and discursive fabric," then addresses a formative episode in the filmmaker's childhood that—like his visits to the heavenly projection booth—seems to have been of such importance to Bergman that he mentioned it publicly on more than one occasion.[33] In this case, however, the anecdote serves to reaffirm Bergman's heterosexually expressed desires. Bergman, as quoted by Staiger, claims: "When I was ten years old I received my first, rattling film projector, with its chimney and lamp . . . It showed a girl, lying asleep in a meadow, who woke up and stretched out her arms, then disappeared to the right."[34] Describing this event as an "originary moment," a formative, causal event in Bergman's early life, Staiger argues for the centrality of this very heterosexually informed memory in understanding Bergman's erotic investment in film: "If I were pursuing a psychoanalytical account of Bergman," she asserts, "this story is gold for its evocation of the elusive female object of desire."[35] By using the phrase "female object of desire," Staiger is obviously suggesting much more than a director merely self-fashioning a heterosexual reputation (perhaps with some curious degree of belatedness, since the quotation dates to 1960). In fact, she is maintaining a stance implicit in virtually every English-language critical argument about the director, asserting the profoundly heterosexual definition of Bergman's life and work.

Staiger is undoubtedly correct to conclude that Bergman's erotic interest in women is of paramount concern in any broad attempt to understand his work, and her more specific point, that Bergman was trying to "self-fashion" a biographical image of himself as heterosexual, is astutely observed. Still, despite the objectified female form emanating from the young Bergman's toy projector, and despite the fact that the films screened at the Maxim or Castle (or whatever it was called) were also most likely heterosexual in nature, Bergman's twice-told tale of going "up to heaven" to watch films beside a queer projectionist does not relate to the issue, broadly speaking, of content, but to that of one's perspective, and this is of primary importance. Even without the insights provided by psychoanalytic film theory's concepts of "spectatorship positioning," one can understand how a motion picture filled with objectified female forms might still be regarded as utterly queer if seen from a queer spectator's viewpoint. For example, any number of "terrible" Hollywood B pictures, including many that could be defined as heterosexually erotic, easily become "wonderful" camp classics when watched in the company of a particular kind of "aging homosexual." In a neat distillation of Alexander Doty's important formative work on queer spectatorship, Harry M. Benshoff suggests that there is a "sense that any film viewed by a gay or lesbian spectator might be considered queer," since any film can be viewed, as Doty himself puts it, "outside the relatively clear-cut and essentializing categories of sexual identity under which most people function."[36]

One of the challenges I had in writing this book, one that I hope does not remain as a significant challenge for the reader, was to clearly chart the precise spectator *positions* I am addressing at any given moment. Feminist scholars working on psychoanalytic theories of cinema in the 1980s thought deeply about the terms they were using and the assumptions those terms implied, positing various definitions of spectatorship as an endeavor and "the spectator" as a historical or hypothetical subject position. Once one began distinguishing between what Miriam Hansen called "the hypothetical spectator constructed through [a] film's strategies," on the one hand, "and the contemporary female spectator with a feminist consciousness," on the other, one had to consider allowing for innumerable others—different or simply more precisely conceived—as well: a female spectator without a feminist consciousness, a lesbian spectator with (or without) a feminist consciousness, a gay male spectator with or without a feminist (or radically queer) consciousness, and so on.[37] Doing so, in the years since the debate began, has allowed for provocative new meanings to emerge, and surely, one would not be presumptuous to suggest that Bergman's projection-booth anecdote can be interpreted as suggesting the value of just such a strategy of spectatorship. If that is the case, one of the questions this study concerns itself with seems obvious: what do Bergman's films and, by slight extension, the other European art films his work was in dialogue with (and regularly compared to) become when watched from a queer and, it should be noted, largely white, vantage point? The challenge, of course, comes in keeping so many overlapping positions of spectatorship clear as one discusses them. I hope I have managed to do so in the pages to come without being unnecessarily wordy or pedantic.

A question related to the one Bergman's projection-booth anecdote suggests is equally important: how does spectatorship function, indeed how does human subjectivity function, when one is obliged—or at least encouraged—to experience the cinema from the perspective of the other? Bergman's projection-room story could be rewritten to ask us to consider what it might mean for a young man to watch a film beside a generically (if there is such a thing) female projectionist, a lesbian one, or, in the interest of this study, a radically foreign one? Experiencing something as intimate and personal as a well-crafted and presumably mainstream narrative film from a decentered position of alterity, as the young Bergman claims to have done—a homosexual's projection booth rather than the (general) public sphere of a theater auditorium—suggests one of Sigmund Freud's definitions of the uncanny: the "unhomely home." Of course, the strong sense of the uncanny found in

Bergman's films makes them particularly apt texts to speak about how the sensibility of the uncanny is itself a profound metaphor for a mode of queer film spectatorship—specifically, queer *foreign film* spectatorship, which promises a strange, eerie, but finally enchanting state of being that can ultimately be claimed as one's rightful domain. These dynamics will begin to be addressed in Chapter Three and will be further developed in Chapter Four.

Chapter Four also contains the fullest development of my argument about Bergman's queer spectator—more specifically, Bergman's queer and heretofore male-identified spectator—although, as in earlier chapters, I occasionally broaden or narrow my scope to include other kinds of spectators. I consider the queer male-identified and again largely, if not exclusively, white spectator, or spectator position, to be distinct from the heterosexual male spectator posited by feminist film theorists of the 1970s, as well as from other spectatorship positions (female, lesbian, black, etc.) that have subsequently been posited and have extended psychoanalytic film theory's understandings about how the cinema works in concert with myriad other ideological practices responsible for engendering human subjectivity.

A number of GLBTQ film scholars have contributed exemplary work to an understanding of gay or queer forms of cinematic spectatorship, including Patricia White, Brett Farmer, and Robert Corber.[38] One of the strengths of all three of these scholars' work is its focus not just on lesbian spectators or gay male spectators, but also on specific forms of lesbian or gay-male spectatorship that emerge through specific kinds of narrative cinema (and generally in specific historical moments): primarily ghost stories, gothic mysteries, and melodramas in White's monograph; musicals in Farmer's book; and film noir in Corber's tightly written chapter on the subject. For my part, I will argue for a form of queer-male spectatorship with a vexed, ambivalent relationship to masculinity, a spectatorship directly elicited by the aesthetics and narrative strategies of the art cinema and epitomized by the films released under Bergman's name in the 1950s and, especially, the 1960s.

I am aware that "straight" approaches to psychoanalysis, meaning classic Freudian perspectives, are hardly considered cutting-edge for many in the contemporary film-studies community. Even the more recently fashionable Lacanian approaches to film analysis have been declared exhausted—often, it should be said, by scholars who never utilized them. Nevertheless, throughout much of this study, I rely on the unreconceptualized psychoanalytic work of Sigmund Freud. I use Freud's work not so much because I think Freud was right about all things regarding human interiority, although I think he was right about a number of very important things, but because his was the perspective through which many of the more educated Western queer filmgoers, certainly many of those watching the European art cinema in the 1950s and 1960s, would have interpreted those films. Needless to say, film artists like Bergman were familiar with Freud's theories as well. While good work has been done in criticizing the homophobic nature of the Cold War–era American psychoanalytic movement, in contradistinction to the more radical European and pre–World War II traditions, the fact remains that many relatively self-accepting, intelligent gays, lesbians, and queers throughout the 1950s and 1960s were intrigued with and conversant in Freud's original psychoanalytic literature.[39] For example, a single issue of the *Mattachine Review* from 1960 offers two articles dealing with homosexual dynamics from a psychoanalytical perspective, while a review of John Huston's Hollywood biography *Freud* (1962) in a later issue shows the (presumably queer) critic's impressive knowledge of the film's subject and his palpable excitement that "[it] smoothly and frankly handles oral fixation and the full impact of infantile sexuality" while dramatizing "cases [that] lead to the Oedipus theory."[40]

Beyond any justifications based on historically anchored senses of a spectator's cultural groundings, however, I remain convinced that Freud's insights into the oscillations of identification, infantile sexuality, polymorphous perversity, constitutional bisexuality, shame, and, again, the sensibility of the uncanny, to name only a few, are central both to an understanding of Bergman's queer work and to the still-vital project of queer theory as a whole. Nevertheless, in what I hope is an appropriately queer fashion, I refuse to commit myself to a single, unidirectional method. I approach my psychoanalytic investigation of Bergman historically while also developing my historiography of Bergman's queer spectator according to psychoanalytic insights. Ultimately, I hope to suggest some of the ways in which cultural and historical forces affect subjectivity, as well as the ways in which subjectivity changes in order to change history, sometimes for the better.

You know, if you took away the
homosexual audience from the arthouses
. . . you wouldn't have much left.

Pauline Kael,

in conversation with

Francis Davis (2001)

Chapter One

"Foreign and Refreshing"
The Art Cinema's Queer Allure

In a 2005 episode of the animated television se-
ries *The Simpsons*, Lisa Simpson wins a set of tickets to a new foreign
film by being the first (and only) caller to the local National Public Ra-
dio station. Arriving at a foreboding downtown venue called the Limited Appeal Theater, the Simpsons find their city's art cinema decidedly
different from the typical suburban multiplex. Bart, Lisa's mischievous
older brother, comments on this strange new environment as he walks
past posters for the current attraction, *Kosovo Autumn*, and then one
for an upcoming feature ominously titled *Oppenheimer's Elevator*. "Instead of video games, they have *weird* free newspapers," he notes, picking up a copy of one from the counter. After briefly studying the periodical, titled *Queer Focus*, Bart asks his mother: "Mom, am I a butch or a
femme?" Distracted by a concession stand that seems to offer only fresh
apples and mineral water, Marge absentmindedly responds: "Honey,
you can be anything you wanna be." Intrigued and happy, Bart continues reading as his oblivious mother stands by.[1]

The fear playfully alluded to here is that by encouraging children to learn and grow, parents might facilitate access to ideas that the parents might not really understand themselves. Speaking more to my purposes in this study, the lighthearted segment alludes to the connections between post–World War II queer-informed urban culture and what one may call a "foreign imaginary"—a perspective on the self's relation to the other that is exceedingly close to what has, in more recent years, perhaps too generally been thought of simply as a queer identity.

In a study of the "homosexual form of existence" that emerged in the Western world in the late nineteenth century, the Danish sociologist Henning Bech discusses the challenges faced by members of urban homosexual microcultures, who found they desired, counterintuitively enough, specifically *heterogeneous* social and sexual experiences. Although he connects homosexuals' yearning for foreign encounters with noted affinities for avant-garde values—the queer modernist's self-conscious desire to be in the vanguard of cultural history—Bech concedes that these wishes also involve "a sheer lamenting of the lack of a place to be, as an abstract desire for another country."[2] Ultimately, in arguing that the profoundly urban character of the modern homosexual identity in fact *dis*courages voyages to too-exotic locales—"it should not be forgotten that the homosexuals are civilized people capable of forfeiting the benefits of civilization only with difficulty"—Bech points to compromise environments born of "a series of innovations and re-sittings . . . in the space of the city."[3] These include "railway stations, zoological gardens, botanical gardens, parks and natural history museums."[4]

Bech focuses on the contradictions between an "anti-civilizatory fulfillment of homosexuality and the homosexual's need for the benefits of civilization," and yet he ends one section (not surprisingly titled "Another Country") of his larger project with reference to a development that can hardly be thought of as a queer, dialectically resolved return to nature—the "liberated zones" of the contemporary metropolis: the "Castro in San Francisco, Greenwich Village in New York, the Marais in Paris or the city centre of Amsterdam."[5] Whatever might be missing in those enclaves, Bech suggests, whether it be another country or simply a country setting, "could be made up on holidays to Ibiza, Mykonos and Haiti."[6] By extension, art-film theaters can be seen as having occupied a place of pride in these largely queer urban districts—from the very beginnings of their histories—while also serving a related and important function in the development of modern homosexual identities. It is the founding assumption of this chapter that a brief exploration of this vital aspect of urban homosexual life, along with an assessment to determine the implications and meanings of the connection between the "foreign films" shown in those venues and their urban "queer spectators," is necessary in order to contextualize the figure and filmmaking of Ingmar Bergman as a transnational film auteur. Indeed, answering such a question is crucial in the quest for any complete large-scale understanding of twentieth-century queer identities.

The most obvious point at which to begin this investigation, it seems, is on that noted common ground of queer male (or, in the vocabulary of Cold War America, "male homophile") subjectivity and twentieth-century urban subjectivity. Referring to Bergman's comments about "how as a child he used to wander in the city of Stockholm," ultimately taking his place in the projection room "manned by the aging homosexual," Maaret Koskinen notes that "what stands to the fore in this quote is how sexuality is associated with the city."[7] I would not argue that Koskinen should have said that, "homosexuality is associated with the city" for Bergman since Bergman also mentions "corsets and douches, prostheses and mildly pornographic printed material" visible in "the store windows" he passed by, but I would hasten to suggest that it would certainly be fair to argue that for Bergman, the city represents a place where transgressive, otherwise forbidden, or occulted expressions of sexuality can emerge and grow.

For his part, Henning Bech developed his project according to phenomenological sociology, and as a result, his work stands largely apart from the traditions associated with GLBTQ historiography and theory, both of which present problems for him (he rejects those approaches) and for his scholarship (which can effectively be contested from the perspectives he rejects). And yet, most scholarship on the rise of modern queer consciousness shares Bech's conviction that urbanity is a necessary correlative to twentieth-century homosexual subjectivity. According to the influential argument of the historian John D'Emilio, the large-scale migration from rural to urban societies, beginning during the Industrial Revolution in the 1800s and peaking near the end of World War II, was a necessary development for the construction of modern homosexual identity formations.[8] Subsequent histories, such as George Chauncey's *Gay New York*, have enriched this perspective by offering necessary detail and nuance, and although a growing body of work on rural queer lives necessarily questions any monolithic understanding of queer urbanity, it would be difficult to deny that "the homosexual," as a socially prescribed identity formation, has been strongly informed by constitutive urban qualities.[9]

Citing Georg Simmel, Mary L. Gray teases out the differences between urban and rural forms of contemporary queerness in ways that reflect historical patterns of cultural taste: "Cities are built on a pride in what . . . Simmel theorized as 'the aggregation of so many people with such differentiated interests' produced by the 'conditions of metropolitan life' . . . Rural communities, on the other hand, organize around an appreciation for solidarity expressed through blending in."[10] This distinction raises interesting questions about the queer strategies of assimilation that tend to be encouraged in rural areas, in contrast to what might be called assertions of (arguably less complex) forms of gay self-distinction found in any number of urban environments. It also offers insight into the logic behind an urbanite's particular receptiveness to the sense of difference occasioned by the radically challenging modes of art-cinema practice: an alien form of filmmaking (compared to dominant Hollywood film genres) usually focusing on people from distinctly different cultures. To put it simply, diversity begets diversity. Obviously, to assume such an axiom as a point of departure requires subsequent attention to detail and nuance. One must keep in mind that not all bohemian pleasures offer the sense of queer resonance that many homosexual urban filmgoers were able to find in the never really monolithic entity of the (largely European) art cinema, and that many people living queer urban lives who found their hunger for heterogeneity satiated in other ways had no interest in engaging with imported forms of cultural discourse.

That said, there is ample evidence with which to argue that the European art cinema in toto was recognizable as a queer discourse, at least to the precisely positioned queer American spectator at the time of the movement's strongest impact. I will argue that this perception was hastened and maintained primarily as a result of four complexly interconnected factors: the perception shared by innumerable people at the time, both homophobic and queer friendly, that queerness and foreignness were uncannily interconnected manifestations of disturbing and tantalizing forms of otherness; the greater visibility of homosexuality in European culture, in more or less direct and more or less positive ways—including its artistic self-representations—than elsewhere, particularly the United States, throughout the middle of the twentieth century; the painterly traditions in European cinematography, which granted a homoerotic effect to a significant number of films centered on "sensitive" and "soulful" male characters, in stark contrast to the differently employed Hollywood cinematography of the Cold War era; and the European art cinema's profound commitment to narrative and thematic ambiguity, which has allowed for innumerable queer interpretations of a significant percentage of the form's films, both canonical classics and long since forgotten subcultural hits. I end this chapter with a brief discussion of one of the only Bergman films, largely ignored, to be marketed as a queer text.

Flash-Forward to the Past: Twenty-First-Century Queer Retrospectatorship

Suggestively re-creating the kind of power that the best examples of the European art cinema offered to queer spectators, William E. Jones's short, resonant feature *v.o.* (2006) operates according to a simple formula. In it, scenes from 1970s and early-1980s American gay pornographic films are combined with dialogue and narration culled from a number of nonpornographic foreign-language features. One might assume the title of Jones's work alludes to the "voices" heard "over" the images of mustached men shown hustling and cruising through various urban landscapes while wearing cowboy boots and skin-hugging jeans. The filmmaker's website, however, tells us otherwise. The abbreviation, we are told, "stands for *version originale*, a French term used to denote films exhibited theatrically in their original languages with subtitles," just as Jones presents them here, "as opposed to dubbed."[11] Using only nonexplicit "bridging" sequences—the very material many porn fans would just as soon skip past—found between the films' hardcore footage, *v.o.*'s visuals can be seen also as part of a different sort of bridge, one spanning the bygone era of pregentrification queer America and a distant culture gleaned through the multiply mediated form of subtitled art films.

Although Jones claims to have combined image and sound somewhat arbitrarily, the juxtapositions are especially resonant. The first sequence in *v.o.* combines one of the most clichéd porn scenarios with an equally recognizable art-cinema staple. As a young pizza deliveryman waits in a foyer for his handsome customer to find some cash, he listens to an antique Victrola playing on a nearby table. Simultaneously hackneyed and seductive, the music—Pachelbel's Canon in D Major—underscores Jones's addition of a sound track evincing a soothing French-speaking voice. As the camera slowly zooms into the beckoning orifice of the Victrola's horn, a lap dissolve transports the spectator to a candlelit bedroom. There, through transparent curtains in a discreet long shot, we see two men, presumably the delivery boy and his customer, lying on the bed making love as the subtitled dialogue acknowledges

Figure 1.1. Two worlds brought together in *v.o.* (William E. Jones, United States, 2006). Copyright William E. Jones. Used with permission.

its hypnotic intent: "And now you must clearly visualize the negative agent that is aggressing you. With all your strength you are destroying it. It is getting weaker and weaker, smaller and smaller. It is now disappearing. Feel your victory throughout your whole body. Don't hesitate to smile and to let it flow through you in positive waves" (Figure 1.1). A dream within a dream, the sexual reverie turns out to be only the delivery boy's wistful fantasy. Inspired by the voice of a simultaneously internal and alien tongue in concert with the foreign but familiar classical music (further distanced from its origins by being played on the "low fidelity" antique record player), the young man momentarily envisioned a curious kind of erotic transcendence while humbly waiting to be paid.[12] In doing so, he had been encouraged to feel a "victory" and to "smile."

The remaining fifty-plus minutes of *v.o.* develop several intertwining paths of empathetic engagement for a queerly positioned spectator. The queer male spectator can relate to the porn films' diegetic characters as one can relate to anyone on a motion picture screen, characters who, in this case, not only are having socially unsanctioned forms of sex with other men in urban settings, but are also, as urbanites, exactly the kind of homosexuals who regularly watched theatrical presentations of gay pornography. This, of course, is just what *v.o.*'s spectator, in one sense, is doing. As a result, there are a number of shots of characters walking in front of "skid row" adult movie theaters, if not going inside. Further connecting the spectator and the characters, *v.o.*'s homosexual male spectator has a much more direct and yet complicated sense of identification with the film than he would have had if Jones had chosen to use clips from a wider array of gay adult films, such as "period piece" pornography like the widely seen *Centurians of Rome* (John Christopher, 1981; "Centurians" is the filmmakers' spelling).

Complicating the equation, Jones's older spectators might remember that many of the "adult" theaters associated with the productions

Jones shows us enjoyed earlier incarnations as art-film venues, and that they likely would have presented the kind of motion pictures—such as Jean Renoir's *La Chienne* (1931)—that Jones now has his spectators listen to, sounding like the Ghosts of Cinephilia Past on the multilayered sound track, as they watch the porn-film footage. They might also remember that there was more than an incidental overlap between art-cinema and gay-porn audiences, and that originally, while patronizing urban art houses, they would have listened to the strangely soothing sounds of the foreign voices that we too, as *v.o.*'s spectators, now hear on Jones's sound track. Not for the first time, then, an artist posited what the academic world belatedly investigates: the processes through which American queer subjectivities were profoundly influenced by a rough sexual subculture associated with street drugs and skid row and also by a kind of intellectual arts culture that might seem to have been its utter antithesis.

Indeed, by the mid-1970s, art-house cinemas and porn theaters were uncanny doubles in a number of different ways. Urban, independently owned and operated, they were usually older venues looking as if they had seen far better days. The complex associations between the avant-garde, foreignness, and queerness are distilled in the name "The Paris": on the East Coast, the name of an art-house theater, whereas on the West, that of LA's most notorious gay adult theater.[13] I am not concerned with the artistic legitimacy of the films shown in Southern California's Paris. Its New York cousin, for its part, holds the distinction not only of hosting the American premiere of Ingmar Bergman's *The Seventh Seal,* but also of being the theater whose 1950 screenings of Roberto Rossellini's scandalous short film "The Miracle" (1948) resulted in the United States Supreme Court ruling that grants constitutional protection to motion pictures as a form of speech. (Perhaps the latter distinction aligns the Manhattan venue more closely to—rather than farther from—its California counterpart, at least to any surviving "Miracle" detractors.) The fact that Manhattan's Paris offered filmgoers in the country's largest city the initial engagements of a number of imported films dealing directly with homosexual themes and characters in the pre-Stonewall era indicates the strength of these associations.[14] In the final analysis, it might be beside the point to wonder whether the kind of queer man seen in the porn films Jones samples attended François Truffaut or Federico Fellini screenings between turning tricks. Instead, *v.o.* raises a slightly different question: were some of the patrons of New York's Paris analogous to those of Los Angeles County's Paris? Put more generally, how does queer subjectivity and desire overlap with art-film spectatorship? And how, in the years when the exhibition of homosexual pornography was legally proscribed in even the most permissive large U.S. cities, did the art cinema function, virtually on its own, to cinematically represent queer forms of being?

Word Is Out: Queerness and Foreignness

To answer the question posed at the end of the previous section, one can turn to the so-called homophile publications produced in New York, Los Angeles, and San Francisco in the late 1950s and 1960s, such as One, the Ladder, and the Mattachine Review, and see that they regularly focused on European art films in columns, arts reviews, and feature articles. Many of the films were discussed because of their real or purported gay or lesbian content, while others seem to have been of interest simply for flying the flag of sexual freedom. Still others, as we will see, were mentioned for reasons that might, at first glance, seem somewhat elusive. The San Francisco–based Mattachine Review reprinted what comes across as a subtly pro-gay review from the Los Angeles Times about an obviously pro-gay French farce, The Ostrich Has Two Eggs (Patelliére 1957), a film that showcases a bourgeois patriarch reacting buffoonishly to the realization that his eldest son is gay.[15] On the other side of the country, those on the mailing list of the New York Mattachine Newsletter were urged in two consecutive issues to see The Time of Desire (Holmsen 1954), an "explosive, daring homosexual film, beautifully photographed in Sweden," in which a central "lesbian love affair" survives, after a brief heterosexual dalliance on the part of one of the women, to constitute part of the narrative's sapphically "happy ending."[16] In fact, the second mention of this film was to promote its inclusion in the organization's Second Annual Film Festival, in the fall of 1960.[17] Sophisticated and undeniably queer in their plots and themes, both The Ostrich Has Two Eggs and The Time of Desire merit rediscovery and further critical attention.[18]

Among less centrally queer (though better remembered) films, the New York Mattachine Newsletter offered a full review of Louis Malle's new-wave comedy Zazie dans le metro (1960), discussing the American release prints' less than frankly subtitled dialogue regarding the sexuality of one of its main characters—the eponymous heroine's drag-queen uncle.[19] It also printed a lengthy paragraph on Club des Femmes (Jacques Deval, 1936), "an old French film seen in a New York revival" and featuring a melodramatic plot that "runs the gamut from unmarried motherhood to more or less repressed Lesbianism."[20] There was also a positive review of *The Confessions of Felix Krull* (Kurt Hoffmann, 1957), which goes out of its way to mention a "delicate proposition" offered to the young protagonist by an "aging Scottish nobleman" in "a touching scene a little reminiscent of the mood of [Thomas] Mann's *Death in Venice.*" Noting the sense of "dignity" with which the filmmakers handled that potentially risible homosexual proposal, the critic happily reports that throughout the greater part of the film, the handsome young lead (Horst Buchholz, rechristened, with somewhat diminished dignity, "Henry Bookholt" for his American debut) can be seen "in all sorts of wildly improbable but delightful situations and in various degrees of 'deshabille.'"[21] More telegraphically, readers of the Los Angeles–based *One* were alerted to "homo bits" found in the Jean Gabin underworld import *Razzia* (Henri Decoin, 1955), the excision of a minute of footage (presumably some of the noted gay content) from a television broadcast of Federico Fellini's *I Vitelloni* (1953), and Canada's outright banning of Ingmar Bergman's *Smiles of a Summer Night* (1955),[22] an essentially heterosexual film that might have been popular among lesbian filmgoers for, among other things, a curiously extended scene of Ulla Jacobsson and Harriet Andersson rolling around together playfully on top of a bed.[23]

At roughly the same time, the *Ladder*, a publication exclusively devoted to a lesbian readership, offered its readers an annotated list of films of potential interest; ten European productions (out of thirteen films mentioned) were described, including another Ingmar Bergman film, *Thirst*. In the following issue, letters to the editor identified five additional European films (out of eight new films mentioned) of potential queer interest.[24] Considering how central Hollywood cinema has been to the queer film-studies literature of the last thirty-five years, it may come as a shock to realize that in what Laurajean Ermayne introduced as "the first attempt to create a checklist of lesbian films," the United States produced what amounts to only 28.5 percent of the films included.[25] The United States does not even rank as the best-represented nation on the list: one film is credited to England, two each to Sweden and Italy, three to Germany, and six to the United States. At the top of the list, however, is France, with seven productions.[26]

One also finds an instance in which the homophile press condemned a European art film that would become a cult hit in post-Stonewall queer American culture, an example curiously counterbalanced by a film that, even though it later would be vilified from a queer perspective, was embraced by early critic-activists: *One's* Dal McIntire attacked

Fellini's *La Dolce Vita* (1960), which, in his view, presented homosexuality "in its most ludicrous, derisive aspect," while both the *Ladder*'s Robin Richards and the *New York Mattachine Newsletter*'s E. Bruce, defended Ingmar Bergman's *The Silence*, a film criticized as sexist and homophobic in post-Stonewall-era queer discourse.[27] Bruce argued that "the sexual daring here," including the "homosexual desire of the [film's] older for the younger sister" and a scene of "auto-eroticism," is not "sensationalism, but is necessary to the development of Bergman's theme."[28] One might argue that it is hardly surprising that the publications of pre-Stonewall-era homophile organizations would eschew the in-your-face camp of Fellini for the despairing drama of a pitiable Bergman lesbian, since, in recent years, the progressive natures of the Mattachine Society and the Daughters of Bilitis (the organization behind the *Ladder*) have been summarily challenged and their leaders and members dismissed as apologetic would-be assimilators: self-hating at worst and merely liberal at best. But a survey of their early publications strongly suggests that such a summation is largely overstated and based on generalizations that require reappraisal.

In his excellent study of Cold War–era male homosexuality, Robert Corber claims, for instance, that the Mattachine Society "discouraged gay men from engaging in camp and other controversial practices that reinforced negative stereotypes," while their newsletter repeatedly mentioned camp aesthetics, sometimes in disparaging ways, but at others in clearly approving ways.[29] For instance, one of the newsletter's writers promoted Andy Warhol's subversively campy *Tarzan and Jane Regained . . . Sort of* (1964),[30] while another wrote a thoughtful, albeit critical, article on appearances by the drag queen Mario Montez in the New York underground filmmaking of Andy Warhol, Jack Smith, and Bill Vehr.[31]

The two-page story about Montez is particularly interesting in that the writer, Peter Sereel (likely a pseudonym), begins by making an explicit comparison between the mid-1960s European art cinema and the concurrent New York–based queer underground: "Antonnioni [*sic*] has Monica Vitti; the French New Wave has Jeanne Morreau [*sic*], and it appears that the Underground Cinema of New York has its Galetea [*sic*] in . . . Mario Montez."[32] The comparison comes across as ironic once it becomes clear that Sereel does not much like Montez as a performer or appreciate the now-celebrated films in which she appeared (including Smith's *Normal Love* [1963] and Warhol's *Mario Banana* [1964].) Nevertheless, his critical voice is not assimilationist, nor is it reactionary. In fact, Sereel expresses admiration for drag performance styles more verisimilitudinous than Montez's—"that wonderful heavy eye-lidded (Dietrich-Garbo) tradition"[33]—and although he criticizes the work of Warhol, Smith, and Vehr, he does so by comparing them with a radical underground filmmaker he enthusiastically recommends, Kenneth Anger.[34] All told, even if much of the writing in these early periodicals shows distaste for the gleefully deconstructive nature of the Warhol-Smith-Vehr–Charles Ludlam strain of 1960s queer urban culture, it nonetheless exhibits a level of eclecticism and political sophistication that would be welcomed by all but the most radical queer readers today. More importantly, perhaps, it suggests the extensive overlapping of two never really discrete groups of queer urbanites: underground queers and art-house queers.

The *Ladder*'s review of Bergman's *The Silence* anticipates queer theory's validation of negative affects and emotions by contrasting the film's embrace of estrangement with its seeming rejection of the destructive intimacies of family structures, making a number of interesting assumptions in the process. Noting that "one of the main characters is a lesbian tormented by desire for her heterosexual sister," Richards concludes that although "the lesbian offers a rationale for her choice in sexuality, this film is not about lesbianism." Instead, she argues,

> *The Silence* explores several alternatives. On one hand we are shown acceptance of alienation when the heterosexual sister says in effect that it is so nice not to understand [the language of] her male lover. On the other hand we are shown the terrible love/hate that may come from understanding, as between the sisters.[35]

Concluding with a more positive assessment than those of most latter-day lesbian-gay-queer critics, who would accuse Bergman of presenting a homophobic vision of a tragically tormented and incestuously driven lesbian, Richards encourages feedback from her readers, inviting them to share "their impressions of . . . this beautiful and controversial film."[36] No letters were printed in subsequent issues, which, considering the *Ladder*'s willingness to engage in various internecine homophile controversies in its pages, suggests, at the very least, that the critic's positive reaction did not engender a firestorm of outrage.[37]

Two of the review's almost offhand assertions seem most remarkable half a century later. Startlingly, considering the gay-lesbian-queer movement's history of identity politics, in which one's minority status is the primary concern in every political or cultural endeavor, Richards refuses to interpret the film along gay-straight lines by, for instance, contrasting a biologically driven heterosexual woman with an intellectual, sexually "frigid" lesbian. Such a juxtaposition—one many critics find unavoidably central to the film—allows for both homophobic and queer claims to be made, using the film as evidence, but Richards shows no interest in pursuing either. Instead, she points to the heterosexual sister's "acceptance of alienation" as being, in fact, a potentially "nice" thing. In other words, Richards asks her queer readers to consider a heterosexual character's perspective in order to dialectically generate understanding for a queer tradition of embracing an erotics of estrangement or, as I would suggest, foreignness. Furthermore, she clearly rejects the value of the lesbian sister's incestuously motivated, but otherwise not so queer, commitment to remain ensconced within her biological family (clinging to her sister, helping raise her nephew) and, as she puts it, to suffer the inevitable "love/hate" that results.

The strategies of fluid, counterintuitive identifications exemplified by Richards's review have been defined and assessed in the years since Laura Mulvey's "Visual Pleasure and Narrative Cinema" first posited, in 1975, that mainstream motion pictures have created and offered only a male, essentially sadistic—and though she did not specifically say so, heterosexual—spectatorship position, one from which every filmgoer has been obliged to regard the cinema.[38] Considering the strong engagement many women and homosexual males have had with the cinema, it was hardly surprising that any development of Mulvey's ideas would have to account for, at the very least, against-the-grain readings of films ostensibly made with a very different spectator in mind. As Marilyn Johns Blackwell points out, feminist theorists such as B. Ruby Rich and Judith Mayne have, in the wake of Mulvey's initial analysis, accounted for a dialectical process inherent in female spectatorship, one suggesting "the possibility for the female spectator of a constructive engagement in the cinematic experience, a way of overcoming and even utilizing the androcentric structures of film in the development of feminist awareness."[39] For her part, Rich has posited a conception of the female spectator, borrowed from Bertolt Brecht's description of the exile, as the "ultimate dialectician." According to Rich, the dialectical practice of an exile, informed by the "tension of two different cultures," parallels the consciousness of a female occupying a male or masculine spectatorship position. Rich claimed that "for a woman today, film is a dialectical experience in a way that it never was and never will be for a man under patriarchy," a position laying the ground for the possibility that homosexual men might approach films dialectically as well.[40]

Dialectical processes are unarguably central to queer spectatorship. Indeed, one can say they are central to queer subjectivity. Surprisingly, however, this obvious point has, until recently, only sporadically or indirectly been addressed. In contemporary scholarship, Marcella Althaus-Reid has conceived of a sadomasochistically informed dialectic structured around the sexual top and bottom in her reading of Christianity's conception of God, Jesus, and "the world";[41] as a consequence, queerness emerges at the center of her thesis on religion's dialectical workings.[42] Both Henning Bech and Elisa Glick have developed productive models of queer subjectivity based on dialectical tensions between presence and absence and between the private self and the public self, among other possibilities.[43] Each of these three binaries (active-passive, presence-absence, private-public) are also involved in the dynamics of spectatorship, particularly queer spectatorship, and they all intersect with a binary fundamental to any film viewer's negotiation of the challenges of foreign-film spectatorship: dissimilarity and affinity.

The Other's Other: Finding Oneself Elsewhere

Raised in a heteronormative, homophobic society, twentieth-century American queers were as likely as anyone else to learn that the homosexual is, by definition, an exemplar of radical otherness, that is, foreignness. Many Cold War–era queers surely read Donald Webster Cory's pro-gay monograph *The Homosexual in America: A Subjective Approach*, first published in 1951 and advertized for purchase in the *New York Times* throughout the 1950s by a mail-order bookseller, the Union Library Association. Cory mentions that "it is a curiosity worth noting that in many lands the description of homosexuality has been associated with things foreign," telling his reader that the English word "buggery" is derived from "Bulgar," or someone from Bulgaria, and that in the nineteenth century, the French repeatedly referred to homosexuality as *"l'amour allemand"* ("German love"), just as English speakers have often called it "Greek love." He also points out that oral sex acts are named in English by the Latin borrowings "fellatio" and "cunnilingus" and have been sometimes called "French love," and that the word "turk" has functioned as a common slang term for a pederast.[44]

One need not have read Cory to be familiar with the oft-noted intersection of homosexuality and foreignness, which reflects a homophobically motivated process of disavowal. In fact, the association of homosexuality and foreignness offers nearly as many variations as there are descriptions of homosexuality itself. From the example of distant, now-lost Sodom to that of homosexuality's currently posited absence in the Iranian homeland (at least according to Mahmoud Ahmadinejad), punitively regarded homosexuality is righteously and rightfully (re)located elsewhere. In the homophobic imagination, it can be conceived of only as an invading, alien menace, a menace that encroaches upon straight and "moral" communities. Less regularly noted than these demonizing exteriorizations, though hardly unknown throughout Western history, however, has been a positive sense of a queer elsewhere imagined, both before and after the concretization of modern homosexual and heterosexual identities at the end of the nineteenth century, by queerly oriented individuals.

The relatively recent appropriation of the term "lesbian," originally referencing the people of the Mediterranean island of Lesbos, by female homosexuals may have been, in part, a counterdiscursive practice in which a pejoratively intended term, not unlike "sodomite," was embraced as a symbol of one's rightful home. Conversely, many other examples of positively regarded queer foreignness, such as the "Magical Land of Oz"—widely celebrated by mid-twentieth-century American homosexuals as their own imagined utopia—and the "Somewhere" used as a song title in Leonard Bernstein's *West Side Story*—widely appreciated as expressing oppressed homosexuals' yearning for a distant, *non*homophobic homeland—had no previous derisory articulation. One would be hard-pressed to quantify a queer tendency to identify with realms of foreign existence, but informal evidence and theoretically augmented explanations for the phenomenon are ubiquitous. Furthermore, this tendency's power is attested to in almost all areas of queer and GLBT studies. The literary critic Michael Lucey, for instance, positing a connection between queerness and the practice of tourism, has suggested that we "imagine trading the constant pressures of homophobia . . . for some new alienation."[45] That is just what Robin Richards had suggested in her review of *The Silence* in the *Ladder* more than thirty years before, when she virtually posited her own theory of "positive estrangement."

Cold War–era homosexuals had ways of spreading news across their communities about films of gay and lesbian interest other than through the homophile press, and there are indications that many art films that may not have been mentioned in *One* or the *Mattachine Review* nonetheless attracted sizable queer audiences through word of mouth or, in some cases, inferences drawn from mainstream advertisements that only queer spectators would have made. Having been the general manager of Berkeley's Cinema Guild repertory and art cinema from 1955 to 1960, the critic Pauline Kael was likely speaking with firsthand knowledge when she pointed out, in a retrospective review, that "although it doesn't have any overt homosexual content," the Italian drama *Amici per la pelle* (Franco Rossi, 1955) attracted an almost exclusively homosexual audience during its American release.[46]

The story of this particular film, focusing on the tender and finally painful friendship between two preteenage boys, builds, like the plots many European imports that attracted queer audiences in the United States, upon a delicate, inchoately understood desire inherent in the specter of foreignness. In a reductive summary, the *Washington Post* addressed this dynamic in terms compelling enough to have no doubt piqued a queer filmgoer's interest: "On the threshold of adulthood, Mario and Franco meet at . . . a private secondary-level school. Franco, being the son of an officer in the Italian foreign service, has the advantage of travel and greater wealth behind him, but Mario, coming from the home of an artist who runs a ceramics factory, is his equal."[47] Admittedly, complementary differences in same-sex friendships hardly ensure homoerotic tension. Indeed, they often function as assurances that *non-sexual* motives are behind enthusiastic homosocial bonds, bonds that can appear as a distinct counterpoint to the imagery of queer narcissistic desire found in many late nineteenth- and early twentieth-century artistic traditions. But in this instance, the juxtaposition of a somewhat effeminate boy who is marked by foreignness and a more masculine adolescent who is nonetheless defined according to a tradition of artistic endeavor puts two signifiers of midcentury queerness in direct, formative dialogue.

The American distributor Lopert Films first released *Amici per la pelle* in the United States as *The Woman in the Painting*, and they might well be accused of trying to discourage a gay male audience's attentions by eschewing an idiomatic translation of the Italian moniker—*amici per la pelle* translates as "friends of the skin," the equivalent of "best buddies" in English—for one that suggests female-centered gothic mysteries such as *Laura* (Otto Preminger, 1944). (Of course there is ample evidence that film noir, and in particular *Laura*, struck its own specific chord with gay men in the mid-twentieth century.)[48] Conversely, a faithfully translated title might have given potential ticket buyers the incorrect understanding that the film was made for, rather than about, children. Also countering the latter consideration, Lopert's publicity material seemed designed to raise expectations for a motion picture focusing on some aspect of a deviant nature, something angrily

Figure 1.2. Newspaper advertisement for *The Woman in the Painting* (Franco Rossi, Italy, 1955). Lopert Films. *Washington Post*, July 10, 1958.

disavowed by its American critical advocates.[49] The *Washington Post's* Leo Sullivan urged readers not to let "the title or the rather lurid ads mislead [them]," calling the Italian import "the nicest little film." After describing the story line as simply as possible, Sullivan confidently concludes with an appeal to the reader's agreeability: "As you see, it's a simple tale."[50] Subsequently, upon the film's belated New York debut, the *Times'* Howard Thompson referred to the tagline adorning the advertisements—"the story of a strange obsession!"—as "baloney," insisting with an almost reactionary fervor that the "boys share a happy, wholesome relationship" (figure 1.2).[51]

It was not unreasonable for critics to argue that the U.S. distributor's advertising misrepresented the film to a certain extent, or at least had the effect of threatening to scare away ticket buyers who might otherwise have been attracted to it, and perhaps this explains what Kael ultimately noted: the film's unfortunate inability to attract a wider audience. The "strange obsession" referenced in the ads is little more than one boy mourning the death of his mother, the titular (in the United States) "woman in the painting," and although this is a crucial element in the film, it hardly summarizes the story as a whole. Looked at today, however, the promotional materials hardly seem lurid or unwholesome. With its imagery of two nervous boys, an eerie old house, and an agitated middle-aged man standing beside a mysterious portrait, one might be led to expect not a Continental noir throwback, but rather, the Italian cinematic equivalent of the Hardy Boys mystery novels that were popular at the time. That, too, might well have disappointed some potential ticket buyers had they seen the film, but such an attempt to frame a straightforward drama as a more commercial film was, and remains, commonplace in the promotion of commercially released motion pictures. Something else may have rattled the critics' sense of propriety regarding a film focused on children, something that served to attract a homosexual audience at the same time. At the time of the film's release, the word "strange," as the film historian Jenni Olson has demonstrated, was often used in film promotion as a thinly disguised euphemism for queer, one that specifically emphasizes its association with all things foreign.[52]

Hetero-Narcissism; or, Homosexuality

While the homosexuality of celebrated American writers such as Walt Whitman, Herman Melville, Willa Cather, and Thornton Wilder has gradually been incorporated into most readers' understanding of their lives and work—with Whitman in particular, but also Melville, a homosexual sensibility is recognizable in the work itself—the heteronorms of the nation long kept those artists, and their legacies, from being framed according to any real, robust sense of queerness. On the other hand, while hardly themselves "openly gay," as one would use the term today, Marcel Proust, André Gide, Jean Genet, and Thomas Mann were fairly direct in their depictions of homosexual perspectives, and this was evident in English-language translations widely available to the post–World War II American reader. Inevitably, this marked those European artists, and many others, as ambassadors, welcome or not, from a decidedly decadent, palpably queer Europe.

David Gerstner has shown how, in a related dynamic, dominant aesthetic traditions were seen by many within the immigrant-fueled American working classes of the mid-1800s as reflecting European or, more specifically, British "imperialism and its effeminized cultural affect." As a result, American "artists and cultural pundits . . . were . . . eager to define the masculine characteristics of American arts and artists in terms of a masculine *national* sensibility."[53] Although by the end of the nineteenth century, "American male artists found themselves negotiating the angst of homosexuality as an artistic 'stereotype' and art itself as a 'feminine' activity," the belief that artistic effeminacy was non- or even anti-American surely remained a part of the cultural equation.[54] If, as Gerstner persuasively argues, the "masculine" "tradition of realism and democratic idealism guid[ed] nineteenth-century American arts toward a unique brand of national aesthetics," the U.S. cinema that emerged "during the twentieth century proved to be the ideal medium through which male artists embodied and projected. . . their narcissistic imaginary of masculinity and creativity." Gerstner concludes, "The cinema was thus *America's* art."[55] I would add to this only by suggesting that a profoundly *European* cinema, popular at a time when homosexuality was associated with a geographic elsewhere generally, and "decadent" Europe in particular, surely carried with it the earlier associations of European cultural effeminacy to which Gerstner referred and thus, in another way, carried with it associations of queerness.

One could sidestep the perhaps simplistic argument positing an intrinsically perverse Continental tradition that called out to the repressed queers of a very different, puritanical nation, and focus instead on the minor American tradition of nineteenth-century homoerotic narratives, which confirms a strong New World tendency to locate homosexual desire within heteromorphic, cross-racial, cross-cultural, or transnational same-sex couples. Discussing how Melville's formative experiences at sea informed his homoerotically resonant novels *Typee*, *Billy Budd*, and *Moby-Dick*, Robert Martin writes, "For 19th century homosexuals, in search of both justification for themselves and a possible realization of their desires, the journey to an exotic landscape offered the possibility of locating a place where there might be others like them."[56] The sought-after foreign men may have been like them (also homosexually active), but also, crucially, not like them: different in language, race, culture, even in their understandings of masculinity and femininity, sex, love and friendship. In effect, Melville's foreign experiences (like those of the world-traveling Gide and Genet) were reimagined and recounted back home for a reader who, for complex and inchoate reasons, found it "necessary to locate the desired partner of the same sex in a distant, exotic setting."[57]

Obviously, not all forms of homosexual desire are contingent upon couplings marked by various forms of alterity. Were that the case, one of the assumptions Michael Warner summarily debunks in his 1990 essay "Homo-Narcissism; or, Heterosexuality"—specifically, that same-sex desire can be explained as a form of narcissism—would have seemed even less plausible than it currently does.[58] But one does not have to believe sexuality to be a dialectical practice attempting to resolve narcissism with the self-transcending lure of an other-directed empathetic desire in order to understand how hetero-erotic forms of homosexuality have earned their appeal. To be sure, there is an undeniably problematic presence of Orientalism within Western homosexual subcultures (as there is in dominant heteronormative Western imaginaries), and yet the ways in which cross-racial and cross-cultural (and by extension, cross-generational and cross-class) eroticism functions in a homosexual dynamic can be argued to involve a simpler, and perhaps potentially less problematic, dialectical relationship than the comparable heterosexual paradigm. In the heterosexual case, a doubly othered partner is involved; a sexual object choice is made that is twice removed from the sense of humanity accorded a "fellow being," to cite the term Simone de Beauvoir famously used to define how Western men have regarded only each other in *The Second Sex*.[59] A same-sex other, for its part, presents a fundamental sense of difference, but also a fundamental form of simultaneity, one that signifies both a shared identity and the acknowledgment of a deeply ingrained foreignness within the self.

With this in mind, one sees how the inchoately queer American subject of the mid-twentieth century corresponds to the foreigner discussed by Julia Kristeva in *Strangers to Ourselves* (and to a lesser extent in *Na-*

tions without Nationalism). Responding to increasing tensions between immigrant and native populations in Europe, particularly in France, in the late twentieth century, Kristeva has exposed and articulated daunting social challenges with impressive critical and theoretical rigor. Arguing that the cultural expressions of militant nationalism and militant ethnicity have emerged as much from intrapsychic as interpsychic dynamics, Kristeva summarizes a central problem: "Living with the other, with the foreigner, confronts us with the possibility or not of *being an other*."[60] Interestingly, the phrase "being an other" is emphasized in the original text, even though the hatred of the other her passage explains suggests that it is "the possibility or not"—the social stakes involved in either being or not being thought of as an other—that encourages political strife and physical violence. Ultimately, however, Kristeva is less concerned with identifying the causes of social outcomes than with proposing radical possibilities inherent in internal psychic contradictions. Speaking of a foreign national's resistance to the "symbolic and legal [forces] holding [him or her] back," Kristeva claims, "In that sense, the foreigner is a 'symptom': psychologically he signifies the difficulty we have of living as an *other* and with others."[61] One might add that the foreigner, along with associated emblems of foreignness, also offers an opportunity to address that very difficulty. By implication, foreignness can be seen as a concept that has significant valence for working out a fundamental otherness inherent within queer subjectivity, within the queer self.

Softer Lighting, More Affection: The Men of the European Art Cinema

A positively conceived connection between foreignness and queerness was surely understood by an anonymous editor of the *New York Mattachine Newsletter* when he or she cited Edith Oliver's *New Yorker* review of Andrey Tarkovsky's *Ivan's Childhood* (1962) upon its 1963 American release under the title *My Name Is Ivan*. Although it is not exactly clear what Oliver meant to denote when she applauded the "open affection among the men" in a Soviet film focused on a World War II reconnaissance patrol, the fact she specifically aligned the presentation of multiple instances of unmistakable, gentle male physical affection with a radical elsewhere, calling it "foreign and refreshing," seemed apt enough to the Mattachine Society's newsletter editor.[62]

While few combat-zone films carry the kind of homoerotic charge that might appeal to members of a homophile interest group, the sexually segregated settings involved offer obvious opportunities for emerging queer energies, and the ways in which those settings can articulate or evoke such energies are both more and less obvious than anticipated. To connect those energies with the queer lure of foreignness previously adumbrated, recall that the military environments in which such films take place regularly function as ideal settings for specifically cross-cultural same-sex intimacies. World Wars I and II brought together citizens of many nations as allies and, in more dramatic and deadly scenarios, as face-to-face (or body-to-body) adversaries. Although Soviet soldiers, to return to Tarkovsky's film, would have been unlikely to encounter their British or American peers until very late in the war, one must remember that the Red Army brought together people from a variety of lands and cultures—Russia, Ukraine, Belarus, and Central Asia among them. *Ivan's Childhood* emphasizes foreign relationalities in an exchange between two characters, one from Siberia and the other from the environs of Moscow, who discuss the differences between their homelands in dialogue redolent of both shy curiosity and enthusiastic interest. In counterpoint, a female officer responds to a flirtatious male compatriot from her own hometown as little more than an annoyance.

The Mattachine Society's newsletter cannily identified the queer pleasures of Tarkovsky's film, and one would be hard pressed to find an American military-themed film set during war or peacetime, produced before or after *Ivan's Childhood*, even those explicitly addressing homosexuality in the military, offering quite the sustained charge of erotic frisson to the Western viewer as its Soviet cousin.[63] Indeed, Tarkovsky's film continues to offer palpable homoerotic pleasures for the receptive spectator a full half century after its debut. Watching *Ivan's Childhood* in the twenty-first century, one is reminded of a more recent Russian film, *Father and Son* (2003), and the controversy that greeted it after its premiere at the Cannes Film Festival. At a postscreening press conference, its director, Aleksandr Sokurov, was reportedly so "outraged by questions regarding the movie's blatant homoeroticism" that he responded with an "angry lecture on the [sexual] preoccupations of the decadent west."[64] Tarkovsky, one imagines, would have reacted similarly, even as *Ivan's Childhood* seems nearly as "wildly eroticized" as those "western critics" found *Father and Son* to be.[65] It is perhaps no accident that the Sokurov and Tarkovsky films both focus on communities of military men: *Father and Son*'s protagonists are a retired soldier and his cadet offspring, while *Ivan*'s three central characters are a twelve-year-old male orphan (Nikolay Burlyaev) working as a reconnaissance scout and the two officers who come together with him to become something of an unofficial family.

Crucial to both films' homoerotic sensibility is the fact that they are noncombat films (the former is part of a cycle of Soviet films often referred to as "quiet war films") with relatively passive, though physically affectionate, military men center screen. But in no small part, the two films' sexual allure also results from the ways in which the male actors are lit and photographed, reinforcing a sense of passivity, at least to an American spectator, which is in strong contradistinction to the ways men were typically lit and photographed in the classical Hollywood cinema. In John Alton's 1949 book on the craft, the eminent studio cinematographer described how the process operated in American commercial cinema with blunt efficiency: "In the illumination of a close-up there are two main groups, feminine and masculine. . . . While in feminine close-ups we strive for beauty, in masculine pictures it is the character of the individual that we accentuate."[66] In a subsequent chapter on the importance of lighting for the "feminine" face, Alton coins the term "beautilluminate" to describe the nonutilitarian role that lighting should play throughout a woman's life, whether she is in front of a camera or not.[67]

Beginning with American motion pictures of the 1920s, 1930s, and 1940s, the image of women was concretized by using the rich, eroticizing chiaroscuro patterns that the artists Rembrandt and Caravaggio had conceived for their subjects centuries before, while male protagonists increasingly became more functionally illuminated through what cinematographers refer to as "flat," or high-key, lighting. Although Laura Mulvey barely mentions lighting as a factor in her formative essay on the objectification of women in mainstream film, she does helpfully suggest that opposing visual strategies have been used to express an "active/passive heterosexual division of labor"; Hollywood's "active male figure," she posited, has been underscored by "deep focus cinematography," while the "woman as object," as exemplified in the cinema of Josef von Sternberg, is an effect of the exact opposite approach: a one-dimensional "play[ing] down [of] the illusion of screen depth."[68]

It is virtually de rigueur, in any fair-minded citation of "Visual Pleasure and Narrative Cinema," to point out that Mulvey added nuance and qualifiers to her sweeping claims in a follow-up essay, "Afterthoughts on 'Visual Pleasure and Narrative Cinema' Inspired by *Duel in the Sun*," and countless other scholars have found exceptions to her thesis, when not arguing explicitly against it. Furthermore, adept queer audiences and film historians have been repeatedly delighted to see the pattern Mulvey initially identified broken (or ignored) by gay classical-era Hollywood filmmakers like James Whale, whose male lead in *Waterloo Bridge* (1931) is lit for the camera as though he were the passively incandescent sex goddess paired opposite a much more dowdily presented Mae Clarke.[69] Additionally, male performers in precode Hollywood sound films (1928–1934) were regularly accorded a sensual sheen evocative of softness, delicacy, and passivity that would be focused almost exclusively on women by the mid-1930s. The masculine version of this sheen, visible on a solitary male figure or in the strongest of heterosexual couplings, was read as homoerotic by many queer spectators.

The silent American cinema was informed by a number of widely popular, elegantly objectified men, many of whom were gay or bisexual, or were rumored to be—Rudolph Valentino, Ramon Novarro, Ivor Novello, William Haines. Richard Maltby suggests that the addition of synchronized sound to classical Hollywood filmmaking compelled the eventual change from sensual sheen to flat lighting for male leads: "The passionate melodramatic male sexuality of Rudolph Valentino and John Gilbert proved vulnerable to the dictates of a sound cinema intolerant of its feminization of the male as erotic object."[70] Although Maltby does not posit a reason why, exactly, sound cinema would have been "intolerant" of a "feminine" male sexuality, one might imagine that the added realism provided by a full diegetic soundscape simply amplified the threat of homosexuality that attended such feminized male imagery, imagery that in its silent-film manifestation managed to present itself somewhat more comfortably, and alluringly, in an exotic silence. (Perhaps the vaguer gender coding of early Hollywood cinematography simply solidified into the crude form that we see on the screen today.) Still, the early sound era offered some fleeting yet indelible images of male pulchritude within Hollywood productions: John Darrow in *Hell's Angels* (1930), Philip Reed in *Female* (1933), James Murray in *Baby Face* (1933), and Buster Crabbe in *Search for Beauty* (1934), among others. Maltby, pointing out that such practices of eroticization were obvious, and finally unsettling, even to the general film-going public at the time, quotes an assertion from a 1932 fan magazine: "The feminine public is wearying of rather pretty and too polished young men."[71] It can hardly be a coincidence that the practice began to change the following year. The excision of Murray's transfixing encounter with Barbara Stanwyck before *Baby Face's* commercial exhibition in mid-1933 and the shelving of *Search for Beauty* after an abortive release in early 1934, not to mention the wild popularity of the very macho, very unpolished Clark Gable (which Maltby discusses), portended the end of that era of unacknowledged homoeroticism in mainstream American cinema, one that has never really been repeated. But the tradition of gender-blind cinematographic eroticization, arguably less sexually connotative in the minds of the art-cinema directors who have presided over it, has continued in the European productions of art-film auteurs who have considered themselves heirs to the late Renaissance Italian and Dutch masters of oil and canvas.

Tarkovsky, for his part, regularly used the historical legacy of the European visual arts—his best-known film, *Andrei Rublev* (1966), is an unconventional biography of the celebrated fourteenth-century icon painter—to rich and varied emotional effect throughout his career. His work repeatedly invokes the absent presence of mimetic representation in ways that, depending on one's perspective, strongly evoke spirituality or erotic longing. In almost every interior nighttime scene in *Ivan's Childhood* (and the film has many), the male body is accentuated with perfectly positioned back lighting. Used most practically to create a sense of three-dimensionality by effectively separating a figure from its background, a strategically calibrated backlight can also create a "halo effect" atop a character's head, which is generally thought to convey a sense of erotic enticement when seen in mainstream film. In applying it across a greater part of the human form, classical Hollywood cinema regularly used it to outline the female form with a border of empyrean radiance. In classical painting, however, such liminal illumination has long been employed as a signifier of spiritual interiority, one shining through as a luminous second skin, and European filmmakers exploring Christian subjectivity through the rhetoric of classical art (such as Tarkovsky and Sokurov) would be as likely to illuminate men (and boys) as women in such a way. Indeed, to the extent that male filmmakers reflect a longstanding sense of Judeo-Christian androcentrism, their male characters are actually more likely than their female ones to be granted a sense of spiritual interiority. Perhaps not surprisingly, the only woman in Tarkovsky's war film to be accorded such illumination is the Madonna-like figure of Ivan's dead mother, seen in dreams and flashbacks.

Explicitly evoking the visual arts at the level of narrative, *Ivan* features a scene of quiet import in which the young orphan studies a confiscated German book illustrated with Dürer engravings from the fifteenth and sixteenth century. From across the haunting expanse of time and place, the images allow Ivan to see his mortal enemies, at least in the instance of an engraving of a benign-looking "German doctor, or writer," as fellow human beings. (Ivan initially scoffs at the idea that Albrecht Dürer's German could be a man of letters. "They have no writers," he says. "I saw them burning books on the square." After he is told the "writer lived about 400 years ago," Ivan reconsiders. "Well, then maybe.") The doubled sense of geographic-political and temporal foreignness here, ironically allowing a heretofore-proscribed identification and even a sanctioned form of attraction, is a constant in a film in which every instance of palpable erotic desire is underscored by multiple estrangements. The most potentially risible examples, of course, are those between the two adult officers, Captain Kholin (Valentin Zubkov) and Lieutenant Galtsev (Yevgeni Zharikov), played by actors who were thirty-eight and twenty, respectively, at the time of the film's production, and the twelve-year-old Ivan.[72] But here too, generational expanses both heighten and excuse otherwise unauthorized attractions.

Ambiguous Narratives, Forthright Readings: Reading for Maximum Queerness

Although criticized by some members of the film-theory community for its lack of any ideological critique, David Bordwell's *Narration in the Fiction Film* contains a chapter on the art cinema that offers a helpful paradigm for a political reading of what its author defines as "art-cinema narration." Indeed, intentionally or not (and likely not), a queer, or at least tantalizingly ambiguous, resonance tellingly recurs as Bordwell catalogues a rich list of art-cinema characteristics. Bordwell posits that in the art film, "personal psychology may be indeterminate" and that "the art-film protagonist is presented as sliding passively from one situation to another."[73] He argues that "'inquiry into character' becomes not only the prime thematic material but a central source of expectation, curiosity, suspense and surprise" and that in many paradigmatic examples of the movement (Fellini's *La Strada* [1954], Agnes Varda's *Cleo from 5 to 7* [1962], and Bergman's *The Silence*), "scenes are built around chance encounters, and the entire film may consist of nothing more than a series of them, linked by a trip . . . or aimless wanderings."[74] Such attributes cannot help suggesting, for the post–World War II queer spectator, a historically specific sense of queer relationality—the habits of disaffected homosexuals searching for their lost reflections, the closeted queers' search for their equally guarded kindred spirits, the drawn-out experience of cruising urban landscapes for fellow travelers.

In utilizing a neoformalist approach to narrative—putting narrative assumptions and inferences (as constructed in a perceiver's mind) in relation to plot and style—Bordwell puts his finger on the primary way by which art-cinema characteristics can be understood as reflecting queer subjectivity, even if he does not identify it as such: by way of ambiguity. In discussing the art cinema's habit of encouraging connotative interpretation through narrative ambiguity, Bordwell himself offers some richly connotative prose.

> Art-film narration solicits not only denotative comprehension but connotative reading, a higher-level interpretation. . . . Uncertainties persist but are understood as such, as *obvious* uncertainties. Put crudely, the procedural slogan of art-cinema narration might be: "Interpret this film, and interpret it so as to maximize ambiguity." . . .
>
> As I have described it, art-cinema narration might seem to encourage what Veronica Forrest-Thomson calls "bad naturalization." She observes of Wallace Stevens, "His obscurity is a kind of coyness, an attempt to stay one step ahead of the reader and so gain a reputation for daring while ensuring that the reader knows exactly where the poet is and how he can take that one step to reach him."[75]

By favoring connotation-based interpretation as a "higher-level" form of understanding while also exalting ambiguity over certainty, the conditions of the art-film as elucidated by Bordwell very nearly reflect a pre-Stonewall ethic of queer subjectivity. Veronica Forrest-Thomson's phrase "bad naturalization," along with her insinuating description of Wallace Stevens exhibiting "coyness" in the way he leads the reader to "take that one step to reach him," allies the practices of modernist narrative ambiguity with the category of (homosexual) seductiveness. Bordwell would undoubtedly protest such a reductive reading (and it would be a problem if posited as the only reading), but I suspect he would agree that when one has the freedom to freely interpret more or less ambiguous narratives, one tends to interpret them in ways that serve one's own desires. To understand all this is to further understand just how a film like *Ivan's Childhood* can be read either as a film about father, brother, and son figures finding one another in the theater of war—it certainly wouldn't be the first or the last of that type—or, just as easily, as a film about queer subjectivity and homosexual desire, or perhaps better still, as both.

Supporting the first possibility, Mark Le Fanu interprets the film according to the logic of heteronormativity: "The special bond which grows up between the two adults and the child [in this film]. . . . [is a] parental bond."[76] And yet, perhaps distressfully sensing the same-sex coupling this implies, he is quick to add that the bond is "some-what modified, in that there is already such a relationship between the captain (a handsome, strong, not particularly 'educated' man) and the lieutenant, about eight years his junior."[77] Setting aside for a moment the fact that the actors who played the adult roles were eighteen, not eight, years apart in age (and, to my eyes, look it), one still wonders why Le Fanu does not consider the twenty-year-old lieutenant to be an older-brother, rather than parental, figure for a boy who is obviously less than ten years his junior. I wouldn't want to make any claims about Le Fanu's conscious or unconscious attitudes, but I do think it fair to point out that his assessment of the dynamic between these characters, as well as of that between the two adult males and the young female doctor courted by both, is more than a little convoluted.[78] Describing the three males, he writes: "The face of the captain is handsome and thoughtful, while the features of the boy . . . are girlish and refined; those of the lieutenant, though older, are scarcely less so." Immedi-ately thereafter, he boldly states that a "curious quasi-sexuality exists in the encounters and parings of the three principals," but less than two lines later, citing a concurrent sense of "delicacy" in the men's behav-ior toward each other, and, more understandably, in the film's three fe-male characters (Ivan's mother and his childhood playmate—seen in flashbacks and dream sequences—and the doctor), Le Fanu asserts that the males' "relationship is plainly *not* 'homoerotic.'"[79] Not wanting to belabor shortcomings in a good film scholar's fine work, I simply as-sume that Le Fanu's definition of "homoerotic" is different from mine (and likely that of most queer spectators of the Cold War era). Teasing out the implications of this discrepancy, however, allows one to see the logic behind the appeal of a foreign component in queer desire.

If the desire between the film's males is mediated by differences in age or gender characteristics (an older masculine man attracted to younger, feminine males: one barely a man, the other barely ap-proaching puberty), then the ancient logic behind pederasty, in which males who have not yet achieved the status of citizen can, with soci-ety's approval, be penetrated by older men, justifies comfortingly near-subliminal same-sex attractions.[80] From this perspective, it can be ar-gued that the energies circulating between the three protagonists in *Ivan's Childhood* are tantalizingly "quasi-sexual" but not unacceptably "homoerotic." With this in mind, Le Fanu's claim that "the scene in which [the female doctor] appears has the sort of gratuitous unexpectedness—the possibility of going 'either way'—that one associates with such adventures" can be acknowledged. To put it more clearly, the improbably young doctor (Le Fanu calls her a doctor, but English subtitles on various editions of the film refer to her as either a "nurse" or a "medical assistant") represents the heterosexual choice the men in such fictions may or may not make. Remarkably enough, Le Fanu later seems to suggest that Captain Kholin or Lieutenant Galtsev might well choose to marry the doctor based on "the need, on the part of whoever is doing the adopting, for a wife, or at least a nurturing feminine presence."[81] In other words, one of the men might want to marry the woman only as a way to justify adopting Ivan. This suggests the logic of Vladimir Nabokov's Humbert Humbert in *Lolita*, who marries the mother of the twelve-year-old girl he desires sexually as the most efficient way to get close to her. As Le Fanu can hardly say directly, the happiest possible ending for this film, the one that every glance and erotically lit male face and body call out for, would involve the two men raising Ivan together, the trio then living in an ecstatic, Oedipally charged all-male family.

Such queer readings can hardly be called counterreadings, or readings against the grain, considering the maximal ambiguity born of narrative structures that Bordwell has identified in the art-film tradition. The fact that there are more than enough examples of unambiguous same-sex desire, as well as real, undeniable homosexual characters emerging in these films, positively presented or negatively represented, simply gives the queer spectator more justification for interpreting the art cinema's predictably ambiguous characters queerly; their cryptic statements and their puzzling, indefinite behavior can be read in satisfyingly self-affirming ways. Once such a process begins, even less ambiguous, cryptic, or puzzling content loses its code-era-Hollywood innocence. In a different context, Lee Edelman's observations regarding the signification of homosexuality through writing seem apt. If homosexuality has been signified through writing, then "every sexual signifier" is potentially permeable by "an 'alien' signification"; in other words, "once sexuality may be read and interpreted in light of homosexuality, all sexuality is subject to a hermeneutics of suspicion."[82]

This approach authorizes the reading of *La Strada* enjoyed by a group of lesbian spectators who saw the film with me several years ago at a theatrical revival. They were convinced that sapphic desire motivated the benevolent young nun who tries to convince Gelsomina to leave her abusive heterosexual relationship with Zumpanò and live at the nunnery under the sisters' protection. In fact, their interpretation was as sharply observed as it was inevitable. So too is the perspective that allows one to see not just Sergio as (obviously) gay in Fellini's earlier film *I Vitelloni*, but (at least arguably) the moral center, young Moraldo, as potentially homosexual as well. Perhaps even the young boy at the railway station who clearly "idolizes" Moraldo and runs after the train taking him away to Rome at the end of that film is acting on queer impulses. I venture to posit that such an interpretation would be particularly likely for an American spectator informed by the specter of art-cinema licentiousness, and let us not forget that *I Vitelloni* first appeared in the United States under the title *The Young and the Passionate*. According to the straight spectator, such a friendship expresses only the "innocent" brotherly concerns of a strictly platonic homosocial bond.

Much the same has been said about the bond between the eponymous characters in François Truffaut's new-wave blockbuster *Jules and Jim* (1962), but almost any queer male spectator who sees the film can easily interpret their shared love for Catherine as little more than a complicated transference of their same-sex passion for each other. In this reading, by killing Jim when she kills herself, Catherine can be said to be vindictively (and not without reason) depriving Jules of the one he loves: not herself, the person most filmgoers have assumed, but Jim. A queer spectator knows this, and knows as well that there is much more to see in these films than generations of myopic straight filmgoers and critics have been able to see.

With this understood, the films of Ingmar Bergman, who has been considered by many to be as profoundly heterosexual a filmmaker as one could imagine, can begin to seem somewhat less so. And as framed in the Cold War era, according to a particularly suspicion-laden view of deviant Sweden, Bergman seems less straight still. The queerness of Bergman's work manifested itself in subtle ways at the very beginning of his film career, as we shall see in the next chapter, but although it has escaped notice thus far, it appeared much more boldly and clearly in the United States somewhat later: not with the appearance of *The Silence* in the mid-1960s, as one might assume, but in 1958, the year that Bergman's name began its ascent to the top of the American film-culture scene with the U.S. premiere of *The Seventh Seal* at the Paris theater in Manhattan. I contend that one would have to look pretty hard at that particular film to find any overt queer content, which is not to say that a queer spectator would not understand the film queerly, but *The Seventh Seal* was hardly the only Bergman film haunting U.S. theaters that year.

Strange Thirsts

Elsewhere I have discussed the use of the word "strange" in the original American promotional materials for a number of Bergman films of the 1950s—including *Summer Interlude* (1951; aka *Illicit Interlude*) and *Monika* (1953, aka *Summer with Monika*)—to describe nonqueer relationships in those ostensibly heterosexually focused films, citing Jenni Olson's work in order to posit an overlapping sense of Swedishness and strangeness-queerness and, by extension, foreignness and strangeness-queerness in Cold War–era U.S. culture.[83] In one exemplary instance, however, the word was actually incorporated into the U.S. title of a Bergman film, in what may have been an attempt to capitalize on an unambiguously lesbian subplot. Praised by Thomas Elsaesser as the first noteworthy film in the director's oeuvre and as a "breakthrough" for the filmmaker by the Bergman scholar Marc Gervais, the director's 1949 feature *Thirst*—*Törst* in the original Swedish—is generally thought to be one of many early Bergman films to have appeared in the United States only after the Swedish auteur's international success had been secured with the back-to-back releases of *The Seventh Seal* and *Wild Strawberries* at the end of the 1950s.[84] Birgitta Steene, in her exhaustive reference guide to the director, mistakenly lists *Törst's* American premiere as having taken place as late as July 11, 1961, crediting Janus Films (which would end up with the U.S. rights to almost all of Bergman's pre-1960 titles) as its only U.S. distributor.[85] In fact, the film appeared in Washington, D.C., in mid-1956 under the imprimatur of "Helene and Arthur Davis"; bearing the title *Thirst*, an accurate English-language equivalent of the Swedish original, it was advertised as "a great new Swedish hit by the maker of *Monika* and *Illicit Interlude*"—two Bergman films whose American releases had been due, in no small part, to their (heterosexual) erotic frankness. The ads for *Thirst* published in the *Washington Post* upon its initial release, much like the other Bergman promotions found in newspapers at the time, foregrounds a heterosexual form of desire aimed to capture a wide, heterosexual audience. It features a clothed woman lying on her back under the quotation "I thirst for love . . . I am so lonely for a man's touch," with other provocative statements peppering the layout for good measure: "In a moment of thirst . . . all of their morals, their passions, their loves, their desires . . . bared!," "The film that dares to express the secrets of a woman's love-stared soul!," and "Share the intimate details of their private lives!"[86]

Although the film played in the Washington area for more than three weeks, wider circulation by its initial distributor did not follow.[87] Two years later, however, on March 9, 1958, Boston newspapers announced *Törst's* "American premiere" at the Brattle Theatre in Cambridge, Massachusetts, under what would remain its English-language title for almost fifty years: *Three Strange Loves*.[88] As when it had been promoted previously as *Thirst*, advertisements mentioned the film's rapidly ascending director, who had added another international hit to his credit in the interim: "From one of Europe's great directors . . . Ingmar Bergman (*Torment, Smiles of a Summer Night*)."[89] At this point, with its revised moniker presumably chosen by someone at Janus Films— *Törst's* succeeding and final U.S. distributor—the lesbian subplot was identifiable within its titular concerns, and it was precisely within this newly queered framework that the film traveled much more successfully to U.S. art-cinema markets. It appeared in Los Angeles that October (the month *The Seventh Seal* was premiering in New York); had its own New York debut the following year, on March 18, 1959; and secured an engagement in Baltimore a few months later, where it was promoted with the provocative, perversely resonant, tagline: "Two of these loves you will recognize, *the third you won't forget*."[90]

Reflecting the marketing logic behind the title change, the description of the film that was printed in the *Ladder*, which was itself reprinted from "the program of the Coronet Theatre in Hollywood," reads: "The story of 3 women and their strange love lives. One is an adulteress, the second has lesbian tendencies, and the third is love-starved."[91] In fact, Los Angeles moviegoers did not have to be *Ladder* subscribers or regular Coronet patrons in order to be alerted to the lesbian content. It was unmistakably acknowledged in an advertisement that appeared in the *Los Angeles Times*. In it, the third of three thumbnail images shows one of the film's lesbian characters—there are at least two—looking intently at an attractive though distraught woman sitting across from her. Below, a caption reads: "I've found a way to love independent of any man."[92] Although foreign-film distributors did have a habit of overstating their films' salaciousness, in this case the ads were reflecting a film that did test American culture's limits of acceptability. The *Chicago Daily Tribune* reported that "*Three Strange Loves*" was "rejected for showing in Chicago" by the "police censor board"[93] in 1959. With all this in mind, Steene's statements that "the film's depiction of a lesbian relationship . . . was cut by the [Swedish] censors" and that "*Törst* had limited circulation abroad"[94] are quite likely inaccurate as well as potentially misleading for how they characterize the film's fortunes in 1950s U.S. markets: it played widely, in art-film terms, in the United States, and at least some of its lesbian content was not only present but also, in some markets, highlighted.[95] Furthermore, it should be noted that its successful national release occurred only after the word "strange," with all the foreignness and queerness that term suggests, had been incorporated into its second English-language title.

It should also be noted that like *The Silence* a few years later, *Törst* incorporates homosexuality into a film about characters traveling through what are, for them, foreign countries. But if the later, much better-known film can, in one way, seem more centrally focused on queer issues than its predecessor—only one of whose three primary characters is a lesbian—it can also seem to offer less queer interest in another regard; *The Silence*'s overriding theme, most would agree, specifically concerns itself with communication. In the earlier film, on the other hand, only a couple of minor characters manifest unambiguous homosexual desire, and yet, as suggested by both of its English-language titles, desire itself is *Törst*'s primary focus. Furthermore, as its second English-language title would have it, homosexual desire is one of but three forms of desire the spectator is asked to consider, and to consider in active, analytical comparison with the other two. A Janus Films catalogue description identifies the title's tripartite concerns: "There is an hysterical young wife unable to bear children, a disturbed widow in the hands of a cruel psychiatrist, and a lesbian dancer who sets her sights on the widow."[96] Spectators can actually identify at least four significant instances of love manifested in vexed, yet not always strange, ways—hardly a surprise, since the film was adapted from four short stories published as part of an anthology by the Swedish author Birgit Tengroth.[97] Considering the complex web of interrelationships within and across each of the stories, several additional, though minor, "strange loves" can be identified as well.

Much as the distributor's catalogue would eventually put it, the realized screenplay contrasts the tumultuous marriage of a "hysterical" wife, Rut (Eva Henning), and her long-suffering husband, Bertil (Birger Malmsten), who are returning to Sweden from a vacation in Italy by train, with the erotic entanglements of a "disturbed" Stockholm widow, Viola (Birgit Tengroth herself.) For her part, Viola finds herself fighting off unwelcome advances from both her (male) psychiatrist (Hasse Ekman) and a former (female) schoolmate, Valborg (Mimi Nelson), whom she meets on the street on the same fateful midsummer's eve that the bickering Rut and Bertil spend returning to Scandinavia from the south. In the film's complex narrative structure, Viola is linked to Bertil through an earlier affair, as well as to Rut, indirectly through both Bertil and Valborg. Valborg, in addition to having been Viola's former classmate, was also a friend of Rut's from the days when Rut and Valborg attended ballet school together.

Most people who recall *Törst* because of its lesbian content remember the fairly startling scene late in the film in which Valborg attempts to seduce Viola on midsummer's night. But there is another equally remarkable series of scenes suggesting sapphic desire, inserted as a flashback somewhat earlier in the film, involving Valborg and Rut and their erotically informed time together in ballet school. In it, Valborg—seemingly the school's most promising dancer—uses her clout to try to protect the less accomplished Rut from the nearly abusive criticisms of the ballet teacher (Naima Wifstrand)—a woman who is herself strongly coded as lesbian, in her attire and manner as well as by the fact that, although about sixty, she is referred to in the dialog as *Miss* Henriksson.

The acting in the dance-school sequence is particularly strong and impressively subtle, with Wifstrand wordlessly conveying something like jealousy over Valborg's obvious strong attractions to Rut. For her part, as Rut, Eva Henning suggests that she might not be completely closed off to the sexual and romantic possibilities made palpable by Valborg's interest in her. In her voice-over narration, Rut wistfully tells herself: "We had no time for love. Play with it, brush up against it, but don't count on it," and as one never sees her so much as flirting with a man, one can surmise that the love she "played with" as a dance student may well have been homosexual in nature. Finally, despite a couple of unfortunate moments at the end of her seduction scene with Viola late in the film, in which Valborg comes across as something close to Dracula's daughter—in shots that, theoretically, could be considered to be Viola's homophobic point of view—the young lesbian seems, to my queer eyes anyway, one of the most sympathetic and level-headed characters in the film. This is certainly the case in the flashback sequence representing Rut's nostalgic memories of her pre-heterosexualized youth.[98] In a single, remarkable shot, however, in which the faces of Rut and Valborg are reflected out to themselves (and the spectator) via a small dressing-room mirror while the older, ominous visage of Miss Henriksson is framed (and isolated) in a second mirror to its right, a decision is made that arguably leads to lifetimes of frustrated desire for both of the young women (figure 1.3).

A lesser actor might well have played Miss Henriksson as a stereotypically "bitter old dyke," one who lecherously grabs the ankles and thighs of the aspiring ballerinas in the studio (ostensibly in the service of teaching them form), and is now voraciously chain-smoking and drink-

Figure 1.3. A moment of truth in *Thirst/Three Strange Loves* (Ingmar Bergman, Sweden, 1949). Svensk Filmindustri.

Figure 1.4. Valborg fears for her future in *Thirst/Three Strange Loves*. Svensk Filmindustri.

ing in the dressing room while (arguably) endeavoring to disrupt Rut and Valborg's growing friendship through insinuation and out of simple spite. But Wifstrand—equally impressive in Bergman's later *Smiles of a Summer Night*, *Wild Strawberries*, *The Magician*, and *Hour of the Wolf*—deftly inspires both apprehension and sympathy as her character teeters between acrimony and sentimental resignation. Implying that Valborg's interest in Rut is sexual in nature, Henriksson looks at both herself and Valborg reflected in the mirrors and quietly remarks: "I see what fate lies in store for you, my dear. It's there in your eyes, as a promise. A slumbering little devil." Once Valborg tells her she has no intention of renewing her contract to continue studying at the school, Henriksson resignedly states, "Fly little birds, fly," and pours herself another drink. She then concludes: "A drop of port for sad thoughts," and at this moment, a look of sharp concern crosses Valborg's face as she looks at her own reflection. Suddenly Rut steps out of the mirror's frame (and the film shot), leaving Valborg alone in the reflected image just as the solitary old teacher is tightly framed, and alone, in her own looking glass (figure 1.4).

A variety of interpretations are possible. Visually, it seems as if by stepping out of the frame within the frame of the dressing-room mirror, Rut is flying away from Valborg, just as Valborg can be said to be flying away from Miss Henriksson's nest. Furthermore, the look of near shock on Valborg's face at this moment can be thought to come from her realization that what has surely happened to the exceedingly unenviable older lesbian to her left was now beginning to happen to her, that she, Valborg, is destined to become just like her teacher, Miss Henriksson. On the other hand, Rut's voice-over narration that immediately follows tells us that it was Valborg, her contract having expired, who mysteriously left town: "Where did Valborg fly off to? . . . She went on a European tour. . . . What happened to her?" This statement raises several questions. Did Valborg suddenly leave Stockholm because she knew she would get nowhere with the ostensibly heterosexual Rut and hoped to find a woman who would love her fully elsewhere? Or was she trying to escape her own lesbianism by "flying away" from both the old woman who saw her secret desires and the younger one who was stoking those flames? The latter seems unlikely. There is nothing inchoate or tentative about Valborg's feelings for Rut. And considering how disturbed Henriksson's accusations, immediately followed by Rut's departure, make her feel, it is far more plausible that Valborg tragically allowed Rut's departure to inspire something of a self-fulfilling prophecy, reinforcing what the teacher was suggesting, namely, that if Valborg were to stay in Sweden to pursue her lesbianism with Rut, she would fail. Her bird would fly away, and she would end up as the next generation's Miss Henriksson. At the bitter end, Valborg would be able to quench her thirst for love only with a bottle of port while staring at her reflection in a dressing-room mirror.

One can only guess what happened to Valborg in southern Europe and why she ended up returning to Sweden, only to have her pathetic encounter on midsummer's night—trying to seduce an obviously distraught Viola after picking her up off the street and plying her with liquor in her apartment. But as Rut's narration makes clear, Valborg had the bad luck to move southward just as World War II was about to start. Likely as a result, and much like Rut and Bertil, who now find themselves returning home from the south to a bleak future, Valborg seems to have failed in her attempted escape to a potentially freer world abroad—an elsewhere that might, had she not had such bad timing, have allowed her to claim a happier life in the foreignness of another country by further exploring the foreignness of her "othered" sexuality. In an appalling irony, when Valborg has become what she seemed to fear becoming, in the scene in which she tries to seduce Viola, she is last seen with two curls of hair lit to look like the horns of a devil: in trying to escape her predicted fate as a "little devil," she ultimately became just that (figure 1.5).

As with Valborg's southern European travels, we do not know the full itinerary of Rut and Bertil's vacation or what happened to them on their journey through Italy, but we do know that one of their sojourns took place in the Sicilian city of Syracuse. This is of extreme thematic importance, since Sicily was also the ultimate destination

Figure 1.5. Valborg, the "little devil" in *Thirst/Three Strange Loves*. Svensk Filmindustri.

of Alpheios and Arethusa in the structuring myth at the heart of the film, one brought directly into focus early in the narrative when Bertil shows Rut a coin (which he purchased in Syracuse) adorned with the face of Arethusa. Of the many studies of Bergman published in English over the years, only Irving Singer's recent monograph *Ingmar Bergman: Cinematic Philosopher*, addresses this core issue. The myth—which involves both the water nymph Arethusa and the river god Alpheios being transformed into water, followed by the liquid Arethusa fleeing the liquid Alpheios through an underground river—is summarized by Singer: "The two . . . finally resurface in Sicily. There the waters of the two forever intermingle in what is called The Fountain of Arethusa." Applying the myth to the film, Singer smartly concludes that the myth commemorated on Bertil's coin "keeps alive the ideal of marital merging that this couple cannot themselves attain or even approximate." [99]

Given the myth of Arethusa and the theme it serves, the film's pervasive water imagery (the opening credits appear over the image of a spiraling whirlpool, and various exterior shots capture rivers and lakes), not to mention its Swedish and original English-language title, encourages a far more complex understanding of the film than one could otherwise discern. Whether boating across a fjord, showering in a hotel bathroom, constantly drinking whatever alcoholic or caffeinated beverages happen to be at hand, or, finally, jumping into the river to drown (as Viola does late in the film), *Törst*'s compulsive characters, seemingly parched for love, are not simply attempting some sort of aqueous escape. Ultimately, they long for the kind of wholeness that can come about only by merging the masculine self and the feminine self, selves that, in a world divided according to gender lines and compulsory heterosexuality, finally come to be understood as a division between self and other, one that both the Greek legend and this Swedish film see, perhaps foolishly, as reconcilable only on a distant island. That both the solitary Valborg and the claustrophobically close Rut and Bertil return to their homeland with their desires unslaked can hardly destroy the dream of foreign transcendence they seem to have sought, one so many queer spectators, also engaged in troubled attempts at seemingly impossible sexual and gender transcendences, also desired.

Spectators' queer desires, perhaps ones they were only just realizing, were acknowledged in the auditoriums of foreign-film theaters at midcentury around the United States. And as William Jones's *v.o.* later encouraged like-minded queers to look back at earlier, less hospitable eras, they may well have felt a small victory flowing through themselves, flowing "in positive waves" in the dark of the cinema.

Chapter Two

The Cultural Construction
of a Cold War Auteur
Discourse and Counterdiscourse

The day after Ingmar Bergman's death at eighty-nine, on July 30, 2007, an article titled "Five Ways to Think about Bergman as a Genius" appeared on a popular Internet film site. Written by the American screenwriter Larry Gross, whose harrowing *We Don't Live Here Anymore* (2004) suggests the influence of Bergman's 1970s middle-class dramas, it functions as a typical postmortem celebration. As he concludes, however, Gross attempts to tackle an immense issue in two paragraphs, and he ends his essay on a familiar note of naiveté:

The world's post World War II conception of the Scandinavian countries—prosperous, sexy, vaguely liberal and well-educated, cosmopolitan and neurotically suicidal—was more or less derived from Ingmar Bergman's films. There were times when angry journalists or politicians from those countries took exception to Bergman's depiction, as one sided or narrow or unfair. And no doubt, there were things he left out.

But this is, in part what a genius does. He helps to create the taste by which he will be judged. We have a hard time identifying the "truth" about modern Scandinavian life, apart from Bergman's representation or conception of it. That is what it means for a creative vision to have authority.[1]

Such declarations about the artist's power are hardly limited to artist-critics, and if there has ever been a feature-film maker whose work represents the efforts of a strong-willed person, it was Ingmar Bergman. Still, as the film-studies discipline has argued for decades, there is more to one's understanding of a film than the film itself. Furthermore, the image of Sweden that Gross describes predates Bergman's emergence on the world stage, and as I will explain, that image can actually be seen as having helped mold Bergman's "authority," rather than the other way around. At the very least, that dominant twentieth-century view of Sweden can be seen as having formed part of the framework for the emergence of Bergman's "vision" in the first place.

From a different school of thought than that illustrated by Gross (and probably representing the feelings of a larger percentage of contemporary Americans), the right-wing critic and former Reagan administration official William Bennett offered a different assessment of Bergman. "I say too bad about foreign films," he exclaimed with characteristic self-righteousness in 1992. "If they can't make it, tough. I stopped going at the same time I threw away my black turtleneck . . . I went to those Bergman things and felt bad, and felt good about feeling bad, and the '80s was good medicine for that."[2] Essentially, Bennett's statement was a snide observation made in the service of an argument against public funding for arts organizations in the United States. Yet it is emblematic of a discourse, and a discursive utilization of Bergman, that was in operation as early as the late 1940s and is at least as powerful as the ideas that Gross asserts regarding the power of genius. Put simply, Bennett offers an implicit critique of a specific political and cultural ideology that resides squarely on the left side of the political spectrum and often is associated with European introspection and, more punitively, a European decadence ultimately inseparable from modernist understandings of queerness. Ever the shrewd propagandist, Bennett implicitly contrasts this queer-tinged decadence with the supposedly optimistic, conservative, and surely nonintrospective values of the political right that were exemplified by, but have certainly not been limited to, the Reagan era.

If one were to speculate why Bennett invoked Bergman rather than other European filmmakers with dark sensibilities in order to personify Continental masochism, Old World decadence, and, perhaps most insidiously, foreign perversity, the resonance of the Scandinavian auteur's nationality should not be underestimated. Bennett is surely a nationalistic thinker, and Bergman himself has repeatedly been defined through the idea of nation, indeed of nation as essence.[3] It is worth remembering that the height of the filmmaker's fame in the United States—which ran, roughly, from his appearance on the cover of *Time* magazine in 1960 to the director's second consecutive Best Foreign Film Academy Award, for *Through a Glass Darkly*, two years later—coincided with the height of the Cold War. At that time, the director's popularity was often referred to as "Bergmania," a term one occasionally still hears in retrospective surveys today. Another term regularly invoked in that era has fallen from use, even as its connotations remain, unspoken, at the heart of Western conceptions of the filmmaker. According to the *Time* cover story, Bergman was often referred to during the period of his greatest impact as "the big Swede."[4]

As this chapter shows, Bergman symbolized Sweden in ways that were profoundly connected with the political anxieties felt in the West about that socialist nation in the Cold War, and crucially, he was just such a symbol at a time when, as Robert Corber has shown, homosexuality also was employed as part of a campaign to perpetuate anticommunist hysteria in the United States.[5] Considering the overlapping discourses regarding decadent, socialist Scandinavia, on the one hand, and radical communist homosexuality on the other, it should come as no surprise that a sense of queerness eventually accrued to the image of Bergman himself, one that has been as thoroughly forgotten in subsequent years as the director's most popular international nickname. (As I suggested in the introduction, many of Bergman's own statements almost seem designed to support that impression.) Throughout this chapter, then, I discuss the culturally mediated creation, or "discursive construction," to use a hackneyed term, of Bergman's queer Swedishness (and Swedish queerness) from the perspective of the American (and to a lesser degree, the western European) spectator, be he or she definable as a queer spectator or not. I do this to posit not just the afterimage of queerness this left on possible readings of the auteur's work, but also the more broadly political resonance this supposedly apolitical oeuvre had within Cold War culture, each work of which, in a veritable Foucauldian counterdiscourse, can be seen as having helped create its own productive meanings for both the political and the apolitical queer art-house spectator alike. To do that, one must look at the very first appearances of the director's work in the United States.

Abbreviated histories of Bergman suggest that the auteur burst from near obscurity onto the international film scene in the mid-1950s with *Smiles of a Summer Night*, an award winner at the Cannes Film Festival, which was followed two years later by the one-two punch of art-house blockbusters *The Seventh Seal* and *Wild Strawberries*. Somewhat longer accounts mention that Bergman's gritty *Monika* had appeared with some controversy in the United States a bit earlier, not as an art film, but as a "skin flick" given the dubious subtitle *The Story of a Bad Girl* and shown primarily in drive-ins. The most complete general accounts dutifully trace Bergman's emergence to *Hets* (1944), released in the UK as *Frenzy* and the United States as *Torment*, a noirish melodrama based on the future auteur's original screenplay and directed by Alf Sjöberg. It was followed by the Bergman-directed *Summer Interlude* (1951) and *The Naked Night* (1954)—both as exploitation films—before the recognized triumphs at the end of the decade. (As I point out in the previous chapter, there has never been any acknowledgment of *Thirst*'s appearance in the United States in the mid-1950s.) No historical account, however, begins with, or even fully addresses, what might be considered the natural starting point in a study of the filmmaker's cultural role outside of Sweden: the first feature directed by Bergman to receive international film-festival attention—it was positively received as part of the official competition at Cannes—as well as the first to garner a commercial release in the United States, even if in a very different context from that of most of his later work: 1947's *Skepp till India land*.[6]

Admittedly, a film that seems to promise moviegoers a voyage to South Asia—a literal English-language translation of the title is "Ship to Indialand"—hardly serves any of the standard historical narratives that have been constructed about Bergman's career. That alone, at least partially, may explain its critical sidelining, and the fact that it has been known by a veritable litany of English-language alternatives over the years—*Frustration*, *Land of Desire*, *A Ship Bound for India*, etc.—only adds an off-putting sense of confusion to this modestly conceived adaptation of an undistinguished play.[7] Indeed, considering the director himself would discuss the film with a sense of little more than good-natured embarrassment in later years, it is tempting to dismiss as a fluke its status as Bergman's American debut, and the first American reviews support this.[8] Noting what would be the film's brief appearance in Manhattan, the *New York Daily News* pronounced it to be "as dark in photography as it is dull in story," while the other New York critics, those writing for the *Herald Tribune,* the *Sun,* and the *Times,* were similarly dismissive.[9] Not surprisingly, after three weeks in a single Times Square venue, the film closed, apparently not to be commercially exhibited in any other major U.S. market in subsequent months. A careful assessment of the film's abortive presentation to American filmgoers, however, keeping in mind the historical era and the cinematic context in which it appeared, helps contextualize the queer unconscious of Bergman's American and—finally, through it—international reputation.

Largely set on a salvage boat anchored off a bleak stretch of the Swedish coast, Bergman's third directorial effort focuses on a quartet of characters—a salvage boat's captain, the captain's long-suffering wife, his young mistress, and, most centrally, his abused and deformed teenage son—all of whom take part in an intense and perverse Oedipal struggle. The film has been compared to the brooding ship-set plays of Eugene O'Neill, but whatever its reputation in Europe, *Skepp till India land*'s first appearance in the United States, under the bluntest of its many eventual English titles, *Frustration,* suggests that a different comparison might have been hoped for by its distributor: one between this dark Bergman-directed film and the equally dark Bergman-written film that had appeared to great financial success two years earlier.

For its part, *Torment,* although completed during the war, was not released in the United States until 1947. Therefore, both it and its unofficial sequel, *Frustration,* can be seen as part of the American postwar foreign film boom that included Italian neorealist hits like Roberto Rossellini's *Rome: Open City* (1945) and *Germany Year Zero* (1948)— both featuring unfortunately conceived, albeit intriguing, homosexual villains—and Vittorio De Sica's homoerotic *Shoeshine* (1946), as well as previously unseen films with queer sensibilities such as Jean Vigo's *Zero for Conduct* (France, 1933; U.S. release, 1947). As importantly, their appearance also coincided with a significant number of domestic features characterized by forms of masculinity in crisis.

Male Subjectivity and Marginal Films

In the immediate postwar era, many of the most prestigious of Hollywood's films seemed to operate under a different set of assumptions from those of the escapist late 1930s and early 1940s, and this new cycle of increasingly dark cinematic offerings attracted large and not-dissatisfied audiences. The surprising popularity of the violent and anxiety-laden film noir movement includes the most often cited sub-set of these films, and they certainly exemplify the profound discontent and sense of loss—primarily the loss of innocence—that filmgoers were willing or perhaps even predisposed to confront and accept as spectators. In 1945, a *New York Times* article popularized a theory developed in the psychoanalytic world that such films were simply "in tune with violent times, a cathartic for pent-up emotions." More sensationally, it argued that "after watching a newsreel showing the horrors of a German concentration camp, the movie fan [according to the psychoanalysts], feels no shock, no remorse, no moral repugnance when the screen villain puts a bullet through his wife's head."[10] But that sense of loss and ethical anxiety had a less violently aggressive spectatorial manifestation that would eventually be projected outward by a number of American moviegoers into the increasingly strange, increasingly *foreign* foreign-language films. At the time, however, *Torment, Frustration,* and their cinematic compatriots were not notably different from those domestically produced dark films, except, of course, that for the American spectator, they were, indeed, foreign.

As Kaja Silverman points out, the sense of unease that characterized both films and film spectatorship in that period points to a historically specific cultural phenomenon. Silverman argues that long-held illusions of essential male authority were violently disturbed by what she has labeled the "historical trauma" of World War II and the Holocaust. Her study wisely avoids suggesting that the trauma of the war was necessarily any more horrifying for those who experienced its effects directly than World War I. Silverman also stresses that "World War II, an event of monumentally tragic consequences," should not be thought to have provided "a privileged agency of social transformation."[11] In fact, she asserts the opposite to be true. Nevertheless, although she does not fully elaborate, Silverman claims that the mid to late 1940s was a period "when the forces of destruction and dissolution got out of control of those attempting to orchestrate the war, and served to annihilate . . . the positivities of the masculine 'self.'"[12] For Silverman, this period marked the historical juncture at which "the equation of the male sexual organ with the phallus could no longer be sustained." As she argues, because of "the disjuncture of those two terms," there was "a collective loss of belief in the whole of the *dominant fiction,*" which had been anchored by a sacrosanct belief in the fundamental relationship between the phallus and (male) subjectivity itself.[13] Ultimately, much of the radical argument made by Silverman throughout *Male Subjec-*

tivity at the Margins rests upon this ominous term, "dominant fiction." Silverman takes care to distinguish between this concept and the Lacanian-Althusserian definition of ideology upon which her term's foundation rests. In Silverman's schema, "ideological belief" is "located at a site emphatically exterior to consciousness," maintaining its efficacy only by commanding the subject's belief at "the most profound level" of his or her psychic "constitution" through the "dominant fiction." In short, she considers the dominant fiction to be ideology's "vehicle."[14]

Silverman posits that one of the dominant fiction's basic strategies involves the construction and sustenance of sexual difference, and the films upon which she focuses, and which mark and help define the historical trauma of the era, confront the dominant fiction in ways specifically related to sexual difference and gender roles.[15] She focuses on a number of characteristic Hollywood motion pictures in her study, two of which were playing in New York the week *Torment* appeared: *The Best Years of Our Lives* (William Wyler, 1946), which was enjoying an exclusive engagement at the Astor, and *It's a Wonderful Life* (Frank Capra, 1946), which was then playing in no fewer than fifteen of the city's theatres.[16] Those films were more widely seen in the United States than *Torment*, but the seemingly unassuming Swedish drama was a part of the broader movement of imported (usually European) films with a significant role to play in U.S. Cold War culture. Collectively, they became a part of a long-gestating process of queer subject construction in the second half of the twentieth century.

The Torment of Homosexual Projection

For its part, *Torment*'s queerly read account of a young man's traumatic Oedipal struggle offers its own, differently formulated challenge to the vehicles of the "dominant fiction" in ways that can seem both erotically compelling and deeply unsettling, and not surprisingly, it inspired intense controversy upon its U.S. release. *Torment*'s status as a deviant work was eventually solidified by an official condemnation bestowed upon it in 1948 by the National Legion of Decency. That this occurred just as the film's growing success had inspired the distributor to book it in "neighborhood" theaters, rather than keeping it contained (or quarantined) within inner-city art houses, was most likely the factor that led to picket lines and protesters. That, in turn, only added to the film's appeal.[17] While many early analyses of the film characterize the Sjöberg-Bergman collaboration as a contribution "to the debate at the time about the structure of the Swedish school system and the need for democratic reform,"[18] the *New York Times'* Bosley Crowther offered an interpretation that few others would entertain, but which points directly to its queer subtexts. Summarizing the plot, he wrote: "The story is that of a schoolboy—a lad in his later teens—who is hounded and driven to distraction by a schoolmaster with a black, sadistic bent." Despite Crowther's liberalism, he was essentially in agreement with the reactionary position taken by the Legion of Decency, referring to the film as "dour and unhealthy in tone." Continuing, he claimed, "the subject itself is noxious and, as it is being shown here in New York with obvious cuts by the censors, it is more melodramatic than acute."[19]

Although the film's original Swedish title should more accurately be translated into English as "stress" or "persecution," depending on the context, the American distributor Oxford Films must not have seen any serious problem, and perhaps even some advantage, in framing the property as one suffused by the profoundly negative, even masochistic emotions promised by "torment." More surprisingly, considering it represented the kind of art cinema that most often succeeded or failed based on the appraisals of critics—in other words it was hardly amenable to being framed, like *Monika*, as a skin flick—*Torment* withstood a number of strongly negative reviews in the United States to become an immediate *succès de scandale* and later something of "an early cult film."[20] As a result of what must have been calculated ambiguity on Crowther's part, readers of his review could not quite have known whether it was homosexuality per se that offended him or, more progressively, the specifically "black, sadistic bent" of the homosexuality in the film. Reflecting the increasing, though still largely occulted, homophobia of the era, Crowther only indirectly suggests that the nature of the film's dramatic struggle involves queerness. As a result, one might well read the review today without fully realizing how a homoerotic charge is at the heart of Crowther's discomfort.

In the (supposedly censored) version of the film seen and denounced by Crowther, "no explanation is made for the schoolmaster's monstrous sadism or for his particular obsession for the boy," and this absence leaves a gap in the film's psychology: "Presumably our sensibilities are spared by that neglect, but the logic and purpose of the exhibit—which is far from pretty—escapes as a consequence. What is shown is a lurid demonstration of gross and extreme malevolence and a mildly affecting dramatization of a boy's attachment to a pitifully wretched girl."[21]

There is clearly as much conflict in Crowther's review as there would appear to be in the film it so vehemently dismisses. Crowther seems relieved to be "spared" any footage that might directly confirm the presumably homosexual motivation behind the schoolmaster's "obsession," and yet at the same time, he is critical of its absence, remarking that the film's psychology, at least in the truncated version he saw, does not make sense. In fact, the original version of the film also only implies homosexual sexual desire on the part of the teacher toward his student, although, as with the version Crowther saw, it is strongly implied. Ironically, by suggesting that such a theme is present in the film even though he could not precisely locate it, Crowther may well have raised the issue for his otherwise unknowing readers, ultimately encouraging Manhattan's curious queer filmgoers to see a motion picture they might otherwise have overlooked. And while such an audience did not get the celebration of same-sex love they had gotten fifteen years before with Leontine Sagan's similarly censored and equally controversial *Mädchen in Uniform* (1931)—a film with which urban homophile filmgoers would surely have been familiar, even a decade and a half later—postwar queer spectators got a film offering a number of parallels and inversions of *Mädchen's* well-known narrative, here similarly involving pedagogic homoerotic desire, albeit, in this case, of a black, sadistic bent.

Torment's first image is an extended two-shot of the actor Alf Kjellin as the seventeen-year-old student Jan-Erik Vidgren, and Mai Zetterling as Bertha, the female corner of the film's perverse love triangle, over which the credits are displayed (figure 2.1). In retrospect, the shot must be considered a flash-forward, but it perfectly sets the tone of the film's general anxiety. It also immediately presents an image of male beauty that is very different from those to which most American filmgoers would have been accustomed. The conventionally handsome actor is illuminated with the kind of soft lighting discussed in the previous chapter, which was almost exclusively associated with the presentation of female sex objects in 1940s Hollywood filmmaking. While it is true that Kjellin shares the frame with Zetterling, who would later become an international sex symbol herself (and ultimately a distinguished feature-film maker focused on forthrightly feminist themes), her head is slightly shielded by Kjellin's, and the light that reaches her face lacks the strong angelic luminosity that characterizes her male partner's. In fact, throughout the credit sequence, the spectator has a more or less unobstructed view of Kjellin, while Zetterling is almost always seen slightly blocked or shielded by his shoulder in a three-quarter-profile shot. Unlike the standard techniques used to demarcate sexual difference in Hollywood films, however, and unlike the qui-

Figure 2.1. Jan-Erik and Bertha trembling together during the opening credits of *Torment* (Alf Sjöberg, Sweden, 1944). Svensk Filmindustri. 35 mm frame capture, courtesy of George Eastman House.

etly heroic, though often passive men in *Ivan's Childhood*, Kjellin is not presented as a confident man in the shot's composition. Indeed, both male and female characters are seen trembling in passive anxiety, each bearing the gaze of some malevolent offscreen voyeur. While the taller Kjellin stands slightly above Zetterling, the lack of any sense of courage and fortitude in the young man's face discourages an interpretation of Jan-Erik as Bertha's heroic savior. (Ultimately, he *is* unable to save her.) Rather, the blocking of the actors in relation to the camera serves only to make the comparatively exposed Jan-Erik seem to be more vulnerable than the relatively protected Bertha to whatever threat might exist outside the frame. Instead of communicating a traditional message of "You'll have to get past me to get to the girl," the image can be read as saying something far more unsettling, given the sexual nature of the implicit gaze: "You can have me, but let her go."

After this shot and the accompanying credit sequence ends, the film begins, its first scenes virtually echoing the first sequence of the once notorious, once celebrated *Mädchen in Uniform*. Its first postcredit shot shows a school building below a clock tower reading 8:10, while the subsequent cut to a close-up of the clock's face suggests the urgency of the time. Likewise, in *Mädchen in Uniform*, the spectator saw establishing shots of the girls' military-like Prussian boarding school, with the sounding of trumpets signifying the beginning of the school day. From *Torment*'s shot of the clock, a dissolve takes the spectator to a vertiginous high-angle shot of a boy of perhaps twelve, clearly late, running into the school. In a series of brief subsequent shots, he attempts to mount the marble steps as quickly and as quietly as possible. Suddenly, as if foreshadowing what will ultimately become the film's larger narrative, an older man begins to pursue the tardy adolescent. After a bit of almost comic cat-and-mouse choreography, the student is captured by his elder and delivered for punishment, tears streaming down his face. Correspondingly, in *Mädchen in Uniform*, the spectator sees an equally tearful Manuela, the sapphic protagonist, being brought into an oppressive new school by her authoritarian guardian in its first minutes.

After the boy has finally been absolved of his tardiness by the intercession of a compassionate elderly teacher, the spectator is relocated to an auditorium where the entire student body is singing morning hymns. *Mädchen in Uniform*, again in structural unity with *Torment*, offers an early sequence in which students can be seen performing the same ritual. While a number of *Torment*'s boys convey a typical adolescent awkwardness, with their jutting ears and protruding Adam's apples accompanied by acne and untamed hair, others, in attention-heightening contrast, would register, according to dominant codes of Western cinematic beauty, as strikingly attractive. In the best tradition of glamour-school photography, these more traditionally handsome men are afforded carefully bestowed backlighting, which causes the tops of their heads to exhibit a halo-like glow. Alluding to homoerotic energies among the upperclassmen, the film's first minutes show one young man jokingly asking another whether he approves of his "soprano voice"; his friend does not. Almost immediately thereafter, a tracking shot glides past one of the most pulchritudinous of the film's young men, on whose shoulder rests the forearm of another notably eye-catching male student. Thus a comic, and therefore more palatable, form of homoeroticism is evoked, only to be followed by a subtle, but more arousing image of it immediately thereafter. For its part, *Mädchen* also offers an interest-grabbing moment for a queer spectator near the beginning of its narrative, when a young woman puts her arm on Manuela's shoulder as they walk down the hall. Contrasting *Torment*'s images of same-gendered physicality with a worrisome heterosexuality, a student is subsequently heard whispering to a friend: "Was I scared when my girl said she was in trouble. A bit early to be a family man."[22]

Likewise, *Mädchen in Uniform* begins with events putting homosexual impulses in tension with heterosexual ones. Following the arm-around-the-shoulder image of Manuela and her new schoolmate, spectators of Sagan's film are confronted with a sequence in which other schoolgirls gaze at erotic images of male bathers.

As *Mädchen in Uniform* continues, however, heterosexual themes essentially vanish from the narrative, finally focusing on a struggle between what B. Ruby Rich has described as a repressive form of tolerance toward homoeroticism, on the one hand, and a more radical celebration of same-sex love on the other.[23] *Torment* remains a far more troubling film for its queer spectator, necessitating a much more complicated reading. Nowhere does it assert the utopian possibilities of homosexual desire suggested in Sagan's German classic. Indeed, the simplest queer response to *Torment* might be to label it homophobic, but as with a number of other features offering a homophobic perspective, *Torment*'s homophobia is not without complicating elements of erotic and psychological ambivalence. More importantly, it maintains a spectatorial elasticity that makes possible various alternative readings and allows for the possibility of different negotiations within the structure of phantasmatic projection that the film ultimately reveals.

After singing, the boys and young men of *Torment* begin their classes, and the film's most intense scene begins. In advanced Latin, the upperclassmen find themselves grilled by a despotic instructor—the third vertex in the drama's perverse love triangle—who is never named but is referred to as "Caligula" by his beleaguered students. An awkward boy is standing with a small book in his hand, trying to translate a paragraph aloud, and when he admits the passage is too complex for him, the teacher offers to "be lenient" and give the boy a "chance to reflect." At this point, Caligula moves on to the obviously more sexually attractive (again, according to dominant notions of male beauty in Western culture) Jan-Erik, toward whom he offers no leniency whatsoever. Each question put to Jan-Erik is more difficult than the last. He is expected not only to translate sentences from Latin into Swedish but also to do so with grace and style; when offering an awkwardly phrased translation, he is chided, even though it is technically correct. As the lesson continues, Caligula demands that Jan-Erik explain the grammatical rules involved in the passage he is translating, and at this point, the spectator can hardly avoid being both impressed that the young man manages to answer each question as well as he does and startled by the ferocity with which the teacher continues the interrogation.

This is likely the scene that compelled Crowther to comment on

Figure 2.2. Jan-Erik, penetrated from behind by "Caligula" in *Torment*. Svensk Filmindustri. 35 mm frame capture, courtesy of George Eastman House.

the teacher's "monstrous sadism" and "particular obsession toward the boy." Broadly hinting at the sexual aggressiveness behind his interrogation, Caligula brandishes a long pointer, which he repeatedly jabs toward the young men. Ultimately, in a justifiably famous, though little remarked-upon, image, Jan-Erik is made to feel the tip of Caligula's pointer thrust into the crack just below his armpit from behind (figure 2.2). Caligula subsequently beats his pointer across the top of a desk as if building toward an orgasmic release, screaming, "Faster, faster!" as the young man tries to locate a specific paragraph in the textbook. Once Jan-Erik begins reading that paragraph, Caligula looks over his shoulder and notices that a translation has been jotted into the book's margin in pencil. Catching Jan-Erik in this act of "cheating," although it is far from clear that this is an instance of premeditated dishonesty, Caligula violently and triumphantly chastises the young man, crowing, with obvious relish, about having to give him a demerit only two months before graduation.

With this threat, the possibility is raised that if Jan-Erik receives enough demerits, he may not be able to graduate that spring and will instead have stay at the school another year under the teacher's power, a possibility that only further suggests a malevolent form of desire be-

The Cultural Construction of a Cold War Auteur

hind the teacher's animosity. Such an interpretation makes this film's dramatic core the inverse of that which B. Ruby Rich locates in her reading of *Mädchen in Uniform*, since for Rich, and for most of that film's latter-day queer viewers, the teacher's requited love for her student is a positive occurrence that liberates both women. But the version of teacher-student sexual desire shown in the Swedish film raises the specter of a homophobic presentation of homoerotic energy. Regrettably, despite her progressive perspective, Maria Bergom-Larsson comes dangerously close to embodying the very homophobic perspective she describes in *Torment*'s characterization of the teacher when she writes: "The picture of Caligula is in many ways the picture of a diseased branch on an otherwise healthy tree [the Swedish school system]. He represents something perverted, a piece of unnaturalness, a repulsive animal, something inchoate and childish, a freak."[24]

Of course, Vito Russo, Patricia White, and Robin Wood, among others, have shown that the middle third of the twentieth century was replete with films featuring subtexts that veer, sometimes wildly, between homoerotic and homophobic responses, including at least two films released at roughly the same time as *Torment*: *Out of the Past* (Jacques Tourneur, 1947) and *Rope* (Alfred Hitchcock, 1948).[25] The *New York Times*' reviews of those films did not call them "dour" or "unhealthy," however. Crowther criticized the former only for what he felt to be its overly complicated plot, and the latter primarily for being "thin" and "monotonous."[26] Conversely, one must wonder why a film that seems to have been read as undeniably homophobic to those who sensed the homosexual undercurrents at all, such as Crowther, would later be canonized as an essential work of the art cinema by the openly and seemingly proudly queer critic Parker Tyler. For Tyler, *Torment*'s "happy emergence" in the English-language markets was nothing less than a "welcome" event. He raves: "Jan-Eryk [*sic*] is a more revealing part, a more complete portrait of a budding man, than anything comparable I can think of. It is as if [the actor] Kjellin himself had discovered the sheer pathos of sex, its hurt and its mysterious desire, while still, like Jan-Eryk, receiving his scholastic education."[27] Reading that, one might well ask: in what way can *Torment*'s seemingly homophobic images of "the sheer pathos of sex" and its exploration of "mysterious desire" have pleased a queer spectator while upsetting a straight male viewer and arguably eliciting a reactionary response from a committed second-wave feminist like Bergom-Larsson?

The easiest interpretation of the film would tell us that Caligula is simply a repressed homosexual (or, more plausibly, considering his relationship with Bertha, a bisexual) who cannot have the extremely handsome young man he desires and so begins tormenting him in frustration. The Roman emperor after whom the teacher is nicknamed was noted for his cruelty and for reportedly having slept with both men and women. In such an interpretation, the teacher, as a result of his obsession, bullies the young man in class and eventually extends his persecution into the realm of the student's personal life by pursuing his girlfriend, an act long theorized as possibly an indirect form of homosexuality. Indeed, by the story's end, the teacher has essentially driven his female rival to her death, only to cower in a dark stairwell, begging the young man not to leave him alone "in the dark." Disturbing this simple theory, however, is the fact that the teacher was clearly involved with Bertha before Jan-Erik showed any interest in her. Intriguingly enough, by looking at the film carefully, one finds evidence that suggests the opposite might be true: Jan-Erik might well have become interested in Bertha just after, or at the very moment that, he learned Bertha was Caligula's likely mistress. Shockingly enough, then, the idea is raised that the handsome young Jan-Erik becomes interested in a young woman because she is linked sexually with his queer teacher.

This possibility is introduced in a scene after that in which Caligula disciplines Jan-Erik for his supposed cheating in class. The young man, along with his closest friend, nicknamed the Sandman, stops at a tobacconist's shop. Here, Jan-Erik sees Bertha, working behind the counter, for the first time in the film. He pays very little attention to the young woman, even though, as their subsequent encounter demonstrates, he knows her well enough to call her by her first name. As the two students are leaving the shop, however, Jan-Erik literally bumps into the incoming Caligula. Clearly, the schoolmaster is in a hurry to get to Bertha's counter, but it is also clear to the spectator that while Caligula is essentially unaware of Jan-Erik's presence in the shop, Jan-Erik is taken aback by the teacher's sudden appearance. From the doorway, Jan-Erik turns around and looks right at Caligula and then just past him in time to gauge Bertha's expression at the moment she first notices Caligula's presence. Although Bertha's face is turned away from the camera, and thus the spectator cannot know with certainty how she responds to what she sees, the young woman must have registered recognition at the moment when her tormenting older lover comes into her place of work to, essentially, harass her. (Her head is very still, suggesting she might be taken aback, perhaps even frozen at the sight of

The Cultural Construction of a Cold War Auteur

the teacher.) What the spectator does clearly see, however, is Jan-Erik's expression, and at this moment he suddenly, and for the first time, seems interested in Bertha.

Although Jan-Erik's suspicions about the possibility of a relationship between Bertha and Caligula are limited to this one moment, the spectator gleans additional information as the scene continues to unfold in the shop after Jan-Erik and Sandman leave. Once alone with Bertha, Caligula moves toward the counter to buy a pack of cigarettes. There he begins talking to her in an overly familiar and flirtatious way. Although Bertha maintains a professional decorum while dealing with this "customer," a strong seed is planted in the spectator's mind that Caligula must be more than simply a customer to Bertha and that she is more than an anonymous shopgirl to him. It would take a second viewing of the film, or a spectator with an amazingly reflective memory, to realize that Jan-Erik's interest in Bertha might have begun at that crucial moment when he saw her looking at Caligula as her lover. Upon remembering this, one might well dismiss the idea, reminding oneself that Jan-Erik does not actually bond with Bertha until he sees her alone and drunk in the street later that night and then takes her home. Even then, with the two alone in her apartment, it is Bertha who essentially seduces Jan-Erik. Finally, one might also consider Jan-Erik's interest in the lover of his authoritarian teacher to be a displaced Oedipal struggle in the most conventionally heterosexual sense, and Jan-Erik's father, as we shall see, turns out to be only somewhat less authoritarian and despotic than Caligula. Perhaps by sensing that Bertha is the lover of his father figure and sadistic mentor, Jan-Erik suddenly relates the young woman psychically to his own mother, a transposition that would logically make her more compelling to a normatively developing Jan-Erik.

With Bergom-Larsson's study as a notable exception, most English-language readings of the film published in the first two decades or so of "Bergman studies" have simply ignored the kinky sadism that offended Crowther, focusing instead on the film's antiauthoritarian theme by making comparisons to the then-recent Nazi era.[28] In more recent years, however, *Torment* has in fact been discussed in terms of its Oedipal subtext. For instance, in a study of Bergman almost entirely devoted to arguing for an Oedipal motive behind the filmmaker's oeuvre, Frank Gado writes of Bertha and Jan-Erik's affair, arguing that "the ostensibly sexual bond between this mistress and her young lover is actually that of a mother and son."[29] Nonetheless, just as there is evidence to suggest that Caligula is only incidentally a repressed homosexual attracted to a heterosexual Jan-Erik, the film provides other evidence suggesting something beyond a traditional Oedipal crisis, something that would be far more troubling to a critic like Crowther, and far more delightful to one like Tyler.

Referring to what he considered to be Bergman's youthful "immaturity" as reflected in the film, Robin Wood argued that *Torment* "is very strong in wish-fulfillment: Jan-Erik [eventually] denouncing and striking Caligula before the headmaster; Jan-Erik denouncing and walking out on his father; the headmaster coming round to find him and make amends for the hurt he has been done, for which the school system is partly responsible; Caligula whining and pleading for pity on the staircase."[30] Wood remains one of the most astute critics of Bergman's work, but at the time he was writing his monograph on the director, he was still a closeted homosexual who, by his own later admission, was "desperately trying to reject and disown his own homosexuality."[31] This may have caused him to glean part of the truth—*Torment* does involve wish-fulfilling plot developments—without being willing to discuss the film's queer thematic core. At the time, Wood considered the wish fulfillment operating in *Torment* to involve the act of repeatedly striking back against adult authority. And yet, from a queerer perspective it can be said to be a wish fulfillment involving a young man fantasizing that he is the object of a powerful teacher's homosexual obsession.

Within the structure of such a person's fantasy projection, the Oedipal journey takes on a different character, one likely understood by *Torment*'s original queer spectator. The teacher (regardless of his "real" repressed or unrepressed sexuality) becomes a persecuting homosexual in the student's fantasy, whose function it is to represent that desire for Jan-Erik. Ultimately, the teacher also becomes the figure that must be vanquished in order for the young man to complete his Oedipal journey, one that may or may not end in heterosexuality. Such a process of spectatorship, in which homosexual desire circulates through an obviously villainous queer character, is so loaded with the possibility of spectatorial self-hatred that a number of gay film critics have implicitly rejected it.[32] A queer reading of Freud, however, explains how such apparent homophobia may be less problematic for the spectator than previously thought.

In "A Child Is Being Beaten," Freud charts the changes in six of his patients' early fantasies, fantasies in which each patient imagined "children were beaten, or were punished and disciplined in some other way, because of their naughtiness and bad behaviour."[33] By laying out how these patients shifted in their fantasies from imagining themselves the

The Cultural Construction of a Cold War Auteur

adult beater to the child being beaten, Freud charted a psychic process of identificatory instability that bridges and defines the seemingly oppositional sexual impulses of sadism and masochism. Building on this foundation, Jean Laplanche and Jean-Bertrand Pontalis suggest that the field of fantasy can most accurately be thought of as an oscillation rather than an identification. Considering the skeletal form of Freud's basic seduction fantasy in which "a father seduces a daughter," they explain that "the indication here of the primary process is not the absence of organization, as is sometimes suggested, but the peculiar character of the structure, in that it is a scenario with multiple entries, in which nothing shows whether the subject will be immediately located as *daughter*; it can as well be fixed as *father*, or even the term *seduces*."[34]

Torment's queer spectators therefore can be understood to easily shift their identification from the sadistic Caligula to the masochistic Jan-Erik—enjoying in both cases what spectatorship theory would define as secondary cinematic identification (identification with a character on-screen)—to finally locating it within the field of a sadomasochistic dynamic between the two. The last location is emphasized by the film's compellingly homoeroticized form of primary cinematic identification: the identification one has with the seemingly desiring, loving camera itself. Such a network of identification is reflected in *Torment* at the diegetic level, where it becomes clear that Jan-Erik sympathizes with Caligula just as he, Jan-Erik, tellingly enough, finds himself drawn toward Bertha. After the encounter at the tobacconist's, the issue of Caligula's aberrant nature is brought up, and Jan-Erik's response regarding his tormentor is telling. Sandman says, "Caligula's a real monster." Surprisingly, considering how ruthless he was to him earlier that day, Jan-Erik responds: "I don't know . . . Peculiar, more than anything." The sense of tenderness in Jan-Erik's voice is perhaps meant to paint the protagonist as a wholly good and decent person, typical for someone whose role in the narrative is to move from innocence to disillusionment. Much as Guy's comment that Bruno is a "queer fellow" in Hitchcock's *Strangers on a Train* (1951) seems more a projection of Guy's own effeminate bisexuality than anything else, it becomes apparent, as *Torment* unfolds, that the "peculiarity" Jan-Erik sees in Caligula has its undeniable corollaries in Jan-Erik's own subjectivity.[35]

Like a good aesthete, Jan-Erik is a sensitive violinist, and his heart melts at the sight of Bertha's small kitten, with which he tenderly plays. Most intriguingly, unlike other students at the school, Jan-Erik seems to have no emerging heterosexual libido. In what might seem to a straight spectator to be mere conservatism, he tells Sandman that he has no desire to sleep with girls at this point in his life, preferring to save himself for a one and only true love—gender not defined. He also maintains that his eventual companion must be of spotless virtue. More than a few queer spectators can recognize in the former comment an excuse many used in adolescence to explain away a lack of heterosexual behavior in high school. As for the latter, the justification that "no girl I've met is pure and good enough for me" is equally familiar to young gay men engaged in a process of denial, as is the idea that a queer adolescent would be drawn to a woman so sexually pure as to essentially take sex out of the picture. Although Bertha's status as a "fallen woman" makes her, in one way, the opposite of the virginal women in whom Jan-Erik claims to be interested (raising an obvious question about the motivations for his interest in her), she does nonetheless radiate, according to Gado, "a curious asexuality," one so noticeable that "several critics have remarked" upon it. Indeed, this asexuality is so pronounced that it leaves the film's spectators to wonder "what there is that could cause Jan-Erik to sacrifice everything for her sake."[36] For his part, Gado takes for granted that Jan-Erik's strong desire for his mother, coupled with the fact that Bertha occupies the mother's position in the film's displaced Oedipal structure, explains his attraction to her. The film suggests another possibility.

When Jan-Erik next meets Bertha, she is anything but an image of feminine beauty. Her makeup is smeared, and she is clearly intoxicated, giggling to herself (or perhaps sobbing) as she attempts to descend a long public stairway. Nevertheless, despite her insobriety, she has taken the trouble to adorn herself with one fashion accessory: she is wearing a small porkpie hat, one that, except for its size, looks like a typical man's hat of that era. (It is certainly not the kind of pillbox, toque, or "off the brow" headwear that signified femininity at the time.) Subsequently, just as Jan-Erik takes Bertha back to her apartment, a figure that seems to be Caligula's suddenly appears, walking down the staircase. While this event is pictured in such a long shot that it is almost impossible to tell whether Jan-Erik and this figure make eye contact, the fact remains that just as the young man begins to take actions leading him into a woman's bed, his homosexual tormentor, or someone resembling him, appears.

The shot ending the next scene in the young woman's apartment is perhaps the most curious, and telling, in the film. At the precise moment the drunken and unattractively self-pitying Bertha has managed to seduce the virtuous and virginal Jan-Erik, in a plot development that

The Cultural Construction of a Cold War Auteur

seems as sudden as it does implausible, the camera tilts down toward the bed on which they are beginning to make love. It discreetly stops before reaching the two, stopping above their unseen heads, where there rests a photographic image of a dapper, mustached Errol Flynn, in classic matinee-idol form, presumably cut out of a magazine and taped to the wall by Bertha. Just below it is a clipped-out photograph of a muscular, clean-shaven boxer stripped to the waist, his gloved fist extended upward toward the image of the other man. In fact, cinephiles of the era would likely have recognized that the boxer is also Flynn, in character in a publicity photograph for *Gentleman Jim* (Raoul Walsh, 1942), a film released two years before the production of *Torment*.

Having the camera focus on this bit of set decoration is an odd way to end this crucial scene, to say the least. The final image offered the spectator after the camera turns away from a scene of lovemaking that the censors could not have allowed to be shown in 1940s cinema, even Swedish cinema, could have been any number of things. (Perhaps the most famous of these kinds of evasions remains the cutaway shot of the airport beacon in *Casablanca* [Michael Curtiz, 1942].) More regularly, the cliché has been that the camera pans to a fireplace (suggesting burning passion) or to billowing drapes in a window frame (suggesting the sense of limitless freedom associated with romantic bliss). To end this particular scene this way, with its image of two (at first glance) seemingly different homoerotically positioned men, one with his arm phallically jutting toward the other man's head—men who are, one finally realizes, one and the same person in different guises—gives the spectator something puzzling and erotically suggestive to contemplate. The film's strategies of secondary cinematic identification put the spectator in Jan-Erik's position in virtually every scene in which he appears, and in this scene, in which Bertha seems far too intoxicated to be a focal point of our identification, he is the only character with whom one could possibly identify. Thus, the homoerotic image could hardly be taken to represent anything about the woman's consciousness.

Indeed, the scene has played out according to the strategies of male cinematic identification at the heart of classical filmmaking, first identified as such by Laura Mulvey, in which the woman is little more than an object (eroticized or, in this case, decidedly uneroticized) to the man's subject.[37] For the spectatorial logic of the sequence, the photos of Flynn suddenly appearing in close-up just as Jan-Erik begins to make love to Bertha suggests that we are looking at a representation of Jan-Erik's sexual desire, regardless of the gender of his actual sex partner at the moment. On the other hand, for the spectator's primary cinematic

Figure 2.3. The images next to Bertha's bed in *Torment*. Svensk Filmindustri. 35 mm frame capture, courtesy of George Eastman House.

identification (the spectator's identification with the camera), the images might simply represent the realization that behind this instance of heterosexual lovemaking is an emerging conflict between two men, who are in fact different versions of the same man (the "real" Jan-Erik and the queer Caligula he has constructed in his own mind), over the woman (figure 2.3). Since the upper image of Flynn, like Caligula, is mustached, and the lower version, like Jan-Erik, is clean shaven and younger, it is easy to see a correspondence between the two men and the corresponding photographic images, with the dominating force visualized in the photo of the more mature-looking Flynn positioned above the younger force, which is seen "fighting back." And since both Caligula and Jan-Erik are, at this point in the narrative, sleeping with Bertha, it is likewise appropriate, in such an understanding, for these pictures to be positioned above her pillow on the wall. But completely unlike Caligula, the mustached Flynn is, like the boxer, someone who would appear to most spectators to be a very attractive man. This creates a strange homoerotic dissonance for the spectator and offers a suggestion that behind the eminently—and, for the era, necessarily—rebarbative image of homosexual desire personified in the film by Caligula,

The Cultural Construction of a Cold War Auteur

there might reside, at the film's subconscious level, a much more enticing and inviting layer of obsessive gay fantasy.[38]

Considering the Oedipal logic of the film, with Caligula as a substitution for and demonic exaggeration of Jan-Erik's stern actual father, the intimation that behind the seduction of a father figure's woman resides a homoerotic desire for the father comes close to putting the entire Oedipal complex under a queer shadow. Put simply, the film can be read, in one of its most radically oscillating positions, as suggesting that the homosexual desire belongs to Jan-Erik, and to his allied spectator, in much the same way that Sabrina Barton has argued that the drama of *Strangers on a Train* is, in fact, the "straight" Guy's queer fantasy.[39] From this position, one feels that Caligula's monstrous sadism is both a displacement of the negative components of that desire as they are struggling to be recognized within Jan-Erik and the spectator, as well as a strong projection of a homosexual form of the Oedipus complex, with all the concurrent and challenging implications for a new understanding of heterosexual desire.

Sigmund Freud distinguished between heterosexual and homosexual forms of the Oedipus complex as early as 1923. Calling the latter the *"negative* Oedipus complex" in contra-distinction to a heterosexual *"positive* Oedipus complex" (emphasis added), he wrote: "Closer study usually discloses the more complete Oedipus complex, which is twofold, positive and negative, and is due to the bisexuality originally present in children: that is to say, a boy has not merely an ambivalent attitude towards his father and an affectionate object-choice towards his mother, but at the same time he also behaves like a girl and displays an affectionate feminine attitude to his father and a corresponding jealousy and hostility toward his mother."[40] *Torment* supports such a dynamic in the scene following Jan-Erik's seduction of (or by) Bertha. Returning home, he attempts to enter unnoticed, in an action mirroring the film's first sequence. Having made it into his room, he is shocked to find his father sitting on his bed waiting for him. As if some unspoken, perhaps unspeakable, understanding has existed between the father and son, one that is now threatened, the elder gets up silently and ominously walks out, leaving a son to retire in a postorgasmic state in a bed only just vacated by his father.

From their psychoanalytically informed perspectives, both Wood and Gado consider Jan-Erik's story to be an expression of various strategies of Freudian wish fulfillment, but *Torment*'s final plot twists challenge their heteronormative analyses. Back at school, Caligula approaches Jan-Erik and, on one of the film's thematically rich staircase sets, uncharacteristically apologizes for his previous behavior: "I don't want you to dislike me. You see; I've had some problems. I've been sick. Very sick. I've been watching you, Vidgren. You treat me with such aversion, antagonism." Jan-Erik, noticeably uncomfortable, replies: "I don't want that. I don't know what to say. I have no such feelings, sir." "Yes, you have," Caligula retorts. "You must not look at me that way anymore." As Jan-Erik struggles to formulate a response that will be either socially appropriate or psychically acceptable on his part, Caligula reverts to demonic form. "I forbid it!" he screams, and the young man rushes away, very nearly traumatized by his tormentor.

Bergom-Larsson well describes Caligula's psychological motivation in this scene: "Caligula's habit of using his bad nerves and his illness as an excuse for tormenting his pupils . . . also indicates a pathological swing between dominance and sadism on the one hand and subjection, self-abasement and masochism on the other."[41] Of course, as Caligula suddenly embodies the masochistic side of the sadomasochistic dynamic, his queer motivations, or rather Jan-Erik's as they have been projected onto Caligula, become even clearer. At one point in this scene, in what is perhaps the most obvious suggestion the film makes about its homosexual subject matter, a pair of students pass by, and once out of Caligula and Jan-Erik's (but not the spectator's) sight, look at each other knowingly as one of the two puts his hand on his hip in the manner of a "swishing" homosexual. Even if virtually none of the critics who have written about *Torment* seem to have noticed the homoerotic bond between Jan-Erik and Caligula, these two students certainly did.

In the film's second half, as Jan-Erik continues his relationship with Bertha, the young woman repeatedly tells him of the other, sadistic man in her life, one whom she nonetheless refuses to identify. It seems implausible that Jan-Erik would be unable to surmise the identity of this fiendish tyrant, even if he has forgotten their encounter in the tobacconist's shop, and the fact that Bertha mentions him repeatedly while always steadfastly refusing to tell Jan-Erik the man's name should have raised his suspicions. In what finally seems to be a willed form of ignorance, Jan-Erik continues his improbable affair without acknowledging either the real or the psychic presence of Caligula in their triangle. Finally, as if in a sudden rupture of the wall of repression that has been in place throughout the film, events quickly change. After a period in which it seems as if the young couple is free of their tormentor, Jan-Erik visits Bertha. Finding her drunk, he realizes she has again consorted with his unnamed rival. Uncharacteristically, Jan-Erik leaves her, and it seems doubtful that he will ever return. Adding to the pressure, an emboldened Caligula intensifies his attacks in class upon Jan-Erik. "I think you're going to fail Latin," he tells him in front of his peers, "fail badly. Do you know what else I think? I think you're too delicate to take examination." In yet another sexually connotative moment, he puts his hand on the back of Jan-Erik's head and pats it.

Again on the central staircase, Jan-Erik later faints, and he is taken home and put to bed. In what is perhaps the most striking image of traditional male beauty in the film, his angelically lit face is shown glowing not only from the soft lighting focused upon it, but also from the blanket of perspiration covering his skin (figure 2.4). It is comparable to the celebrated homoerotic image of Alain Delon lying in bed and gazing toward the camera in *Rocco and His Brothers* (Luchino Visconti, 1960), only in this case, the suffering seen on the young man's face continues the sadomasochistic aesthetic largely missing in Visconti's analogous close-up. Segueing into the young man's dream, the spectator is startled to see Caligula sitting on the foot of Jan-Erik's bed, in the same place his father sat on the night of his sexual initiation. Making explicit the young woman's psychically exterior position within the men's relationship, Bertha is also present in the dream, but to Caligula's left, and not on the bed. She looks as unattractive as ever, her wet eyes deep in their shadowy sockets as if she were drunk and had been crying.[42] Holding his phallic pointer again, now situated between his spread legs, Caligula tells his student: "I must put you to death, Mr. Vidgren, for being inadequately acquainted with dead languages. When you are dead you will find yourself more and more at home." In what is surely the most obvious of the film's metaphors, Caligula then raises a fountain pen and, in an orgasmic act of shocking directness, flicks it toward the young man, splashing ink on his face. If the homosexual resonance of that ejaculatory gesture is almost too obvious, the line of dialogue preceding it is only comparatively subtle.

As Leo Bersani has argued, male homosexuality, at least when it involves anal intercourse, has been both historically and psychically connected with an abdication of power that, in the social order, is thought to occasion a kind of "death." The image of the sodomized male, his "legs high in the air, unable to refuse the suicidal ecstasy of being a woman," foregrounds for Bersani this abdication within the Western social imaginary. By metonymic extension, male homosexual activity in general represents, "the grave in which the masculine ideal . . . of proud subjectivity is buried."[43] According to this logic, surrendering to the pull of homosexual desire in any form is to embrace a kind of liv-

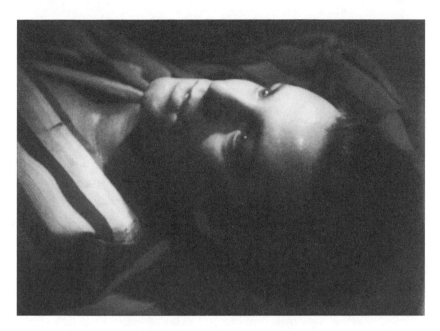

Figure 2.4. Jan-Erik suffers in soft lighting in *Torment*. Svensk Filmindustri. 35 mm frame capture, courtesy of George Eastman House.

ing death, a death suggested in the film by the "dead" language Caligula teaches.

Not long after recovering from his undefined illness, Jan-Erik decides to visit Bertha, presumably out of concern and perhaps to apologize, but when he arrives, letting himself in with the key Bertha once gave him, he finds himself greeted by her corpse lying across the bed. Gado dismisses this late development as "melodramatic" and "a wholly unnecessary bolt from heaven."[44] After discovering the body, Jan-Erik somehow notices Caligula cowering outside the apartment on a landing so deep in shadow as to make his discovery seem utterly improbable. In a reversal of their personalities, Caligula is trembling in fear, and Jan-Erik is seething in fury. Certain that Caligula is responsible, Jan-Erik accuses him of Bertha's murder before running to alert the authorities. Caligula, realizing he is about to be arrested, has the presence of mind to turn himself in, and is exonerated after the autopsy reveals that Bertha died of heart failure precipitated by alcoholism. Jan-Erik refuses to recant, however, and again accusing his teacher of murder, physically attacks Caligula in the headmaster's office. Not surprisingly, he is expelled, now just days before graduation.

In light of these wild events, Gado considers "the plot . . . to have es-

The Cultural Construction of a Cold War Auteur

caped beyond Bergman's control."[45] But he then offers what is, initially at least, a psychoanalytically plausible explanation for those events:

> Bertha's demise . . . represents a wish to escape from the complex effects of Oedipal guilt by eliminating its cause and, thereby, removing the impediment to development toward a "normal" manhood. In this instance, of course, Jan-Erik does not actually kill Bertha, but in the realm of dream beneath the refracted image on the realistic surface, the events subsequent to her death indicated that just such a wish has occurred. The presumption of Caligula's direct or indirect responsibility for her death should be seen as an attempt to deny guilt by shifting the blame to the accusing father/conscience.[46]

This interpretation is sound, but it ignores two complicating details. First, one can hardly forget the intense dream sequence, in which Caligula told Jan-Erik: "I must put you to death, Mr. Vidgren . . . When you are dead you will find yourself more and more at home." With that in mind, Bertha's death, as it relates to the fantasy structure of the film, can be read as another fantasy substitution. It marks the moment when Jan-Erik begins to take the woman's place as Caligula's dead lover. The film's odd final scenes solidify this seemingly undesirable fantasy conclusion.

Upon his expulsion from school and the subsequent graduation of his classmates, Jan-Erik is visited by the kindly and understanding headmaster, who had interceded to rescue the younger boy in the film's first sequence. Defying logic—how is he paying the rent, and why haven't Bertha's effects been taken away by the landlord?—Jan-Erik is now living in Bertha's room; her pet kitten is now his, her belongings are his belongings. In her place, but without her, the "dead" boy has never looked more at home. This scene is one of those described by Wood as being "very strong in wish-fulfillment," but structurally, it is not simply, as Wood puts it, "the headmaster coming round to . . . make amends."[47] Replacing, in the final scene, the demonically homophobic image of Caligula with the positive image of the schoolmaster, allows the queer spectator to experience, through Jan-Erik, the acceptance of a new subject position born of a painful, indeed very nearly traumatic, Oedipal complex. And while both the "negative" homosexual side (Caligula) and the "positive" heterosexual side (Bertha) of Freud's complete bisexual Oedipus complex have been expelled from the narrative, to be replaced for a time by a simple homosocial relationship with the schoolmaster, positive forms of queerness have hardly been rendered impossible. Indeed, everything throughout the film develops in a way that exposes the existence of a negative Oedipus complex while radically enough suggesting that, at least in some instances, the positive Oedipus complex is a symptom of, rather than an evolution out of, more elemental and, in some cases, stronger homosexual desires.

Silverman considers the always-privileged positive Oedipus complex to be the "normative psychic response . . . to the dominant fiction," the one that provides "the structure through which we 'ideally' live our necessarily imaginary relation to kinship" in the larger social world beyond the family.[48] If so, this film, one of the titles that introduced the European art cinema to U.S. filmgoers, surely had a role to play in challenging the imaginary relationship between the subject and a social order promulgated by the no longer tenable conflation of phallus and penis, heterosexuality and developmental destiny, and the "inevitable" desire of a man for a woman.

The Frustration of Heterosexual Displacement

Considering the success of *Torment*—in spite of, or more likely partially because of, its controversies—it hardly seems surprising that an American distributor was attracted to a natural successor like *Skepp till India land*. Film distributors certainly must have read an encouraging short notice published in *Variety* in 1947: "Transition of the Martin Soederhjelm play into celluloid has made a good film. Ingmar Bergman's crisp direction and scripting plus fine camerawork of Goran Strindberg are principally responsible for making this picture a crack tale of a salvage boat and four persons whose lives are tied up in the ship's destiny. Holger Lowenadler's portrayal of the captain is neat thesping and others in cast measure up to his standard. Okay for the U.S. mart."[49]

Despite *Variety*'s approval (coming from an unnamed critic who had seen the film at its Stockholm premiere), Film Classics—a small Broadway-based company noted for successfully marketing a mixture of foreign films, quality independent American films, genre movies, and rereleases of older Hollywood studio titles[50]—still seems to have felt that the low-budget effort required a carefully constructed framework in order to attract an American audience. Furthermore, a careful assessment of the *New York Times* advertisement for the film suggests how the distributor wanted its new acquisition to be marketed, with its newly christened titular affect as a focal point (figure 2.5). On the upper-left side of the advertisement, one sees the image of a het-

Figure 2.5. Newspaper advertisement for *Frustration* (Ingmar Bergman, Sweden, 1947). Film Classics. *New York Times*, August 26, 1949.

erosexual couple in an intense embrace. (One learns upon viewing the film that it is, in fact, the disturbing image of a violent yet finally pathetic rape attempt.) As one's eyes move across the diagonally positioned title and down to the bottom right-hand corner of the advertisement, they finally rest on a handsome—although, curiously enough, hunchbacked—young man who is seated before a provocatively posed, bare-legged young woman. Assuming (rightly) that it is the same couple seen in the ad's upper-right-hand corner, one can glean the development of a story that moves from violent sexual desire to a promised state of sexual release and peace—in other words, from sexual frustration to respite. And yet the fact that the man has a visible hump on his back suggests little hope of a completely tidy resolution. If the titular frustration is in fact being foregrounded as erotic and salacious, connected with traditional power relationships between the genders, the advertisement connects this with an unmistakable emblem of malformed male subjectivity.

The venue for *Frustration*'s premiere, Times Square's once-infamous Rialto Theater, is also a crucial determinant in understanding its first domestic impression. Beginning in 1933, the Rialto was managed by Arthur Mayer, a former Paramount Studios executive ultimately best known, as Mayer himself would proudly admit, as Broadway's "Merchant of Menace."[51] For the most part, his theater offered previously released Hollywood films, which were presented in double bills and marketed in the most sensational manner conceivable.[52] Because of this, and the fact that Mayer's early programming focused sharply on the terror and fantasy genres, the Rialto gradually became known as "New York's last bastion of commercialized horror in celluloid."[53] By the late 1940s, however, changes in the film industry, including, as Barbara Wilinsky has pointed out, "increased costs of studio film rentals . . . and the decrease in the amount of film product from the studios (especially less expensive B films) . . . motivated exhibitors to search outside of the mainstream industry to fill their screen time."[54] According

Queer Bergman

to *Variety*, Mayer considered changing his theater to an art-film venue by the fall of 1947 but was hoping to do so in a way that would retain as much of his older clientele as possible: "[Mayer would] like to latch on to foreign pix which are steeped in a reminiscent flavor of action and sex so that the drop-ins continue to haunt his theatre."[55] Clearly, Mayer wanted *Frustration* to be seen, at least for interested audiences, as a continuation of his exploitation programming. The "cheap sensationalism" noted by the *Times* in the Rialto's lobby display for the film, along with the simple, blunt newspaper advertisement, was surely intended to attract an audience at least as interested in sexuality, shock, and melodrama as in European artistry.[56] Considered together, these factors must have convinced Mayer or his booking agent that *Frustration* would fit the Rialto's new policy of presenting films that straddled, or perhaps blurred, the line between exploitation fare and the art cinema.

Envisaging the feature's potentially dual audience, and perhaps encouraged by *Torment's* success, Film Classics may have expected a particularly successful release. The first signs of trouble, however, appeared when *Variety* offered a second review of the film, one contradicting its earlier endorsement: "*Frustration* is a slow, murky film with no appeal for the U.S. market. This Swedish import unwinds its tortured tale with arty pretensions in its long closeups and underlighted lensing but the result in [*sic*] soporific. . . . The over static story and the hamminess of the thesping will depress the customers."[57] The discrepancies in the two reviews can be explained by the differing tastes of (presumably) two different critics, but one can also imagine annoyed Film Classics executives wondering how a film praised for "fine camerawork" could suddenly be criticized in the same publication for "underlighted lensing," and why one initially credited with "brisk direction and scripting" was now being castigated as "slow" and "soporific."

Indeed, as far as the film's pacing was concerned, the distributor had cut seventeen minutes of footage before the film's U.S. debut. But while the editing was not drastic, the changes would have served only to heighten the film's sense of anxiety, dread, and pessimism far beyond that of the director's version, giving it, in fact, more of the atmosphere of the kind of horror film Mayer liked to show. Not unrelated to this subtle shift in emphasis was the fact that the reedited version helped construct the image of a wretched form of solipsism, one that resonated with the Sweden imagined within America at that time. An idyllic, nonexplicit love scene was cut from the film, as was the ending of an earlier scene in which the captain's son, Johannes (Birger Malmsten), and the captain's mistress, Sally (Gertrud Fridh), lie down on the floor of a deserted windmill to (presumably) have sex. These two excisions may well have been made to avoid censorship problems in certain cities, but it is noteworthy that they were removed even though the ugly scene in which a drunken Johannes attempts to rape Sally was not only retained for the U.S. version, but also highlighted in the newspaper advertisement.

Less drastically, and completely inexplicable for decency considerations, a scene was cut in which the entire group of salvage-ship workers eat dinner together in the vessel's galley and praise the captain's wife, Alice, as a good cook. With that brief scene's removal, the film loses the only real moment of communal joviality among its major characters. When compared to similar scenes in a number of other Bergman films, this seemingly unremarkable moment of happiness can be seen to have an important structural role in the director's work, lightening the mood of often-dark dramas while suggesting that, however rare, life does provide individuals with palpable moments of grace.[58]

Most drastically, however, the film's prologue was removed. Presenting an older Johannes returning home many years after his wretched adolescence, it casts a crucial light on the rest of the unfolding film, which then continues in flashback, with the spectator always aware that the younger Johannes will somehow break free from his abusive father and become a world-traveling sailor. During the prologue, the happy, confident, and appealing adult Johannes is introduced in uniform as a naval officer disembarking from an impressive ship. In a contrived development, he comes across a despondent Sally, after which memories of the events that led him to fall in love with her but finally to leave her come flooding back as on-screen memories that make up much of the rest of the film. According to the narrative's logic, only after remembering his harrowing coming-of-age seven years earlier can Johannes take Sally away with him, out into a better world, as a naval officer's wife.

While the American version ends with the same happy denouement found in the Swedish original, the erasure of the prologue makes Johannes's inexplicable return and his retrieval of Sally in the film's final moments seem as unconvincing as it is sudden. The excisions, at least those not involving potentially censorable material, may well have been justified by Film Classics as an attempt to cut the film for American audiences' supposedly shorter attention spans, but in the process, they radically darkened the tone of a film that was only ninety-two minutes long originally.[59] Finally, by removing the flashback structure of the film, the American distributor effectively erased the film's dramatization of a person's ability to come to terms with and master his or her traumatic past. American spectators first see Johannes not as a successful naval officer returning home to reclaim his sweetheart, but as a virtually hopeless teenager working for his despotic father on a hell-on-earth salvage ship, literally cowering in the shadows as the crew ridicules him both for his physical disability and, more generally, for his inadequate masculinity. After a seemingly uncharacteristic attempt to take charge of the crew in his father's absence (in what had become the film's first scene) and thereby to demonstrate, as much to himself as anyone else, a sense of his own independence, the son immediately finds himself humiliated again, now by his father, who suddenly appears on the scene.

Adding contemptuous emotional injury to a son he has just insulted, Alexander Blom brings Sally onboard as his mistress, announcing that she will be living on the cramped vessel with the family and crew. When an outraged Johannes asks where this interloper is expected to sleep, Blom deposes the boy from his room, telling him that he will henceforth be sleeping with the other crewmates. "The crew's bunks are better suited for you and your hunch," the captain tells his utterly humiliated son.[60] When Johannes is subsequently informed that he will not be allowed to get his naval papers processed in town the following day, thereby causing him to miss a crucial deadline, he realizes he will, in effect, be forced to remain under his father's control well into the foreseeable future. With no other avenue for rebellion open, Johannes gets drunk below deck, and it is at this moment that the otherwise timid young man attempts to rape Sally. In the tradition of countless Rialto thrillers, Malmsten performs the scene as a trembling Dr. Jekyll suddenly regressing into a demonic Mr. Hyde, but Johannes's attempt to rape Sally is as feckless as his earlier threat of suicide, and his mother (Anna Lindahl) quickly intervenes. Before she does, however, the image of Johannes attacking Sally has been strikingly displayed.

Remarkably, the most erotically lit and centrally positioned piece of normally hidden skin on display in this shot does not belong to the assault victim. As highlighted by a strong beam of light that creates a dark shadow running down Johannes's spinal column, the sexualized image of the small of Johannes's back is instead the image's focal point (figure 2.6). More than anything else, it strongly suggests the hidden cleavage between the buttocks just below the visible indentation, thereby alluding to that unseen fissure's metonymic and metaphoric associations. In other words, as presented, the image of this would-be rapist, rather than connoting a phallic power associated with violent hetero-

Figure 2.6. Johannes attempts to rape Sally in *Frustration*. Nordisk Tonefilm. 35 mm frame capture, courtesy of George Eastman House.

sexual masculinity, suggests its very opposite: Johannes's penetrability. Furthermore, the pronounced image of Johannes's hunched back higher up on his torso can be regarded only as a deformed and essentially useless phallic presence. Once the young man's mother has interceded and stopped the assault, the sense of emasculation that the image as a whole suggests becomes unavoidable. As blocked by Bergman and lit by his cinematographer, Johannes's attack offers both a compelling deconstruction of the psychic resonance of the iconography of rape and a related, uncannily homoerotic subtext in the film.

Frank Gado points to what he calls a pervasive "*anxiety* about homosexuality which radiates from [Bergman's] uneasiness about his masculinity," but by considering "all public indications of his private life [to] have been vigorously and unstintingly heterosexual," and concluding that "the dreamlike patterns of his fictions afford no evidence of being the product of a homoerotic imagination," he posits that the core issue in the filmmaker's oeuvre involves an amalgamation of "sexual conflicts traceable to his mother."[61] In other words, Gado psychoanalyzes Bergman by using an understanding of heterosexual Oedipal guilt already fully deconstructed in *Torment*. Unfortunately, such a line of reasoning points to the limitations inherent in any psychoanalytic project that fails to incorporate the nuanced understandings of the Oedipus complex developed by queer theory.[62] Although what generally reads to American (and western European) queers as homoerotically beckoning imagery is largely absent from Bergman's later films, homoeroticism, in fact, repeatedly appears in the director's earlier work, perhaps partially as an application of lessons learned by watching Sjörberg bring his first script to the screen. Indeed, it seems telling, if only as part of the kind of psychobiographical approach Gado practices, that simultaneous with Bergman's tentative but direct confrontations with homosexuality in the 1960s, at the level of dialogue and plot, there occurred a concurrent, perhaps compensatory, decline in the traditionally homoerotic imagery in the films: when the delicately handsome Birger Malmsten was at the center of Bergman's frame repeatedly in the 1940s and early 1950s, homoerotic desire was a visually palpable presence that dared not speak its name.[63] As soon as the subject of homosexual desire began being addressed more openly in Bergman's films, the comparatively unenticing visages of Max von Sydow and Erland Josephson (unenticing at least according to my understanding of the Western homoerotic imaginary operating throughout the twentieth century) took over.

In *Frustration*'s sexual dynamic, what is presented as Johannes's deformed masculinity is meant to be regarded not with a mixture of dread and loathing, but, more compellingly, with compassion and even erotic investment. Moreover, as in *Torment*, Johannes's Oedipal struggle with his father over Sally can easily be read as part of a negative Oedipal complex, with a mother figure (both his actual mother and Sally in turn) being fought over as a substitute for and symbol of the dark sadomasochistic desire between father and son. Few images in the film have more erotic resonance than that seen in the wake of a particularly brutal assault upon Johannes by Alexander, with the son cowering on the floor as if waiting to be raped by his father. In predictably sadistic fashion, the father refuses to oblige his emasculated, masochistic son. It seems hardly coincidental that immediately following this "rejection," Johannes attempts to take control sexually by trying to rape Sally. Since he obviously could not rape his physically superior father, he attempts the "next best thing": trying to violate his father's lover. At that moment, he tells the young woman something with a particularly queer subtext: "Mother once asked me if I had a girl friend . . . I said no, I was much too particular. But if ever I should meet a hunch-back girl, I might lose my head."

The Cultural Construction of a Cold War Auteur

Such a remark offers a number of connotations: perhaps most obvious is the indirect inference to emasculation expressed by the phrase "I might lose my head." More pointedly, Johannes suggests that he has been celibate by choice and that he sees his "deformity" as a determinant of his sexual subjectivity, a deformity that compels him to imagine a partner with the same minority status and, by extension, the same sexual subjectivity. Although it follows a rather complex form of metaphorical "logic," this clearly loaded reference must have resonated strongly with queer spectators at the time, who were routinely being told their sexuality was a kind of birth defect. Although never stated in these terms, Captain Blom, with his failing vision, is the only character besides Johannes to suffer from a handicap. Quickly going blind, he metaphorically exemplifies one side of the narrative's thematic struggle between an (in)ability to imagine (literally, "image") the world, on the one hand, and the desire and dread of journeying into it physically, on the other. But the claim that the only sex partner suitable for a person with a "hunch-back" is another person, like his father, marked by physical defect, gives the metaphor a homosexual Oedipal connotation as well. Perhaps the most strikingly sexualized image in the film, one that serves to link father and son sexually, will be the central image of the film's climax.

After Johannes finally stands up to his abusive father and he and Sally have become lovers late in the film, the young man finds himself underwater in a diving suit beneath the hull of the salvage ship. In a decision either foolhardy or unconsciously self-destructive, Johannes has asked his enraged father to handle the air pump that will keep him from suffocating at the other end of the oxygen tube. In a sequence fusing Oedipal tensions with implied sexual stimulation, Blom holds the pump handle between his legs to send the air down into his son's lungs. Cutting to an expressionistic silhouette of the captain operating the air pump, the image offers a pronounced visualization of masturbation (figure 2.7). Therefore, an overdetermined image of sadomasochism, passive aggression, and Oedipal rupture confronts the spectator when Blom stops pumping the air in an attempt to suffocate his son. Johannes survives the attempted murder, inspiring the captain, now suffering his own sense of emasculated shame, to attempt suicide. Leaving both his now physically paralyzed father and his mother behind, Johannes is able to claim his manhood and eventually to return and claim Sally. In other words, the film ends with the normative, heterosexual Oedipal trajectory fulfilled.

Nevertheless, the queer spectator cannot have been unimpressed by

Figure 2.7. Alexander Blom's sexualized shadow in *Frustration*. Nordisk Tonefilm. 35 mm frame capture, courtesy of George Eastman House.

the force, conviction, and eroticism with which this father-son conflict played out. From the position of the queer male watching *Frustration*, its traumatic incestuous struggle cannot easily be forgotten, especially when it is sutured by such a sudden and unconvincing conclusion in what, in the U.S. version, can seem to be only a hastily added and unconvincing epilogue. But even while taking the film's thematic journey to its intended heteronormative conclusion, the queer spectator can have a satisfying sense of enjoyment in watching a "deformed" child gain a measure of self-respect as he leaves his dysfunctional traditional family to journey far beyond where his father would have dared to go.

Throughout the greater part of the film, both the father and his son dream of lands beyond their country, but in what could be taken, in any contemporaneous political reading of the film, to represent Sweden's lack of international commitment, they are unable to venture abroad. It is a sign of the monstrous patriarch's encroaching madness that he sees the outside world as a two-dimensional mindscape that ranges from clichéd picture-postcard images to outright Orientalist danger, visible in his collection of exotic artifacts. Johannes, on the other hand, sees the world for what it is, first through the ships passing on the sea's horizon and then, in the film's triumphant conclusion, moving beyond a passive form of spectatorship by becoming a participant in a positively portrayed multicultural world after he leaves home and joins the Swedish Navy.

Despite the satisfying though abrupt conclusion of the American version of Bergman's film, its appearance in the United States in 1949 went almost unnoticed. When one compares its release to that of *Torment*, one wonders whether Film Classics' biggest mistake in marketing the property was to fail to promote it as a new film "by the writer of *Torment*." This was a mistake that would not be repeated by the Times Films Corporation when, seven years later, it presented *The Naked Night* to U.S. filmgoers, forthrightly billing it as: "Directed by Ingmar Bergman, creator of the screen masterpiece *Torment*."[64]

The Cultural Construction of a Cold War Auteur

Studying the response accorded *The Naked Night* in the United States, only the fourth Bergman-directed feature to appear in the country, one sees a pattern that brings both *Torment*'s and *Frustration*'s earlier appearances, and those of virtually all the director's subsequently released films, into new focus, one demonstrating that the director—often regarded as an individual genius who transcended his national origins— had, in fact, been characterized as part of a discursive construction of Cold War–era socialist Sweden. This dark and brutal film about a sadomasochistic, codependent relationship between a self-hating circus owner and his calculating mistress was virtually hissed off Swedish screens after receiving vitriolic reviews, including one from Stockholm's largest newspaper comparing it to "vomit."[65] Nevertheless, it received American distribution shortly after its European premiere, and was introduced to American audiences with a promotional campaign highlighting its darkest themes. Although the film's Swedish title, *Gycklarnas afton*, translates as "The Clowns' Evening," Times Films gave it the more prurient title, even putting it into the tagline: "Desperately they fought the desires, the passions that dragged them down deeper and deeper into *The Naked Night*."[66]

Newsweek's review is particularly noteworthy for what can ultimately be seen as a broadly imagined discursive construction of Sweden, one characterizing the country as licentious, masochistic, and emotionally dysfunctional. Although it makes repeated reference to the film's blink-and-you-miss-them images of skinny-dipping—the headline reads

"Splash in Sweden"—the review otherwise regards the "somber" and "melancholy" *Naked Night* as proof that "the Swedes never make happy movies."[67] Calling the male protagonist "a sorry figure of mediocrity who even fails in his ultimate attempt at suicide," the uncredited critic spoils the film's denouement in order to bring the recurrent subject of Swedish suicide into a three-paragraph review. While the critic writes, not inaccurately, that the characters "move through their lives with the graceless steps of people knowingly predestined for failure," he or she ignores the film's riveting montage editing and its stunning chiaroscuro cinematography. Less surprising than the critic's silence on the film's impressive style is the complete lack of attention accorded its trenchant portrayal (to the point of black comedy) of various class-based professional hierarchies, exemplified by the prejudicial treatment afforded the circus performers by members of other social groups.

Such simplifications were ubiquitous in the presentation of Bergman to American audiences during the Cold War; so too were similar characterizations of Sweden at the time. And just as stereotypes about Sweden were used to guide Americans' understanding of Bergman's films, stereotypical images from the auteur's work were used to guide inchoate understandings of Sweden. In a lengthy article about the country first printed in the British magazine the *Spectator* in 1962 under the title "Goodbye to Summer," Desmond Fennell offers a paradigmatic example. His essay contends that Sweden, a once-great Christian nation, tragically lost its way in the twentieth century, claiming this in spite of the fact that it was economically prosperous, clean, and outwardly impressive in almost every way. Fennell implies that Sweden's material achievements were due, in part, to a newly secular society organized around an infantilizing socialist economic system, and he strongly suggests that the price Swedes paid for their Pyrrhic victory is deep-seated, toxic unhappiness. In a typical remark, he states that in Sweden, only "religion and shame are things you must feel ashamed of." He suggests that in this godless culture, in which the people have determined that "'there is no world but this,'" bitterness and hatred have become primary emotions. "It is the democratic life, it is the enlightened life, it is the rational life, it is the fully employed, wealthy and civilized life," Fennell asserts, "but it is still," he concludes, "hateful." And this odious sort of life leads to only one conclusion: "The fascination of death as the biggest event is met by a longing for death as a release from the pain of living."[68]

In keeping with the *Spectator*'s format, Fennell's screed is accompanied by rough drawings illustrating his thesis. Readers are provided with a sketch of solipsistic Swedes dining alone in restaurants, as Fennell ominously claims they tend to do.[69] One also finds an image of a Swede who, presumably no longer believing in Christ, worships the sun during what Fennell describes as the pathetically short Swedish summer.[70] In what critics of the country often labeled the skinny-dipping capital of the world, it is unsurprising that this drawing shows the atheistic Swede disrobing in order to worship the sun in the nude.[71] Finally, one is presented with the inevitable result of a God- and competition-free environment: a grim illustration of a miserable wino in the gutter, representing what Fennell and other conservative critics of the time claimed to be the nation's huge problem with alcoholism.[72]

When Fennell's essay was reprinted as an opinion piece in the *Washington Post*, the editors faced a challenge, since their format called for photographs rather than the *New Yorker*–like line drawings used by the *Spectator*. And yet, photographic proof of the kind of abstract problems Fennell posited for Sweden remained elusive. Therefore, in this reprinted version, the article was accompanied by images from two of Bergman's early films as a form of supporting evidence. With a new, even more critical headline, "What Shall It Profit Fat-Cat, Joyless Sweden?," the essay and its illustrations conspire to prove an argument that Sweden was an economically prosperous but nonetheless miserable society (figure 2.8).[73] But if the Bergman film stills served to anchor a specific image of Swedish unhappiness, they did so indirectly. Indeed, the choice of photographs suggests a subtlety lacking in the *Post*'s vulgar headline. Looking downward on the full-page article is an image from *Monika* in which the male and female protagonists stare toward, almost directly into, the camera. The young man, Harry, and his teenage lover, Monika, are uncharacteristically disheveled, so much so that someone who had seen the film might have not recognized the photograph as having come from it. Directly below that photograph is a still from *Summer Interlude*, which also offers an image of a heterosexual couple, in this instance in profile. Unlike Harry and Monika, this young man and young woman are well kempt and smiling, clearly, tenderly in love.

The two photographs might, at first glance, seem rather ineffective images with which to visualize the unhappiness Fennell claims to have found in Sweden, and yet there is a subtle logic to their presentation. The image of the happy lovers in *Summer Interlude* seems to be contradicted by the larger image above it. It becomes nearly impossible to consider the tranquility of the lower still apart from the disturbing, spatially superior image of hungry discontent above it. In this way, the pho-

What Shall It Profit Fat-Cat, Joyless Sweden?

By Desmond Fennell

Big Bottle, Free Love
Replace the Lost Values
Of King and Religion
In A Welfare State

Lars Ekborg and Harriet Andersson in "Summer With Monika," in which
a young man and woman yield in lust and nature simultaneously.

Maj-Britt Nilsson and Birger Malmsten in "Summer Interlude," a film
set in the Stockholm archipelago, where tens of thousands of Swedes go
every year to live out the myth that summer is a time for the realization
of perfection.

Figure 2.8. The "discursive surround" for Ingmar Bergman's *Monika* and *Summer Interlude*. *Washington Post*, February 25, 1962.

tographs suggest something that a number of critics of Sweden at the time took great pains to argue. While, at one level, the country seemed happy and peaceful and friendly, at another, higher—one is tempted to say superstructural—level, a towering discontent overwhelmed the society.

In her sour, sarcastically titled 1961 travel memoir *A Clean, Well-Lighted Place*, Kathleen Nott begrudgingly acknowledges the "handsome façades of Stockholm" before spending the greater part of her book suggesting that a sinister, phantom Sweden lay behind it, one involving the same horrors Fennell describes, along with another common accusation made against twentieth-century Sweden: pervasive, socially sanctioned homosexuality, spreading like a disease in both open and conspiratorial ways throughout the nation.[74] Such suggestions of occulted misery and perversity teeming behind the country's sunny exterior had been made by detractors of the culturally liberal, socialist country as far back as the immediate post–World War II era. A 1948 headline in *U.S. News and World Report* reading "Lobsters for Tourists, Herrings for Swedes" suggests a deliberate and systematic practice of self-misrepresentation.[75] In another article from that year, Evelyn Waugh, of the same nationality and temperament as Fennell, allows that "at first glance [the Swedes] seem to have attained a Socialist paradise," but, on closer examination one notices the dark fact that "the favorite authors of the young are Kafka and Sartre" and that "there is a low birth rate and a high suicide rate."[76]

The charge of a high suicide rate in Sweden, opportunistically raised throughout the Cold War, climaxed at the height of Bergmania. At the 1960 Republican national convention, the outgoing president, Dwight Eisenhower, joined the chorus of disapprobation and characterized the Scandinavian country as a hotbed of drunkenness, sloth, and suicide: "I think they had almost the lowest (suicide rate) in the world but now they have more than twice our rate."[77] The idea that Sweden's economic system, socialist but hardly Stalinist, has any bearing on the suicide rate has summarily been discounted in the years since Eisenhower's remarks, in part because of recent work on seasonal affective disorder. In fact, the charge that Sweden has an unusually high suicide rate was disproved years before, once all contingencies were taken into account.[78] The charge was made so repeatedly, however, that even though Eisenhower coyly declined to identify Sweden by name in his speech, everyone who heard it, and all the journalists who reported on it, knew—and did name—the nation to which he referred.[79]

Looking at the Bergman films released in the United States throughout the first twenty years of his career, cinéastes might feel that Eisenhower's was not an unreasonable statement. *Fängelse* (1949), taking its title from a Swedish noun meaning "prison," was retitled *The Devil's Wanton* in the United States and promoted with a remark attributed to Bergman that put the taboo subject of suicide on newspapers' entertainment pages. "After life comes death," the director is quoted as saying under the headline "Ingmar Bergman on Life . . .": "That's the only thing you need to know. Those who are sentimental or frightened can resort to the church. And those who are bored, tired or indifferent can commit suicide."[80] That sentiment is not an unfair representation of the film's theme or tone. More than sixty years after its release, this crude, early work still stands as one of Bergman's darkest films. Through a complex, often hard-to-follow flashback structure, *The Devil's Wanton* presents the story of Birgitta-Carolina, a Stockholm prostitute who, after turning her "illegitimate" infant over to her abusive pimp only to have it murdered, does, in fact, commit suicide in the cellar of her apartment building. In other words, the advertising campaign, though not the English-language title, is a fair representation of the film's tone. But it erroneously characterizes Bergman's personal perspective. The quotation comes not from the director himself, but from a particularly cynical character within the film. Thus, the American publicity conflated one of the film's nihilistic characters with its director. This suggests that even before the release of a number of Bergman films in which specific characters can legitimately be seen as mouthpieces for the auteur, the "discursive surround" in Cold War American film culture was encouraging just such a conflation.[81]

In looking at how Bergman's work was used in the United States at the time, one should, however, look beyond such pieces of concrete evidence. Remembering Michel Foucault's statement that silences "are an integral part of the strategies that underlie and permeate discourses," one does well to consider those elements of the director's oeuvre that Cold War America chose to ignore or dismiss when Bergman's productions were first being released within the United States.[82] *Till glädje* (1950) focuses on an ambitious musician (Stig Olin) who achieves emotional serenity only after abandoning an egocentric desire to become a superstar soloist, choosing instead to accept a more modest position within his orchestra as second violinist. Surprisingly for a latter-day Bergman spectator, the film strongly reflects and seems to endorse Sweden's socialistic philosophy and communal spirit before concluding with an unambiguously upbeat ending. But *Till glädje*, despite being a more technically and dramatically polished production than *The*

Devil's Wanton (or *Frustration* or *Thirst*, for that matter), with a clearer narrative and more-sympathetic characters, did not follow *Wanton* into U.S. theaters. Even after the success of *Wild Strawberries* (released in America in 1959), which stars one of *Till glädje*'s primary performers, Victor Sjöström, it remained undistributed in the United States. The film, the Swedish title of which literally translates into a very "un-Bergmanesque" "To Joy," had what was perhaps the most modest American premiere of any of the director's commercially imported releases. It quietly appeared on a local television station in New York in 1974.[83]

The Devil's Wanton was not the only brooding Bergman film released in the United States while more optimistic work was ignored. *Det regnar på vå kärlek* [*It Rains on Our Love*] (1946) never appeared in a commercial U.S. release, despite having won the Swedish Film Journalists Club's award for best picture of the year and a notice in *Variety* calling it "perhaps one of the best films any Swedish producer ever made."[84] Popular at home because of its "playful and lyrical style," this "whimsical . . . quaint, amiable film" follows a pair of young heterosexual lovers (Barbo Kollberg and Birger Malmsten) from troubled backgrounds who suffer a series of often-comic travails as they attempt to establish a "respectable" life for themselves.[85] While *Det regnar på vå kärlek* might be considered critical of Swedish society in its illustration of heartless bureaucrats who expect its beleaguered protagonists to negotiate a series of picayune hurdles, the film's generally sunny temperament and its hopeful denouement belie the occasional moments of pessimism. Laura Hubner recently has written that upon finally seeing the film on television, she found that it "radiated happiness."[86] Indeed, its numerous comedic sequences suggest the contemporaneous Ealing comedies produced in Great Britain. Although *Det regnar på vå kärlek* begins with David fresh out of prison and Maggi, not unlike Birgitta-Carolina in *The Devil's Wanton*, struggling as a pregnant former prostitute, its upbeat conclusion offers the very antithesis of the ending of its sister film. Of course, had *Det regnar på vå kärlek* (as *It Rains on Our Love*) and *Till glädje* (as *To Joy*) been the first two Bergman films to appear in the United States, rather than *Hets* and *Skepp till India land* (as *Torment* and *Frustration*), it might have been possible to develop a very different conception of the filmmaker, one less neurotic, but also less queerly critical of Kaja Silverman's "dominant fiction."

As long as the Cold War was a concern in the mind of the American spectator, however, it would hardly have been possible to think of Bergman without at least some residual sense of queerness. He would always be a European filmmaker, specifically a Swedish one, and those designations connoted a queerness that transcended any specific instance of politically motivated reception. The full conflation of what was seen as Sweden's political and economic deviancy and its supposed sexual deviancy most obviously took shape around Dag Hammarskjöld, who became secretary-general of the United Nations in 1953. Rumors that the unmarried forty-seven-year-old intellectual was a homosexual began circulating as soon as he was nominated for the post, encouraged in part by Hammarskjöld's resentful predecessor, Trygve Lie.[87] Most biographers consider Hammarskjöld to have been asexual, but as one puts it, "the homosexual rumor was resurrected from time to time by various detractors when he was under political attack."[88] In published discourse during his UN tenure, accusations usually took the form of innuendo: there were "comparisons sometimes made of him with Lawrence of Arabia, whose homoerotic tendencies are well-known," as well as the odd rumor, reported in the *New Yorker*, that Hammarskjöld once went skiing with a "volume of Proust . . . under his arm."[89] In perhaps the most insidious conflation of Sweden's political stance with a failure of heterosexual masculine potency, the *Chicago Daily Tribune* described Hammarskjöld upon his emergence on the international stage as simply "a political neuter."[90] As that term suggests, imaginings of Swedish sexuality and gender took form not simply around ideas of homosexuality or heterosexuality, masculinity or femininity, but somewhere queerly and inscrutably in between, imaginings reflecting a nation aligned neither with the worldwide communist revolution nor with American or British capitalism and colonialism.

Focusing a keen eye on the queer side of the equation, the era's fledgling lesbian and gay press occasionally remarked on the controversies, usually in the form of quotations from nongay publications that functioned as self-parodies. *One* noted the early battle in Sweden for homosexual rights, reprinting reactionary quotations about it made by Ronald Clark in the British periodical *The People*. "Perhaps I'm just a typically prudish product of the 'decadent west,'" Ronald Clark stated, offering a puzzling contradiction, but his prudishness was uppermost: "I deplore [Sweden's] open acceptance of homosexuality. . . . [Sweden's National League for Sex Equality chairman] Hr. Ove Ahlstrom is a man who openly boasts of the League's 400-membership figure for Stockholm alone. And, as he was careful to explain, Lesbians are also eligible for membership in what I regard as his weird and horrifying League of the Damned."[91]

With the abundance of allusions to a queer Sweden, it is hardly surprising that "Swedishness" found itself attached to gay-themed films having no connection with the country; an example appears in *One's* review of Veit Harlan's notorious West German production *The Third Sex* (1957), which repeatedly refers to the production as Swedish for no self-evident reason.[92] Conversely, a sense of queerness would be attached to many Swedish films with no, or very little, actual homosexual content, none more so than the early Bergman films. As mentioned in the prior chapter, the adjective "strange" often functioned in film advertisements in the pre-Stonewall era as a code word for queer sexuality, and Bergman's cinema received this treatment recurrently. In addition to the previously discussed *Thirst, Sommaren med Monika* (literally "Summer with Monika"), after first being released in a dubbed and cut version with a new jazz sound track as *Monika: The Story of a Bad Girl* for the drive-in and grindhouse circuit, also reappeared at the height of Bergman's popularity as, simply, *Monika*, but with a new tagline accompanying its redefined status as a Swedish-language art film: "the Story of a Strange Girl."[93] Even Bergman's fairly traditional love story *Summer Interlude* somehow seemed strange to Bosley Crowther, allowing its original distributor to highlight that particular mischaracterization in its ads.[94] As a result, this "story of a sad, strange love affair" doubtless attracted numerous aficionados of the nonnormative, both gay and straight, to its screenings throughout urban America; many homophile men, no doubt, were further compelled to see it by the ballet-world setting and the erotically enticing images of Birger Malmsten as its beautifully doomed male object of cinematic adoration.[95]

The acclaimed romantic comedy *Smiles of a Summer Night* clearly merited a wide international release whether it conformed to outsiders' attitudes about Sweden or not (in some ways it did, in some ways it did not), and with it, Bergman finally became a filmmaker whose annual productions were destined for U.S. distribution, whatever their purported sensibility. Following the release of *Smiles*, American audiences were presented with the three films that cemented Bergman's international stardom: *The Seventh Seal, Wild Strawberries,* and *The Magician.* Each is usually viewed as reflecting the brooding sensibility that helped concretize the director's image for years, even though they all contain elements of comedy and romance. At the same time, other Bergman-directed films from the second half of the 1950s, those not easily reflective of a neurotically depressed socialist dystopia, were regarded as anomalies. Offering a gratuitous swipe at what it called Scandinavia's "gloom for gloom's sake," the *New York Reporter* opined that *Brink of Life* (1957), a Bergman film with an antiabortion theme and a happy ending, could be explained only as a calculated and deceptive opportunity for "Bergman (who heretofore has tended to get all snarled up in his own allegorical webs) . . . to prove he is capable of spinning out a lean, straightforward and thoroughly realistic film."[96] The *New Yorker's* review, pointing out Ulla Isaksson's screenplay, carefully distinguished the straightforward maternity-ward drama from what it calls "all-Bergman" films (those written by Bergman himself) such as *Wild Strawberries*. "It may be," the critic wrote, "that the French know how to bring off this sort of thing better than the Swedes."[97] *The Devil's Eye* (1960), with its warmhearted, comedic celebration of chastity, was dismissed in the same magazine as "a curiosity, full of entertaining and occasionally instructive matters, but not apt to become canonical."[98]

Ultimately, the processes involved in the ideological construction of a national imaginary operate in several interconnected ways. In the case at hand, a number of dominant cultural institutions within America utilized Bergman's work very specifically, whether with film stills (literally framed by Fennell's essay, for instance) or with entire films, often retitled, reedited, and selectively chosen for American audiences. The institutions responsible may have been doing so only to further their own specific interests, such as making a profit in the "art film business" or selling movie magazines, but in doing so they tapped into an emerging zeitgeist, as opposed to challenging it, functioning as effective support for the U.S. Cold War position. From the other direction, the "discursive surround" accompanying Bergman's films (all the various reviews, advertising campaigns, and related news articles) played a significant part in shaping the reactions to these films within the country.

The subsequent discourses built and maintained around Bergman have regularly focused on accounts of his harrowing childhood and the religious issues he admittedly grappled with as the son of a strict Lutheran minister. The result has been a portrait of a neurotic, perverse, and spiritually dissatisfied man. All the while, the media largely ignored documentary images and accounts from coworkers of a man reported to be high-spirited (though also quick-tempered) and generally self-assured.[99] Perhaps most important, however, were those issues related to how this constructed Bergman and this constructed Sweden functioned to project away from America all the disturbing thoughts and feelings that U.S. filmgoers might have had about their own culture during a time of barely repressed anxiety. Obviously, if filmgoers were to confront disquieting issues at the cinema, it was more palatable to do so at arm's length through the practice of foreign-film spectatorship. Birgitta Steene noticed this as a "displacement" that was characteristic of 1950s America, calling it the "stereotyping of a counterimage to the officially happy and optimistic American society." Bergman's early films (and I would specify those films chosen for international distribution), she continues, "many of them set in contemporary times and dealing with youthful rebellion or uneasiness with bourgeois autocracy . . . lay bare similar repressed anxieties in a nation that was trying to uphold traditional values in a postwar world."[100]

Even though set in Sweden, Bergman's contemporary dramas like *Frustration* and *Thirst* asked Americans to confront an anxiety that was still too close for comfort and too intense for many. With *The Seventh Seal* (set in the Middle Ages) and *The Magician* (set in the nineteenth century), however, the repressed melancholy of America's postwar era, its nervous anxieties about the Cold War, and the ongoing alienation of twentieth-century capitalist industrialism finally had popular elucidation, and in films set at a reassuring distance across the Atlantic and in the past. Even better, Americans were able not only to have that anxiety projected elsewhere, but also to be told that it was the result of an ideology counter to that operating in their own nation, the just deserts of a society that refused to do what America was doing and was telling that other nation to do.

For queer American audiences, however, who were in a similar circumstance themselves—foreigners in an inhospitable land—the on-screen foreigners could be differently conceived, and a counterdiscourse emerged through films speaking eloquently to those most sympathetic spectators. And if the word "strange" had gradually disappeared from discussions about Bergman's films by the 1960s—even as, in many ways, his films actually became stranger—another word began to appear in relation to the director's work, one with its own relation to queer understandings of psychoanalytic theory and to queerness itself: "uncanny." In retrospect, many of Bergman's earlier films could best have been described by that term too. This development is discussed in the next chapter.

Sometimes I think I'm a lesbian man obsessed by other women. Sometimes I think that my sensations and feelings are extremely feminine and very little of the manly sort. Well, I don't know.

Ingmar Bergman (1971)

Chapter Three

The Uncanny Undefined

In 1965 in "Tangents," a long-running tongue-in-cheek column in *One* magazine, there was a short notice exemplifying the connection between Sweden and a reactionary form of gender anxiety. It was printed under a subheading, "Swedish Males Becoming Feminized":

"Men, it appears, are taking women's place as the 'weaker sex'—at least in Sweden." So begins a Reuters' [*sic*] dispatch published in the *Los Angeles Times* for 7-18-65. The dispatch hastens to explain this statement in terms of a conspicuous decline in the health of Swedish men, and a sharp rise in the death rate for men compared with that for women. Lars Widen, director of Stockholm's Central Bureau of Statistics, is quoted as saying (of Swedish males), "Man has not merely become the weaker sex, but even the much weaker sex." But then the dispatch goes on to generalize: "Doctors and sociologists here have also noted a change in young people. They say the actual facial features of boys have become more effeminate" and that "in larger Swedish cities, it is no longer easy to decide which is boy and which is girl at first sight. Hair is the same length, sweeping down to shoulder level, and clothes are often identical." From *One* in the U.S.A., a broad "ho hum" . . . so what else is new?[1]

Thus, just as previous reports had taken Swedish death statistics out of context in order to make dubious claims connecting socialism with suicide, the Reuters article implies an odd conflation of longevity with masculinity, as well as of long hair with femininity, in order to continue forecasting dire consequences for the ideologically deviant nation.

Sweden was widely referred to as the "land of the middle way" throughout the first decades of the Cold War. In fact, this description was used as early as 1936, when Marquis W. Childs used "The Middle Way" as the subtitle of his study of that nation's cooperative society.[2] By 1947, when the volume was reissued in a revised edition, "the middle way" had found regular and widespread use in, among other publications, "tourist guidebooks and the official literature of Sweden."[3] In 1956, an article in the *New York Times* described "the middle way" as a sociopolitical system featuring "moderate socialism and a middle class society—neither laissez-faire capitalism on the one hand nor nationalized or socialized industry on the other and with the representative democracy of a parliamentary system."[4] While such a definition might initially have seemed innocuous or, for Cold War progressives, even positive, once it was considered in tandem with (or perhaps one should say, once it was intermingled with) fears about Sweden's progress in gender equality and sexual liberalism, the specter of a perverse androgyny was destined to raise its uncanny, undefined face. Indeed, as an intentionally disquieting Cold War–era metaphor for Sweden, the image of androgyny was central.

As if offering supplementary evidence for this fearfulness, or perhaps a perversely wry provocation of it, Ingmar Bergman's productions throughout the period often addressed androgynous forms of subjectivity, alongside a dynamic of genderless sexual desire that could be seen as capable of emerging, at least in theory, from them. Like Freud's work in this area, Bergman's bares the traces of a protracted struggle with repressive patriarchal forces maintaining both gender and solid, concurrently gendered forms of sexuality. The final results of this kind of struggle, whether found in Freud's writings or Bergman's films, require a strongly hermeneutic enterprise, one in which Bergman's queerly positioned U.S. spectators were more than aptly positioned to engage.

Like Freud, but perhaps more consciously, Bergman approached issues of gender deconstruction directly through the affective state of the uncanny: the dark quality that Hélène Cixous once specifically identified as emerging through "the figure of the androgyne."[5]

The Uncanny Undefined

Significantly, the first notable mention of the word "uncanny" in the U.S. press in relation to Bergman's work seems to have occurred just after the domestic debut of the director's first film to explicitly foreground the issue of androgyny, *The Magician*, in 1959. Pointing out the seemingly remarkable fact that Bergman's films often explored female subjectivity with a previously unprecedented sense of engagement in the cinema, the *New York Times* remarked on the director's "uncanny insight into the problems and thoughts of women."[6]

Approaching the concept of the uncanny within the context of European cultural production and its reception, including its relationship with the Bergmanian sense of androgyny, is virtually unthinkable without paying rigorous attention to Freud's cornerstone essay "Das Unheimliche," which was originally published in the autumn of 1919 and had, by the late 1950s, become a landmark text of which Bergman and his spectators must have been at least indirectly aware.[7] Translated into English as "The 'Uncanny,'" it begins with an exhaustive linguistic dissection that is used as an entry into the topic. "*Das unheimliche*" is, obviously enough, the negation of the German word "*heimlich*," which means "homely" (as in "of the home"), "comfortable," or "intimate." *Das Heimlich* is thus, Freud reports, that which arouses a "sense of agreeable restfulness and security as in one within the four walls of his house."[8]

While this concept seems untroublesome enough at first glance, before the reader is given a definition of *heimlich*'s opposite, a more sinister meaning is attributed to the original word: "Concealed, kept from sight, so that others do not get to know of or about it, withheld from others. . . . Deceitful and malicious toward cruel masters."[9] *Unheimlich*, then, is shown to be the antithesis of *heimlich* and, paradoxically, a conflation of much of what the latter means. As Freud put it, quoting his preferred definition, by Friedrich Schelling, "'*Unheimlich*' is the name for everything that ought to have remained . . . secret and hidden but has come to light."[10]

Freud did not devote particular attention to the uncanny or uncanniness as a foregrounded subject until his 1919 paper, yet the term had occurred in his writings as much as ten years earlier. It appears three times in his famous account of the sexually traumatized and repressed—"Rat Man"—and again, several months later, in his speculative account of Leonardo da Vinci's sexual repression and subsequent genius.[11] In the latter case, Freud refers to Leonardo's "infantile" personality traces and his childlike proclivity for playfulness, remarking that these manifestations indicate why that particular artist "often appeared uncanny and incomprehensible to his contemporaries."[12]

Freud's use of the word in those earlier studies was surely not casual; indeed, Freud's analysis of Leonardo is, itself, quite uncanny, even when compared with other cases from the psychoanalyst's career. In it, Freud interprets the "piece of information about Leonard's childhood" that the artist left behind in his notebooks regarding a memory, seemingly from the cradle, in which the infant found himself besieged by a vulture, which came down to the child, opened the boy's mouth with its tail, and struck his lips repeatedly with its plumage.[13]

As Freud lays out his interpretation, the young Leonardo is shown to be remembering not a factual occurrence (how could he be?) but a vivid fantasy, originating at a later date, of the boy performing an act of fellatio. This assessment may not seem remarkable in and of itself, but Leonardo's fantasy of infantile homosexuality is shown to harbor, just behind it, the early state of *jouissance,* in which all persons "once felt comfortable—when we were still in our suckling days . . . and took our mother's (or wet-nurse's) nipple into our mouth and sucked at it."[14] As unsettling as any of the numerous examples of uncanniness that Freud offers in his 1919 essay, this account of a primal memory of a nipple transmogrifying first into a penis and then into a rapacious bird provides the key that explains the uncanny adult Leonardo: a person who harbors in his thoughts and actions the traces of the bisexual, pregendered infant well into his maturity.

Lest one think Freud is engaged simply in a specific hermeneutical enterprise involving a great figure's biography, it should be remembered that a cornerstone insight of psychoanalysis is that each child is born "constitutionally bisexual." In *Three Essays on the Theory of Sexuality* (1905), Freud wrote: "Long-familiar facts of anatomy lead us to suppose that an originally bisexual physical disposition has, in the course of evolution, become modified into a unisexual one, leaving behind only a few traces of the sex that has become atrophied."[15] In other words, in Freud's understanding, both biological males and biological females carry within themselves a trace memory of an earlier evolutionary stage of undivided "wholeness."

In many of his writings, Freud seems beholden to the conventional thought of his day, which suggests that it can only be a person's "feminine" sensibility that desires to have sex with a "masculine" partner, and vice versa. In other words, masculinity requires femininity in its sexual object, and femininity requires masculinity in its sexual object. While Freud would later develop a theory of homosexuality in ways that seem more in line with contemporary understandings, only with the development of queer theory would scholars fully conceptualize homosexual and heterosexual object choices as distinct from—although not completely unrelated to—female and male gender positions.[16] Meanwhile, the notion of bisexuality remained problematic in psychoanalysis; while it stood for a mere masculine-feminine mixture in the person, it was often discussed by Freud as part of a heterosexual-homosexual dynamic in the psyche. Put simply, Freud made the mistake of confusing gendered identity with sexual object choice.

In the fourth edition (1914) of *The Interpretation of Dreams*, Freud makes just this conflation: "We can assert of many dreams, if they are carefully interpreted, that they are bisexual, since they unquestionably admit of an 'over-interpretation' in which the dreamer's homosexual impulses are realized."[17] Bisexuality is seen in this passage to be a state in which one's secondary gender position (for example, the "woman in the man") asserts itself through an attraction to a member of one's own biological sex. Gender divisions are thus very much still at play in Freud's schema, and one could say that this kind of bisexual person, at the psychic level, is no more or no less than a person whose homosexuality is played out heterosexually, as for example, when a man thinks of himself as a woman when having sex with another man. To further complicate the issue, just beyond the two notions in Freud's writing, bisexuality is also understood in psychoanalytic discourse to be an extension of, or a construction out of, what Freud famously called "polymorphous perversity."

The term "polymorphous perversity" first appears in the *Three Essays*. Here Freud makes his revolutionary statement that sexuality is an erotic force that exists beyond the genitals, beyond the procreative function, and beyond, it would finally seem, gender itself. He persuasively argues that everything from thumb sucking to the practice of delaying one's bowel movements until maximum anal stimulation can be felt, are, in fact, sexual practices.[18] In "Polymorphously Perverse Disposition," a subsection within the second of the three essays, Freud writes: "An aptitude for ['sexual irregularities'] is innately present in [the child's] disposition."[19] Later he summarizes:

> In view of what was now seen to be the wide dissemination of tendencies to perversion we were driven to the conclusion that a disposition to perversions is an original and universal disposition of the human sexual instinct and that normal sexual behavior is developed out of it as a result of organic changes and psychical inhibitions occurring in the course of maturation: we hoped to be able to show the presence of the original disposition in childhood. Among the forces restricting the direction taken by the sexual instinct we laid emphasis upon shame, disgust, pity and structures of morality and authority erected by society.[20]

As the growing child travels through the stages in the Freudian epic of normative sexual development, moving from the thumb-sucking "oral stage" (based on the first part of one's body that one can gain control of and pleasure through) and the subsequent "anal stage" (based on that other noticeable part of the digestive apparatus that the child can pleasurably control) to the stage of a "genital" sexual focus, one gradually abandons the earlier stages, at least as they can exist as dominant loci of erotic satisfaction. They remain in trace form in "nonperverse" adult activities such as nail-biting, smoking or gum chewing, and, perhaps, in constipation; otherwise, they retreat into the mists of what Freud calls a person's "prehistory," that part of the child's life that has been hidden by what Freud calls "infantile amnesia."[21] For Freud, "infantile amnesia . . . turns everyone's childhood into something like a prehistoric epoch and conceals from him the beginnings of his own sexual life."[22] In retrospect, this can be seen as an undeniable, strong link between Freud's conception of human sexuality, certainly in its earliest stages, and his mature understanding of the uncanny.

As Freud developed a more specific understanding of what links the uncanny with the child's prehistory, he began with the commonsensical notion that the uncanny corresponds to "what is frightening—to what arouses dread and horror":

> Among instances of frightening things there must be one class in which the frightening element can be shown to be something repressed which *recurs*. This class of frightening things would then constitute the uncanny; and it must be a matter of indifference whether

what is uncanny was itself originally frightening or whether it carried some *other* affect.[23]

Here Freud stresses that despite what one might think (specifically, that an uncanny moment comes when a particularly dreadful or horrible memory from childhood recurs), uncanniness can occur when repressed feelings reappear that were not necessarily frightening in their original form. Obviously, however, these feelings must involve memories that represent something that threatens the subject in the present. Freud continues:

> Our conclusion could then be stated thus: an uncanny experience occurs either when infantile complexes which have been repressed are once more revived by some impression, or when primitive beliefs which have been surmounted seem once more to be confirmed. Finally we must not let our predilection for smooth solutions and lucid exposition blind us to the fact that these two classes of uncanny experience are not always sharply distinguishable.[24]

Lest one conclude that Freud would have us connect all moments of uncanniness with a repressed, forgotten, or otherwise evolved-away-from constitutional bisexuality or infantile androgyny, one should remember Freud's precise position, which was revealed during his debates with Wilhelm Fliess. According to Freud, "Fliess was inclined to regard the antithesis between the sexes as the true cause and primal motive force of repression." In other words, for Fliess, a struggle between the feminine and the masculine impulses in the self were, at a biological level, the sole cause of repression in the psyche. "I am," Freud asserted, "disagreeing with his view when I decline to sexualize repression this way."[25] Freud held to the conviction that a bisexual struggle in the self cannot be considered the sole cause of repression. He also warned against bisexuality being seen as the sole motive for or explanation of dream works: "To maintain . . . that *all* dreams are to be interpreted bisexually appears to me to be a generalization which is equally undemonstrable and unplausible and which I am not prepared to support."[26] On the other hand, Freud did believe that polymorphous perversity, constitutional bisexuality, and the subsequent division into heterosexual and homosexual states represented periods in the individual's past that were oftentimes, though not always, repressed.

To connect polymorphous perversity with constitutional bisexuality and then to connect both of them with a condition in which one is attracted to other gendered people (through heterosexual or homo-sexual desire, or both) and, finally, to put it in relation to the uncanny, one must first contend with Freud's concept of castration. Although it is an organizing concept and central metaphor in Freud's thought as a whole, the castration complex is, more specifically, a necessary facet in Freud's definition of the uncanny. Freud adumbrates the complex in "The Infantile Genital Organization":

> The [male] child arrives at the discovery that the penis is not a posses-sion which is common to all creatures that are like himself. An acci-dental sight of the genitals of a little sister or playmate provides the oc-casion for this discovery. . . . We know how children react to their first impressions of the absence of a penis. They disavow the fact and be-lieve that they *do* see a penis, all the same. They gloss over the contra-diction between observation and preconception by telling themselves that the penis is still small and will grow bigger presently; and they then slowly come to the emotionally significant conclusion that after all the penis had at least been there before and been taken away after-wards. The lack of a penis is regarded as a result of castration, and so now the child is faced with the task of coming to terms with castration in relation to himself.[27]

Freud's understanding of castration anxiety—particularly when cou-pled with its corollary in females, "penis envy"—has caused a good deal of vexation in the decades since its initial postulation. A number of latter-day Freudians, stressing the importance of cultural specificity, see castration anxiety as a result of particularly monstrous Victorian-era repression. Robin Wood's remarks are typical of this stance: "In Freud's time castration anxiety . . . was . . . rooted in practical family reali-ties: Little boys were actually threatened with castration as punishment for masturbation, if not directly ('If you do that I'll cut it off'), then indirectly ('If you do that it will drop off')."[28] This reading of Freud's work—while important to consider—is, if taken alone, extremely reduc-tive, suggesting that many, perhaps all, psychological and sexual con-structs would be radically different were a subject simply raised in a more permissive environment.

Freud's particular genius was his ability to use resonant metaphors, like that of the boy traumatized by the sight of his sister's "castration," to describe virtually universal psychic processes that might otherwise have resisted description, particularly considering the limited vocabulary of his day. In writing of a child "coming to terms with castration in relation to himself," Freud suggests with considerable rhetorical force that what the child is, in fact, "coming to terms with" is the trauma of gender difference: the trauma of realizing one is only half a complete human being, half of humanity, the trauma of realizing that one has an image in the world that, to others, does not reflect the subject's desired wholeness. This is a trauma that is itself, to be sure, magnified by the historical and cultural specifics that Wood alluded to, and that made the threat of literal castration such a nightmare in late-nineteenth and early twentieth-century Europe.

The influence of Freud's writings on this dynamic should not suggest that he was the first to use castration as a metaphor. He was always eager to list the many manifestations of castration as metaphor in myth and literature that predated his theorizations, from Zeus to Sophocles (and in all those cases, castration was never far removed from that kind of murder—patricide—that eventually would be seen as a destruction of a part of the self necessitated by hegemonic subject formation).[29] Proving that castration continues to exist as such a resonant and central metaphor is the fact that it emerges time and again within a kind of collective unconscious as a stand-in for the shock that greets the subject upon his or her traumatic engendering.[30]

In Freud's 1919 essay, he distinguishes between two forms of the uncanny, only one of which explicitly involves the castration complex. He finds one of these two—the one proceeding "from repressed infantile complexes, from the castration complex, womb-phantasies, etc."[31]—to be most often elicited in various forms of literature and cinema, while the other—arising when one is confronted with an event that "seems to confirm to the old, discarded beliefs [one has surmounted]"[32]—is more likely to occur in conscious life. But Freud makes a connection—and he makes it several times—between the notion of cultural or evolutionary prehistory and an individual's personal prehistory, which is erased via infantile amnesia.

Thus, uncanny moments in fiction, those that return someone to the moment of castration as gender differentiation, can be said to effectively connect with, and be inseparable from, the sense of uncanniness that floods someone outside the library or movie theater, where the exposed subject is suddenly found regressing to that homelike yet vastly disturbing state of primitive "prehistory." Bergman's cinema demonstrates this connection with great alacrity and increasing power in a series of films that begins with *The Magician*.

Coming after *Smiles of a Summer Night, The Seventh Seal,* and *Wild Strawberries,* the American premiere of *The Magician* occurred at the zenith of Ingmar Bergman's international fame; *Time* magazine's cover story on him appeared during its U.S. engagement.[33] Indeed, the writer-director's name appears twice in the initial *New York Times* advertisement—"Ingmar Bergman's *The Magician,* Written and Directed by Ingmar Bergman"—suggesting both the auteur's star power at that moment and a strange sense of doubling that emerges as a theme within the film itself.[34] *The Magician* is also significant as the first of the director's films to explore androgyny and thus, not surprisingly, the first (it seems) to inspire critics to explicitly cite the quality of "the uncanny" in relation to his work. Echoing the *New York Times'* use of the word two months earlier to describe Bergman's insight into women, the *Los Angeles Times'* Charles Stinson identified a primary Bergman theme thus: "a tidy and confident scientism vs. . . . the irrational and uncanny aspects of reality."[35]

Beyond the doubling of Bergman's name in the advertisements, as mentioned above, other elements in the U.S. publicity materials promised potential filmgoers a motion picture featuring more popularly understood components of the uncanny: those associated with the horror genre.[36] Approached freshly, the film—titled *Ansiktet* in Sweden and released in the United Kingdom under an exact translation of that word, as *The Face*—might just as honestly have been promoted as an erotic comedy; more than a handful of French and Italian films with less eroticism and fewer moments of comedy have been released in America as sex farces. Ignoring that option, the Janus Films ad features a horror-genre tagline—"[a] haunting journey to the nether-world between reality and the unknown"—next to the image of actor Max von Sydow's shadowed and malevolent-looking face (figure 3.1).[37] But despite being promised a supernatural chiller, the film's spectators had to engage with a feature that moves dexterously from horror to comic romance and back again in a cycle that repeats itself several times. Thus, before an American viewer could assume a position of spectatorship within the auditorium, *The Magician's* "discursive surround" had already pointed the way toward an experience in which Bergman's tonal shifts would be readable as a manifestation of an uncanny duality.

The film's first several minutes are fully in accord with its publicity material while also being characteristic of what American filmgoers had come to expect from a Bergman film. Like *The Naked Night* and

Figure 3.1. Newspaper advertisement for *The Magician* (Ingmar Bergman, Sweden, 1958). Janus Films. *New York Times*, August 27, 1959. Used with permission of Janus Films, Inc.

The Seventh Seal, The Magician begins with a series of shots chronicling a group of silent travelers photographed against a bleak, overcast landscape; in this instance, it is identifiable (through the performers' costumes) as taking place at some time in the mid-nineteenth century. As in *The Naked Night*, the taciturn group seems to consist of itinerant entertainers, and as in *The Seventh Seal*, von Sydow quickly appears on the screen and is positioned as the central performer.[38] But despite what must have felt to Bergman's legion of admirers like a comforting sense of familiarity, the overriding emotional effect of *The Magician's* first scene, like those of *The Naked Night* and *The Seventh Seal*, is one of simmering disquiet. The Munchian landscape, strikingly photographed by Gunnar Fisher, shimmers with muted shades of pervasive gray, and the plaintive notes of a nondiegetic guitar alternate on the sound track with the cries of an angry on-screen magpie. Throughout, the diegetic but invisible sound of the wind is also heard blowing across the hills. From the beginning, then, *The Magician* offers its spectator an eerie sense of the familiar and a familiar sense of the eerie, ones in which the seen and the unseen, as well as various other forms of presence and absence, intertwine. As the plot unfolds over the following one hundred minutes, a veritable catalogue of uncanny images appears, from a disembodied eye and hand to a pair of seemingly dead bodies that rise to their feet to pursue the living. But beyond these explicitly horrific images, others create a subtler sense of mystery and anxiety, and many of these gravitate toward and revolve around discomforting understandings of gender.

The Uncanny Undefined

Figure 3.2. Aman and Vogler in *The Magician*. Svensk Filmindustri.

In the first scene, as one of a series of establishing shots, we see what appear to be two men in tuxedos sitting on the ground and waiting for their horses to be fed. But one quickly notices obvious differences between the two individuals. While the figure on the left (recognizable as von Sydow) strongly connotes masculinity—with his top hat, pipe, beard, and sideburns—the other is visibly androgynous: despite sideburns, the figure on the right is clean shaven and bears a distinctly feminine physiognomy. Nevertheless, in a rather subversive twist on tradition, the second figure occupies a more dominant position in the frame. The bearded personage is stretched out passively on the ground, while the clean-shaven one is sitting up and is, as Marilyn Johns Blackwell points out, "in a position both higher on the hill and more central" within the frame.[39] As the film progresses and the troupe of travelers continues its journey in the coach, a subsequent two-shot of the couple amplifies the smooth-faced figure's feminine features while giving the bearded man the prominent position in the frame (figure 3.2). This not so gradual feminization and subordination of the androgynous character is largely responsible, I would imagine, for the film's reputation as, finally, a conservative and conventional film, a reading to which Blackwell, finally, subscribes.[40]

Although Blackwell bases much of her reading of the film on the conviction that "we do not know that [Aman] is a woman until midway through the film," which is true only in terms of the narrative construction of the story, viewers can easily surmise that the androgynous personage is, in fact, a biological female.[41] U.S. filmgoers who saw Ingrid Thulin as Marianne in *Wild Strawberries*, which was released earlier that year, certainly would have had no trouble recognizing her in this role.[42] Adding to the intrigue of the film's first scenes, we cannot help noticing that a queer aura seems to emanate from the bearded figure's visage as well. The figure himself remains silent, even as his face registers a series of intense emotions. (The more feminine figure, by contrast, is quietly passive.) Furthermore, the hair on his head and chin appears so unnaturally thick and dark—virtually jet-black—that one assumes it is inauthentic. In short, both seated figures appear not to be simply men, but two people, a biological male and a biological female who are purposely taking on forms of male drag. Even if a spectator might be tempted to interpret this image positively—as an act of the kind of subversive gender performativity that Judith Butler would later examine—the scene, and much of the first half of the film, develops in a way that seems very unsettled and unsettling.[43]

Across from the androgynous, tuxedo-clad couple, an elderly woman, referred to throughout the film as Granny (Naima Wifstrand), and a middle-aged, good-natured man named Tubal (Åke Fridell) share the coach and the silent pair's journey. They are as talkative as the others are silent, but when a scream is heard through the trees beside the road, eventually causing the driver, Simson (Lars Ekborg), to jump off the coach box and rush inside, the discussion turns to the supernatural, with Granny murmuring an incantation to ward off evil. The bearded man, whose name one eventually learns is Albert Vogler, leaves the coach, crosses a brook, and walks into the forest toward the source of the scream. This sequence creates some mild suspense as the camera focuses on Vogler's boots as he carefully creeps through the grass, but when he finally kneels down next to a moaning figure, he finds nothing more (or less) horrifying than a sick, drunken actor. The trembling stranger introduces himself to Vogler and explains his malady, though not his reasons for being alone deep in the woods: "My name is Johan Spegel. As you can perceive, I am very ill. Will you offer me a little brandy? Although brandy is my infirmity, it is also my solace . . . I am an actor . . . But my illness has put an end to my career."[44]

As Spegel (Bengt Ekerot) allows Vogler to lead him out of the brush toward the coach, the two hang onto each other with a sense of closeness and indeed intimacy that seems strange between men who have just met: they look into each other's eyes as though trying to see each other's souls, and at this proximity, Spegel can see through Vogler's disguise. The published screenplay describes the finished film accurately:

"Are you an actor too?"
Vogler shakes his head.
"Why then are you disguised, sir? You are wearing a false beard and your eyebrows and hair are dyed. Are you a swindler who must hide his real face?

The Uncanny Undefined

Vogler suddenly laughs.

The dying man opens his eyes and presses his lips together in a shrewd smile.[45]

The two continue toward the coach, but the infirm actor falls into the stream. When, after Vogler picks him up and pulls him out of the water, Spegel says, "This is the last day of life," one does not doubt him. Spegel rests his head on Vogler's shoulder, offering a thematically resonant soliloquy: "I have always yearned for a knife. A blade with which to lay bare my bowels. To detach my brain, my heart. To free me from my substance. To cut away my tongue and my manhood. A sharp knife blade which would scrape out all my uncleanliness."[46] As theatrically clumsy as this passage seems—at least in English translation (Pauline Kael would later quip: "There are times when one would be happy to hand Bergman that knife")[47]—it lays out the film's theme with such clarity that one wonders why so few scholars have dealt with its obvious ramifications in their analyses of the film.

As the narrative continues to unfold, with Spegel indeed expiring shortly after being taken into the coach, the traveling performers find themselves detained upon their arrival in Stockholm. Over the next twenty-four hours, these vagabond performers, who present themselves as a harmless troupe of magicians but are suspected of being a more pernicious form of outlaw charlatans, are interrogated by city authorities who seem both frightened of them as practitioners of the "black arts," on the one hand, and eager to humiliate them, as simple frauds, on the other. Much is made of Vogler's silence by the local officials—Tubal explains to the authorities that he is mute—and the queerly inauthentic gender roles performed by Vogler and the more androgynous figure introduced as his "ward and foremost pupil, Aman" arouse palpable suspicion. Similarly, *The Magician*'s conjoined themes of silence and gender will be interrogated throughout the remainder of the film.[48] Nonqueer art-house audiences might well have found the drama's unfolding project, pitting magic against rationalism as an allegory for the ideological division between art and science, to have been an exhausted subject by the late 1950s. Kael complained that Bergman "uses a 19th-century setting for the clichés of the 20th-century," but noted that "the mysterious images of Max von Sydow as the 19th-century mesmerist, Vogler, and Ingrid Thulin as his assistant, Aman (Vogler's wife, Manda, in male disguise), carry so much latent charge of meaning that they dominate the loosely thrown-together material."[49] Read by a queer audience, these "dominating" images, played out against a story of established authorities persecuting a group of nonnormative outsiders, must have carried an even greater resonance.

Brought into the house of the city's consul, Abraham Egerman (Erland Josephson), the troupe is placed before a tribunal consisting of him; the royal medical councilor, Dr. Vergérus (Gunnar Björnstrand); and the chief of police, Starbeck (Toivo Pawlo)—who, wearing an obvious wig, connotes a somewhat less enticing form of androgyny than does Thulin's character. Granny, Tubal, and the coachman are essentially ignored while the silent, disguised Vogler, and the young androgynous Aman/Manda find themselves under intense scrutiny. When Vergérus first notices the latter, an eyeline match (along with Björnstrand's effective acting as he removes his spectacles) betrays his immediate fascination with this young "Aman."

A heterosexual viewer might assume that Vergérus identifies Aman's true gender, but *The Magician*'s queer spectators might wonder whether the doctor simply has a predilection for feminine-looking young men. The possibility of Vergérus harboring queer desires is further suggested when he allows Vogler to attempt to hypnotize him, finding himself visibly disturbed by the intimate eye contact made by the silent and mysterious queer visitor. Later, when Vergérus creeps into Aman's room late at night, seemingly to seduce her, the fact that he seems pleased to see her dressed as a woman does not negate the fact that he started to pursue her without full knowledge of her biological gender. Moments later, when Vogler enters the room and angrily interjects himself between them, breaking Vergérus's cane and shaking him by the shoulders, the doctor's line is resonant with potential sexual meanings: "Do you hate me? And I like you. This is really quite stimulating."[50] At this point, a queer spectator might have broken into a mischievous, knowing smile at the possible, now multiplying implications. Indeed the smirks and puzzled glances cast by virtually all the members of the consul's household toward both the silent middle-aged man and his young "ward" might be interpreted as something other than the reaction of people seeing through a woman's disguise: the members of this seemingly scandalized household may well suspect that the younger guest is the silent man's pubescent homosexual lover. With that in mind, the entire scenario dramatizing the establishment figures' hostility to—and persecution of—these vagabond, nonnormative "outsiders" takes on a meaning for late-1950s queer audiences that is far more timely than the critics' "straightforward" understanding.

If the visitors' sexualities are in question throughout the early scenes of the film, gender, nevertheless, remains *The Magician*'s central queer concern, one that never, however, becomes completely separated from sexual identification. In a development that Michel Foucault would have appreciated, Vergérus becomes obsessed with exposing the uncanny couple as being simple, straightforward frauds rather than supernaturally gifted performers, hoping thereby to arrest and control the specter of their uncanny personac within the realm of positivist understanding. The intellectual uncertainty that the physician feels when faced with these supposed practitioners of the black arts, and that he spends much of the film trying to dispel, is a strong indication of his own sense of uncanny disequilibrium born of the visitors' presence.[51]

During a moment of considerable dramatic suspense and clear metaphorical inference, Vergérus demands to physically examine Vogler in order to verify his claim of muteness. After obliging his guest to open his mouth and stick out his tongue, Vergérus violently grasps Vogler's throat and squeezes his windpipe in an attempt to locate the man's vocal cords. Finishing the examination, Vergérus says: "I regret to say, Mr. Vogler, that I find no reason for your muteness." As the screenplay describes it: "Vogler has tears in his eyes. He wipes them away with the back of his hand."[52] The furious sense of sexualized humiliation implicit in this examination underscores the film's legibility as a metaphor for uncanny queerness under positivist siege and sharply focuses that trope upon the issue of muteness, willed or otherwise. By extension, the uncanny sense of illegibility that accompanies a refusal of opacity is also suggested.

Much of the rest of the film involves the magician's silent attempt to exact revenge by mortifying the doctor. As this plot development unfolds through the latter half of the film, and as Aman is revealed as a woman, *The Magician* does, arguably, lose some of its queer edge. Ultimately, it becomes a rather conventional comedy of manners in which the bourgeois officials, particularly Vergérus, find themselves the targets of Vogler's complexly devised retribution. A comfortingly traditional subplot, one that finally lessens the film's uncanny impact, shows the "downstairs" servants finding themselves drawn to Granny's "magic" potions and to the coachman's and Tubal's earthy sex appeal. Blackwell, having noted the potentially radical nature of Aman/Manda's androgyny in the film's early scenes, feels that "once Aman is unmasked [as a woman and Vogler's loyal wife], both to Vergérus and to us, the film abandons its problematizing potential and moves forward toward an essentially conservative and conventional conclusion."[53] Those hoping for a more radical understanding of sexuality and gender would have to wait for subsequent Bergman films, but *The Magician*'s denouement nonetheless leaves spectators with a number of tantalizing, and uncanny, unanswered questions with which to contend.

Alone in their guest room, Manda and Vogler are finally visible to the spectator outside their social costumes, and their appearances change from ones signifying degrees of masculinity to ones, at some level, signifying femininity. Suddenly, Vogler is much less hirsute—his beard is gone and his hair shorter, indicating he had been wearing a wig; what hair remains is a willowy, soft blond color. Without his black wig, false beard, and sideburns, and with his face powder and hoop earring more prominent, he suddenly has a pronounced feminine appearance. Manda, who is revealed in her feminine persona in the same scene, is also transformed from a brunette to a blond. More curiously, in contrast with the short black haircut she sported in her male guise, she now has a long, flowing head of hair that cascades down behind her shoulders. Since it seems impossible that Manda could have hidden all her newly visible blond hair under a short, boyish, dark wig, and since there is no immediate logic for the particularities of her husband's public disguise, one is faced with interpreting the changes in their appearances according to a different, more metaphorical logic.

Only in the privacy of their room does Vogler take off a wig and false beard that has allowed him to function as an appropriately authoritative—for his profession—masculine figure in the masculine public sphere. Furthermore, with his sudden lack of facial hair made apparent immediately after suffering a series of humiliations at the hands of Vergérus, Vogler's visual emasculation reflects his private fears about his own lack of mastery. At the end of this sequence, he confesses to Manda, in only his second line of dialogue in the film: "I hate their faces, their bodies, their movements, their voices. But I am also afraid. Then I become powerless."[54] Likewise, Manda has put on a wig that allows her to perform a female role precisely where it is most appropriate—in the private, domestic world of a couple's bedroom.[55] As a result, Manda's newly seen femininity appears to be as much, or even more, a costumed, culturally conditioned performance as her previous androgynous appearance. Blackwell reads this development, not at all unreasonably, as a retreat in the film's radical project: "Back in 'correct' dress, Manda becomes a loving wife, comforting and consoling her husband in his artistic crisis."[56] But there is a queerer way to interpret it. The change in the couple's appearance, revealing lovers who at first appeared to be gay men but who now are suggestive of a demasculinized, lesbian eroticism, points to a number of developments, taken up in subsequent Bergman films, involving the connections between gender, sexuality, and the uncannily amorphous and androgynous matter from which they are constructed.

As the film concludes, with Vogler faking his death in order to appear to resurrect himself from an autopsy table and thereby frighten and humiliate Vergérus, spectators are immersed in a tour de force climax capable of temporarily unnerving them and plunging them into the realm of the uncanny as effectively as it does the once-rationalist physician. The sequence not only dramatizes what, according to Freud, have traditionally "been represented as most uncanny *themes*"—specifically, "apparent death and the re-animation of the dead"—but also does so by offering a veritable catalogue of *effects* noted by Freud for their uncanniness.[57] As this happens, "the distinction between imagination and reality is effaced" in Vergérus's mind: events occur that metaphorically (though only temporarily) castrate this man of science with stunning efficacy.[58] As Vergérus is finishing the paperwork after his autopsy of the man he thinks is Vogler (in fact, it is Spegel's body that he has dissected), he attempts to dip his pen into an inkwell, only to see a disembodied eye in the reservoir. Since, presumably, Vergérus thinks this eye belonged to Vogler, and given Freud's exhaustive discussion of "the substitutive relation between the eye and the male organ which is seen to exist in dramas and myths and phantasies," the subject of castration, at least Vogler's castration, is brought firmly to the fore.[59] Immediately thereafter, a hand detached from Spegel's dissected body is placed on Vergérus's wrist by a hidden Vogler, a sharp reminder of Freud's conviction that "a hand cut off at the wrist . . . [has] something particularly uncanny about [it] . . . [which] as we already know . . . springs from its proximity to the castration complex."[60] This sense of emasculation reaches its height after a bit of trickery on Vogler's part causes Vergérus to lose his glasses, effectively blinding and, as a result, effectively castrating the good doctor.

The fact that Vergérus's castration is directly linked with Vogler's supposed castration-dissection gives the sequence its radical charge. The doctor loses his ability to see only after he has encountered two body parts supposedly once belonging to Vogler. Indeed, he was castrated—in the sense of losing his ability to write—at the moment he found the first symbol of Vogler's castration, the disembodied eye, in his inkwell. Ultimately, Vergérus descends into total, impotent hysterics, having lost his glasses and his sense of reason, when, at the end of the sequence, blurry as his vision must be, he is faced with Vogler (or what he thinks to be Vogler's reanimated corpse), shorn of his signifiers of masculinity, his beard and dark hair—in other words, his phallus. Faced with a queerly androgynous Vogler, Vergérus too loses his masculine mastery: it amounts to a trenchant comment on how another's queerness can threaten one's own sense of normalcy.

After the impressive feat of emasculating the representative of patriarchal social power, the visiting charlatans are obliged to make a hasty retreat. But in a deus ex machina ending, they are intercepted by an emissary from the king who, rather than arresting them, escorts them to the royal palace for a command performance. A number of critics have been unimpressed by the film's final developments, even if not the penultimate horror climax, then certainly this fairy-tale resolution. The sense of the film being resolved with, essentially, a cheat of a happy ending, has caused many to consider *The Magician* a failure, or at least a minor work.[61] Assessing the film's conclusion, Blackwell, in the only English-language analysis of the film that takes account of gender issues, roundly dismisses it: "The end of the film is . . . regrettable both artistically and ethically."[62]

Looked at queerly, however, the conclusion can be read to offer a kind of uncanny conclusion that allows it to rise above what the film's initial reviewers called "an almost prankish dénouement."[63] In a series of hairpin turns, a seemingly horrific triumph on the part of the queer magician turns into his humiliation as his foe, Vergérus, regains his composure, admits that he was only momentarily frightened by an all-too-rational fear of death, and bids farewell to the performer by contemptuously throwing a coin at his feet. But crucially, in the film's final twist, the supernatural, still bifurcated on the side of queerness, does seem to rear its head again as the king's representatives arrive to admit the outsiders into the palace, in an uncanny form of wish fulfillment.

For Blackwell, the film, after a promising beginning in which "the patriarchy and . . . sexual difference as the ultimate reality" are subverted, presents a conclusion with an unambiguous "affirmation of the patriarchy," symbolized by an eager capitulation to the requests of a male monarch.[64] However, Blackwell ignores the potentially (queer) fairy-tale quality of this offscreen king, whose sudden rescuing of the disgraced outcasts might well be read as a supernatural transcendence of the realm of rational logic for an unbounded and preempirical *jouissance*. At the very least, queer, or potentially queer, spectators could well have appreciated the film's ending as described by the same *Los Angeles Times* critic who was one of the first to use the word "uncanny" in a Bergman review: "With a final . . . twist . . . Bergman ends his tale and leaves us confused—just as he intends—not, however, as to the nature of his film but as to the nature of our human certainties. Could they be even frailer than we imagine?"[65]

The Travelers

In the 1960s, the "frail" "human certainties" alluded to in the *Los Angeles Times* review of *The Magician* found themselves under ruthless attack in a series of increasingly uncanny Bergman films that finally seemed to explode the very fictions of sexuality and gender as such. While American audiences received four new Bergman productions (as well as eight previously unreleased titles) between the 1959 debut of *The Magician* and the North American release of *The Silence* in 1964, the latter film can be seen as a direct thematic follow-up to the former in several ways. Like *The Magician*, *The Silence* begins with a group of characters journeying through a seemingly inhospitable landscape; they find themselves unhappily detained in a large foreign city, in this case in a labyrinthine old hotel. In what seems like nothing so much as an uncanny repetition of *The Magician*'s opening scenes, *The Silence* begins with the (re)appearance of an only somewhat less androgynous Ingrid Thulin, positioned much as she was at the beginning of the earlier film, only now she is in a contemporary train compartment rather than a nineteenth-century horse-drawn coach.

Instead of traveling with a man finally shown to be her heterosexual spouse, Thulin's character here is gradually revealed to be accompanying her slightly younger sister and that sister's young son. Like Bertil and Rut in *Thirst*, they have apparently finished a vacation abroad and are now returning home. And like *The Magician*'s Voglers, this family conveys a sense of both exhaustion and apprehension on a journey that seems more an ordeal than an adventure, and as in *The Magician*, as well as virtually all the director's subsequent uncanny films, which include *Persona* and *Fanny and Alexander*, the characters with whom the spectator most strongly identifies are introduced as they struggle to emerge from sleep. Peter Cowie has remarked on this recurrent motif: "Bergman likes to introduce characters as they awake, fresh to the world," but *The Silence*, unlike earlier examples such as *Thirst*, *Wild Strawberries*, and *The Magician*, offers a specific, focused version of a subset of this in which the first characters seen emerging into the waking world are prepubescent boys—and these awakenings repeatedly serve as metaphors for birth.[66] Before Thulin's Ester is shown drifting in and out of sleep, it is actually her young nephew who is spotted waking. Indeed, while the nephew, Johan (Jörgen Lindström), is shown waking from a solid sleep, Ester and her sister, Anna (Gunnel Lindblom), are fitfully struggling to go to sleep, though they are ultimately unable to do so. Therefore, an allegorical drama involving a sexually inchoate person coming into adult life as two older and fully sexually aware individuals struggle, in a sense, to escape life is immediately and efficiently outlined.

Within moments, it becomes clear that Ester is gravely ill; when she is shown coughing up blood, it is easy to conclude that she has tuberculosis. In this regard, Ester, who is initially presented as a double of Manda, is more a corollary of *The Magician*'s alcoholic Spegel, whose wish to divest himself of his body, his sex organs in particular, seems to have contributed to his particular sickness; and like the actor, Ester gravitates toward liquor. But whereas *The Magician* offers no concrete motivation for Spegel's desire to divest himself of his gender (and by extension, his sexuality), Ester's implicit desire to destroy her gender and sexuality by destroying herself has a more specific motivation: she is a lesbian deeply in love with her sibling. It is easy to understand why later homosexual critics would—contra Robin Richards's review in the *Ladder* at the time of the film's release—condemn *The Silence*. Ester's repressed lesbianism also reads as a metaphor for sterility, which itself can seem connected with her imminent death. Since Ester clenches her jaw in repression, and coughs and moans in pain, a condemnation of the film along the lines of Susan Sontag's argument in *Illness as Metaphor* is easily revised to condemn Bergman for using lesbianism-sterility in equally damning, symbolic terms as a metaphor that, like illness, also inevitably raises the specter of death.[67]

In his *New York Times* review, Bosley Crowther suggests the film's tonal qualities when he described its primary setting—"a strange hotel in a strange city"—and concludes that the "mystifying and morbid" film is "almost like death."[68] His reference to the film's engagement in Manhattan's Rialto Theatre, "the old 'house of horrors,'"[69] further suggests the film's eerie and unsettling qualities (much as the setting had done for *Frustration*'s first American spectators fifteen years earlier). Richards's sensitive response (discussed in the first chapter), however, suggests a number of threads that point to the film's uncanny project. Writing that "every line counts in this baffling film," she admittedly describes the experience of the film as a confounding one, with all the negativity that implies, despite—perhaps even precisely because of—the spectator's need to engage in close analysis of it. Collapsing love and hate into something born of understanding, while suggesting that a lack of understanding represents a refuge from the "terrible" qualities coming from knowledge, Richards's review implies that the film's profound and productive sense of ideological incertitude leads to, even as it is born of, its uncanny effects.[70]

Unlike *The Magician*'s uncanniness, which comes from two basic sources, a resonant sense of androgyny and a traditional catalogue of horror-film images, *The Silence*'s overall uncanny effect is elicited with much more sophistication and much more indirectly, largely at the level of style. Indeed, Freud's statement that the feeling of the uncanny is often an "effect of silence, darkness and solitude" aptly describes the way the film works on the spectator.[71] The remarkable monochrome cinematography, achieved with Eastman Double-X film stock developed "to a higher than normal gamma" (according to the film's cinematographer, Sven Nykvist), exploited a previously impossible effect of high-contrast imagery with "more and finer gradations."[72] This makes possible vast pools of darkness in which faintly seen, ghostly details are only barely perceptible. The pervasive use of *temps mort* throughout the film, which creates a purgatorial sense of doom during the characters' sojourn in a dilapidated hotel while waiting for Ester to recuperate, along with an unnerving use of absolute silence on the sound track, gives the film the suspended quality of a trance.

As Richards suggested, this sparseness leads to a hermeneutic impulse within the spectator that results in disquieting feelings of bafflement, particularly considering how many of the film's themes unfold unstably and how many of its symbolic gestures refuse scrutability. Pauline Kael described her negative reaction to this effect found in many 1960s Bergman films: "It is far better to have inner order and outer chaos, because then there is at least a lot to look at . . . even if it is disorganized, while if the movie looks formally strict but the ideas and emotions are disturbed the viewer may feel that the fault is in himself for not understanding the work."[73] Considering the spectatorial position constructed in *The Silence* (and later in *Persona* and *Fanny and Alexander*), however, in which the world is viewed from the perspective of a presexualized child, such a lack of "understanding," one that, for some, might be its own "nice" refuge from knowledge of the social order, functions as a reminder of one's own repressed, infantile bisexuality and androgyny.

Beyond putting the viewer in the uncanny position of a child, the film uses diegetic details to reinforce a sense of infantile helplessness. Unable to understand the language of the inhospitable foreign coun-

Figure 3.3. Johan gazes at a representation of adult heterosexuality in *The Silence* (Ingmar Bergman, Sweden, 1963). Svensk Filmindustri.

try, Johan (like Anna and Ester, for that matter) is faced with an inscrutable world of undecodable symbols. In "The 'Uncanny,'" Freud writes of walking in a foreign city and trying to leave a disreputable neighborhood where "nothing but painted women were to be seen," only to find himself returning to that area again and again as he continues to make wrong turns.[74] Johan likewise cannot seem to escape a particularly mysterious signifier of adult sexuality as he explores the foreign hotel; he repeatedly finds himself passing a rather disturbing image of a "painted" woman on the wall in his wanderings: a nymph being accosted by a satyr in an image that seems to both fascinate and frighten the curious child (figure 3.3).

The film's thin and vaguely detailed plot follows the painful relationship between the sisters: two women who seem, at first glance, to embody oppositional halves of humanity, and from Johan's perspective, the women's psychic battle takes on the gravitas associated with a painful struggle within a divided human soul. By looking outside the murky categories of metaphysics, however, one can more accurately revise the film's theme as it is generally understood—"a struggle within the divided soul"—to one of primarily queer concern: "a struggle within the gendered, sexualized subject." Robin Wood perceptively resisted the problems of a simple metaphysical reading in his late-1960s assessment: "To force *The Silence* into this kind of allegory is to simplify and schematize. If Ester were merely 'soul' she wouldn't have to masturbate, and wouldn't be *physically* attracted to her sister. . . . And if Anna were merely 'body' she wouldn't feel guilt. Each sister, in fact, possesses in a suppressed and perverted form the more obvious attributes of the other."[75]

For Johan, the conflicted attraction he feels for each of the two women, his kind and thoughtful Aunt Ester and his openly sensual mother, speaks of a longing, not for a merging with the (or an) Other,

The Uncanny Undefined

but for a singular wholeness on his part. This longing is illustrated in a number of the film's most remarkable scenes. And yet, although he is obviously fascinated by and drawn to the two women in his life, Johan has a number of unsettling but strangely satisfying encounters with the men he meets while wandering alone through the hotel corridors. Not surprisingly, it was the queer Parker Tyler who became the first writer to dare remark upon the implicit homoeroticism within these encounters:

> The boy fleetingly tries to engage the attention of a male worker, is briefly entertained by a benevolent old butler, then runs into the film's most remarkable invention: a troupe of dwarfs who perform at a local theater. They are all men . . . parading down the corridor to their rooms. . . . As Bergman films it, it is like a religious procession, grand, rhythmic, almost pontifical. And one of the first things we notice is that one of the foremost dwarfs (all still in their theatrical costumes) is in drag as a bride.
>
> Whether or not any of them are homosexual hardly matters—at least, not to the dwarfs. To us . . . the point has relevance which might make it mercilessly true, and in the artistic view, not a little sublime. What the dwarfs proceed to do with the little boy, in the harmless sport which they begin, is to dress him in one of their female costumes. . . . This casual transvestite incident so common to childhood . . . may conceivably be a supreme moment of revelation for the frail, wistful little boy: the golden, glamorous sign of his homosexual future.[76]

It will not, of course, be so glamorous, or seem sublime, if his homosexuality, like his Aunt Ester's, comes to feel like a straightjacket rather than a theatrical costume. But whereas Ester seems defined in tragic terms, Johan's future seems open. (As Blackwell notes, the fact that this film, unlike *The Magician*, ultimately "does not indulge in textual closure" suggests the possibility of a cultural rejection of "patriarchal hierarchy," one that might well benefit Johan's generation.)[77] The fact that Johan is able to easily put on (and later, quickly take off) the dress, gives his exploration of gender performativity far less oppressiveness than Aman/Manda's in the earlier film, and Ester's in this film. The concurrent image of a number of the dwarfs slipping in and out of costumes that also connote gender positions—beyond the wedding dress, a dwarf dons a gorilla costume to counter the boy in his dress—further underlines the mutability of these "little people's" identificatory positions.[78]

Through a number of instances of crosscutting, the dwarfs, and Jo-

Figure 3.4. Anna gazes at a troupe of performing dwarfs in *The Silence*. Svensk Filmindustri.

Figure 3.5. The happy troupe of dwarfs performs a queer merger in *The Silence*. Svensk Filmindustri.

Figure 3.6. Heterosexuals coupling in *The Silence*. Svensk Filmindustri.

han's subjective mutability, are sharply contrasted with the sisters' utterly arrested senses of self. Perhaps the only moment in the film showing a sense of unvarnished shock on Anna's face occurs when she is faced with a lurid image of adult heterosexuality in the balcony of a dilapidated theater where the dwarfs perform. Anna looks with quiet fascination at the band of dwarfs onstage, who seem to merge together and change species to become a comically presented human centipede (figures 3.4 and 3.5), and then, almost immediately thereafter, she turns and looks with revulsion at a frantically copulating man and woman futilely attempting their own form of transcendent merging (figure 3.6). As edited, the sequence suggests a juxtaposition that results in horror, both for Anna (the spectator within the diegetic theater), and ourselves (the spectators of *The Silence*).

The Uncanny Undefined

Later, back in the hotel, when Ester is at her most heartbroken and humiliated, having discovered Anna engaging in rough sex with a waiter she picked up on the street (Birger Malmsten)—sex performed deliberately to shock and taunt the older sister—the dwarfs slowly come down the hotel corridor.[79] Passing her, they can suggest a potential state of happiness existing before adult sexual "maturity" as represented by Anna and the waiter's coitus. In context, the look on Ester's face as she watches the dwarfs passing by suggests her personal longing for a form of gender and sexuality that has not become a prison, one instead associated with the professional performers' "strange," mutable identities.

Read differently, the use of the dwarfs as a metaphor for a precon-cretized form of gender and sexual identity brings up a host of ethical problems. Dwarfs or midgets used as a metaphor for an arrested form of development, upon which "normal" people can project their fears and fantasies, has a long and ignoble tradition in literature and film.[80] But as Blackwell points out, from Johan's perspective, the one the spectator is encouraged to adopt, there is no sense of the dwarfs or their activities being "in any way threatening or distasteful"; indeed, the dwarfs can be seen as "perverted" (or "stunted" in their sexual growth) "only to those who have accepted gender roles as fixed, the adults."[81] In fact, I disagree with Blackwell to the extent that none of the adults in the film seem at all repelled or threatened by the dwarfs, as I see it; only viewers stubbornly reading against the grain of this particular text (perhaps assuming that Bergman must be doing here what other artists, such as Fellini, have done with this particular metaphor) could consider the dwarfs to represent negative stereotypes. Indeed, in comparison with the film's other characters, they are the most well-adjusted figures in the film.

With the dwarfs, counterintuitively enough, representing a state of being before the construction of the arresting shackles of gender and fixed sexuality, *The Silence* becomes a deconstructive critique of the structuring binaries of normalcy and "perversion." Robin Wood's adumbration of this insight is particularly appropriate to *The Silence*: "Freud used the term 'polymorphous perversity' to describe [a] (it seems to many of us) highly desirable and enviable state of being. It is not a felicitous choice of words: surely, if the infant's 'polymorphous' eroticism is natural and innate, it is the 'normal' (i.e., socialized) adult who is 'perverse' (literally 'turned aside')."[82]

If a number of queer spectators have been offended throughout the years that Ester's homosexuality is presented as being as much a vexed subject position as Anna's heterosexual identity, others have given a more nuanced reading. Again it was Robin Wood, writing about Bergman's films in the period before he fully embraced his own homosexuality (and thus from a position of considerable confusion and denial), who managed to offer a perspective on *The Silence* that remains of great relevance in any queer reading:

> Curiously, by the end of the film it is Ester who, for all her sexual disgust ("Semen smells nasty . . . I stank like a rotten fish when I was fertilized"), emerges as the less abnormal of the sisters: Anna's ravenous sexuality divorces sex entirely from love; in Ester's physical approaches to her sister, we can at least feel that the sexual yearning is not finally disjunct from the tenderness and complexity of feelings that go to make up complete human love, that it is not exclusively a matter of unsatisfied appetite.[83]

Wood, who later would apologize for a number of homophobic or seemingly homophobic comments written during the closeted period of his career, would no doubt want to reconsider a statement so moralistically critical of sex without love, particularly one using the word "abnormal" to characterize it. Indeed, his later writings specifically challenge that very idea. Still, he was correct to point out the greater depths of feeling involved in Ester's sexuality, and the spectator's ability to share them, as opposed to Anna's.

Thus, the film's deconstructive practice reverses the commonsensical understanding of virtually every sexual binary presented, not only by suggesting the ethical components of Ester's incestuous and lesbian desires but also by showing Anna's heterosexual activity as little more than an attempt to lash out at her sister and masochistically defile herself. Still, much of Anna's heterosexuality as vindictive performance, indeed much of the film, has been misunderstood by spectators who find that the uncanny, horror-film qualities of *The Silence* can elicit a reactionary form of dread at the very idea of sexuality itself. Hastened by the film's uncanny effect, however, the queer spectator might be more likely to identify with a protagonist, not yet heterosexual or homosexual, not yet a man (or a woman), who faces a profoundly foreign and uncanny universe not with the dread of an adult, but with a profound curiosity and sense of possibility: in other words, with young Johan.

The film is bookended by two images of Johan in a train compartment: the first, after he has awakened into life, matched by the second, as he finally leaves the uncanny, foreign land. The meanings of both images are largely the same, even if they offer crucial differences. At

the beginning of the film, Johan looks at the world as a visual spectacle, something that firmly aligns his subjectivity with that of the spectator while also suggesting both the boy's "innocence" and his sense of
phenomenological curiosity. At the end, he reads a note from Ester that
lists words from the language of the country he is leaving and their definitions. In a sense, during the course of the film, Johan emerges from
a preideological state of overwhelming imagery (what Lacan would label "the imaginary") and begins to move toward a fully symbolic world
compromised by ideology. The fact that he attempts to learn about this
profoundly foreign, overwhelmingly uncanny place through its own
language, as communicated to him by one of its lesbian guests, leaves
the spectator with a great sense of hope for Johan's future and for one's
own not yet necessarily foreclosed future. For those who come to this
understanding through the film, the resulting impact can be felt with
the force of an epiphany.

> If a man stands in front of a mirror
> and looks at himself, he can perhaps feel
> a little bit ashamed.

Ingmar Bergman,

in conversation with

Dick Cavett (1971)

Chapter Four

Staring Down Gender
"Caught Between the Shame of Looking and the Shame of Being Ashamed to Do So"

In the late 1960s and early 1970s, just as the art-film phenomenon was losing its preeminence as a global cultural force, psychoanalytic spectatorship theory began its ascent in Anglophone film studies. There is no need to offer another comprehensive review of the influential theory's evolution here. Suffice it to say, its insights remain useful, certainly when the amendments offered over the last forty years by feminist, GLBTQ, and critical-race scholars are acknowledged.[1] Briefly adumbrated, theories of spectatorship concern themselves not with a *viewer* (a flesh-and-blood filmgoer whose viewing habits can be codified in the kind of statistical analyses favored by sociologists and most historians) but with a *spectator* (defined as a more abstract form of subjectivity attending to a motion picture)—a spectator existing within an ideologically constructed space occasioned by the cinema. With this in mind, theorists more accurately refer to a "spectatorship position"—or, as later critics argued, "positions"—rather than individual film spectators, a position constructed by what the French scholar Jean-Louis Baudry first defined in 1970 as an "apparatus."[2]

Spectatorship theory, as part of a longstanding, broad-based intellectual project attempting to synthesize Marxist understandings of ideology with psychoanalytic models of the human psyche, began from a conviction that social perspectives (how one sees the world as a cultural creature) and psychic perspectives (how one sees the world as an individual) are best understood as conterminous. Furthermore, and most intriguingly, spectatorship theory offered a lucid explanation of how cinema is supremely effective at eliciting one of these two perspectives—either the cultural-ideological or the psychic-personal—in relation to the other, ultimately leading to an increased sense of legitimacy and universality for the culture. In short, the cinema reinforces the ways—or, in the more monolithic formulation, the *way*—we understand the world as a result of the manner in which we have been compelled to see it. This occurs, in large part, through the manipulation of our sexual desires.

By looking at the cinema's ability to replicate many of the components of our dreams as Freud understood them, voyeurism, narcissism, and desire, theorists of spectatorship quickly came to focus upon vital issues of sexuality and gender. Beginning the conversation, Laura Mulvey's "Visual Pleasure and Narrative Cinema" had a truly revolutionary effect. Some of its initial impact was doubtless due to Mulvey's beautifully rendered adaptations of Freudian and Lacanian theory—describing the logic of spectatorship, she writes that "cinematic codes create a gaze, a world, and an object thereby producing an illusion cut to the measure of desire," and that the cinema uses "pleasure as a radical weapon"—and some was due to its dazzling (and well-timed) explanation for that most mundane vexation: sexism in the movies.[3] More importantly, Mulvey's argument offers an understanding of how the cinema perpetuates androcentric values—a (heterosexual) male's perspective presented as the universal human perspective—at the expense of diversified, equitable forms of subjectivity. But the argument that classical Hollywood cinema inevitably creates a sadistic male heterosexual spectator or spectatorship position seemed to deny the undeniable fact of a female—and later a gay male and a lesbian—investment in the film-going experience, and in responding initially to the question of what happens "when the woman looks" (the title of one of the better-known responses to Mulvey), subsequent critics offered their own provocative ideas.[4]

One of the most useful studies for one taking a psychoanalytic approach to Bergman remains Gaylyn Studlar's work on masochism and the films of Josef von Sternberg. Suggesting, contra Mulvey, that some films forestall sadistic heterosexual-male spectatorship to create an androgynous, masochistic, and bisexual spectatorial dynamic, Studlar asserts that "the cinematic spectator passively surrenders to the filmic object of desire in much the same way that the masochist surrenders to his/her object of desire."[5] Both Constance Penley's previously discussed assertion that the experience of seeing *Cries and Whispers* was one "of being emotionally and psychically raped" and William Bennett's heteronormative condemnation of Bergman discussed in Chapter Two ("I went to those Bergman things and felt bad, and felt good about feeling bad") implicitly identify masochism as a fundamental part of the experience to be had with a Bergman film.[6] And yet the disapproval, to put it mildly, that both Penley and Bennett expressed toward the Swedish filmmaker can hardly be explained as a simple rejection of the masochistic possibilities of the film-going experience. In fact, one would not be surprised to learn that, despite their many differences, Penley and Bennett each like the American films of Josef von Sternberg every bit as much as they hate the Swedish films of Ingmar Bergman.

A rejection of a masochism, then, is hardly enough to explain the criticism leveled against some of the most (ideologically) challenging Bergman films; for although the first two Bergman-authored films released in the United States did, admittedly, appear with tellingly sadomasochistic titles—*Torment* and *Frustration*—thereby promising, and generally delivering, a classically masochistic cinematic experience, the title of a Bergman film released two decades later, in 1968—a crossroads year for both the director and world cinema—promises something that, unlike masochism, traditionally has far fewer visible devotees: shame.

From *Torment* and *Frustration* to *Shame*

On December 23, 1968, Ingmar Bergman's final black-and-white theatrical film had its American premiere.[7] Although he continued to make theatrical films until 1982, as well as films for television until 2003, Bergman's segue into a very different form of bigger-budgeted color filmmaking, on the one hand, and intimate television productions, on the other, arguably classifies his twenty-ninth feature as something of a "last film" or "final statement," much as *Weekend* (1967)—released the previous year—had been for Jean-Luc Godard.[8] Coming nineteen years after *Frustration* introduced U.S. filmgoers to Bergman as a director, *Shame* (an ominous, literal translation of the Swedish title, *Skammen*) suggests the continuing eagerness of American film culture to characterize the Swedish auteur's films with as much negativity (some would indeed say masochism) as possible.

Nevertheless, this stark one-word title must have given someone in the U.S. distributor's marketing department pause, for despite the fact that readers and spectators have long expected (and often taken delight in) a certain sense of frustration, and thereby a narratively constructed masochism, in their fictional journeys—going back at least as far as Odysseus's protracted return to Penelope in the *Odyssey*—those eager to submit to a shameful or shaming experience are much rarer. Films trafficking in this particular emotion tend to be rejected by nearly all those who encounter them.[9] This process of rejection has affected the reputation of Bergman's oeuvre as well.

Bergman's detractors have always been able to find enough ammunition with which to criticize his films on both aesthetic and political grounds. Certainly, Bennett's snide assessment was not an exclusively conservative opinion, even during the Reagan era, and although Penley's reaction can also be taken to allude to (and implicitly condemn) a masochistic experience, she describes her displeasure as fundamentally connected with a female subjectivity, while Bennett expresses his without referring to gender. It is hardly likely that Bennett was thinking outside the box of what is surely his proudly held male subjectivity, which raises the question: how is male-identified displeasure felt watching a Bergman film to be distinguished from Penley's feminist or female-identified reaction? Could Bennett have felt "spiritually and psychically raped" as well? From the perspective of queer—rather than feminist—theory, such questions finally seem beside the point.

Indeed, I would argue that those critics who have aligned Bergman's cinema with a form of sadomasochistic spectatorship are in error. Bergman's films do not sadistically offer a masochistic experience, or in the terms of spectatorship theory, construct a sadomasochistic spectatorship position. Rather, they confer shame. The metaphor of rape that Penley employs, hyperbolic as it may seem, makes that clear. But if the female-identified spectator feels the shame of being violated, the feelings of the male-identified spectator need also to be identified. Does he feel shameful guilt for identifying with a rapist, or does he feel the emasculating shame of being made to feel like a woman who is being raped by a man? Or is it something ultimately far more radical? In the introduction to her study of Bergman, Marilyn Johns Blackwell asserts that "a plurality of spectator experience . . . warrant[s] our consideration" when approaching his films.[10] As I have been arguing, this plurality can be charted productively according to subject positions defined by gender and sexuality.

In this chapter, I argue that the shame Bergman's work obliges its spectators—at least a significant percentage of its male-identified spectators, normative or queer—to face represents a valuable and deeply self-revelatory process. I contend that this process assumes and hastens the possibility of a queer subjectivity within what has traditionally been considered to be the exclusively straight-male spectatorship position constructed by classical cinema. Indeed, right-wing male homophobes like Bennett were correct, from the perspective of their stated positions and goals, to attempt to vitiate Bergman's project. As noted antifeminists, they could hardly have been criticizing Bergman's problematic cinematic images of women or his films' enactments of male sexual aggression. Clearly, their attacks were a defensive response to many of those films' attacks on their own tenuously constructed masculine and heterosexually directed gender positions. Regarded from a queer perspective, Bergman's shaming work offers a radical deconstruction of hegemonic understandings of both gender and sexuality. This can be most clearly demonstrated by attending to what is, arguably, Bergman's "signature shot"—a shot of one or two characters looking directly into the camera at moments of dramatic intensity—in five Bergman films released before the director's move into color filmmaking. The films are *Monika, Winter Light, Persona, Hour of the Wolf,* and *Shame.*[11]

Set a few years in the future on an island off the coast of Sweden, *Shame* chronicles a fierce but vaguely defined civil war that has been fought for so long that the civilians have begun to take it for granted. Made during the Vietnam conflict, but equally evocative of World War II, the film offers stark, monochromatic images of burning forests, bombed-out buildings, and corpse-strewn landscapes as it follows the ethical and emotional deterioration of one heterosexual couple. Counterintuitively perhaps, considering my ultimate argument, the film confronts political and historical issues in a largely straightforward way. The Brecht-inspired modernist style found in much of that era's cinema, including Bergman's preceding two films, *Persona* and *Hour of the Wolf,* is mostly absent. Spectators instead find a detached, neorealist aesthetic in operation. And yet despite *Shame*'s docudrama sense of reality, presentiments gradually appear suggesting that Bergman's self-effacing approach may be repressing a great deal of what one might finally call a "queer" anxiety, a sensation that was deconstructed and ultimately made the subject of dark comedy in the director's previous pair of films, but expressed here in ways that can seem troublingly inadvertent on the director's part and, well, shameful.[12]

Late in the first third of what may be characterized, roughly, as a three-act narrative, the island on which most of the film is set suffers an invasion that brings the bloody conflict squarely to the once-quiet enclave. The attempted takeover is thwarted, but as part of an effort to restore order, the community's forces take a number of civilians into custody. Inside a school building converted into a command center, Jan and Eva Rosenberg (Max von Sydow and Liv Ullmann) await interrogation despite their protestations of complete political neutrality. As they sit huddled among a crowd of frightened fellow detainees, a nervous man named Oswald (Ingvar Kjellson) introduces himself and reminds the couple that they met at a charity concert a few years prior. Stating the obvious, he remarks, "Things don't look very good."[13] In the finished film, this line is followed by an unmotivated cut to a long shot of the room that does not quite match the preceding image; consequently, a spectator familiar with classical editing practices might identify it as a cutaway shot bridging two parts of a truncated scene. In *Shame*'s published screenplay, one does indeed find intriguing dialogue ultimately (and perhaps shamefully) removed by the director. In the lost passage, Jan asks Oswald what he might have done to merit arrest, and Oswald replies, "I have a passion for the classics. Art, ethics, philosophy, politics and so on. I'm a humanist, if you don't find the word pretentious." This hardly seems a valid reason for his arrest, and once soldiers escort Oswald out of the room, a heretofore-silent captive offers his theory: "I know that one. He's a queer, he's been seducing schoolboys by the dozen these past three years. It's only right that they should get him, now they're having a decontamination."[14]

Perhaps the most immediate feelings that could have been engendered by this exchange, had it remained in the film, are homophobic. The self-righteous busybody speaking about the "queer"'s habits communicates his own revulsion well enough, and like a number of other (presumably) gay male characters in the cinema of the period, Oswald can easily be regarded as obsequious and weak. He is someone who, if the other detainee is to be believed, seduces "innocent" adolescents and who will not, even in his current moment of crisis, disclose the real facts of his situation to his sympathetic fellow artists; instead, he has chosen to hide behind the euphemism "humanist." On further reflection, however, one might sense an approving kind of comradeship between Eva and Jan and this persecuted man. One might conclude

Queer Bergman

that the same forces that persecute homosexuals within totalitarian regimes may take away the freedom of virtually anyone eventually—our protagonists being a single example—in order to instill obedience in a permanently frightened and therefore manipulable populace. And if considered from a slightly different angle, the scene suggests that anti-homosexual prejudice is a subtle manifestation of the cultural intolerance of difference horrifyingly exemplified by this film's civil war.[15]

More intriguingly, one might take Oswald's self-definition at face value. Maybe Oswald is being persecuted primarily for being an ethical humanist, one interested in philosophical inquiry and free thought, a body of thought he has been teaching (perhaps with an erotic investment) to a younger generation of males.[16] Such activities, persecuted of late and faintly suggesting the dawn of Western civilization and ancient Greece's practice of pedagogical Eros, might be considered to be in direct opposition to the unethical, nonhumanistic, strife-filled world that *Shame* presents. If this is the case, the homosexuality that Oswald personifies is both beside the point and even more deeply connected with the film's theme. Indeed, if this interpretation is accepted, the entire film—that is, with the excised passage restored—could be seen as a lament against a violent attack on ideals that are, in the final analysis, inseparable from queer consciousness.

With these considerations in mind, the appearance and disappearance of the film's one likely queer character raise several questions, which are multiplied when one takes into account the statement that Eva makes immediately following Oswald's "outing." Before any real atrocities are presented in the film's second and third acts—in which many of its characters, Jan and Eva included, commit the kind of shameful acts that are all too common in war-torn environments—Eva turns to her husband and utters the film's most resonant, most oft-quoted dialogue:

> Sometimes everything seems like a long strange dream. It's not my dream, it's someone else's, that I'm forced to take part in. Nothing is properly real. It's all made up. What do you think will happen when the person who has dreamed us wakes up and is ashamed of his dream?[17]

Contextually, this is an odd passage for an everyday-life-amidst-war film, one in which the characters seem more likely to discuss food rationing and kerosene shortages than existential guilt. Of course, Eva's statement could be dismissed as a momentary lapse, a mere allusion to the more characteristically Bergmanesque Bergman films that preceded it. But this passage, this precise instant when a queer character has appeared briefly, only to find himself taken away to a seemingly dire offscreen fate, can function as a key not only to this motion picture (particularly since it marks the first utterance of the titular word "shame" [*skammen*] in the film), but also to a practice of shame construction found across the director's career.

Such shame was always palpable in the Bergman canon, but here its forcefulness is achieved in part by the many departures the film represents from the director's previous (and subsequent) work. Many observers have pointed to the film's newfound realist aesthetic, along with its un-Bergmanesque inclusion of crowd scenes and fairly large-scale war and action sequences, and most controversially, to the unprecedented attempt it seems to represent on Bergman's part to deal with overt political issues of its day. And yet, one can note an important difference without even setting foot in the theater. *Shame,* unlike previous films directed by the Swedish auteur, was and continues to be marketed as "a film *from* Ingmar Bergman," in notable contrast to Bergman films released previously as being "*by* Ingmar Bergman" (emphases added). The distinction is telling. Common practice in film distribution and advertisement in the 1960s, as now, compelled directors (particularly writer-directors) to claim authorship by asserting that their films were created "by" their hand: "a film by Federico Fellini." The preposition "from," on the other hand, has been used almost exclusively in conjunction with a film's producer or distributor: "from the studio that gave you . . ." Furthermore, a text "by" an individual does not necessarily suggest any relationship between a sender and a receiver. A diary "by" an individual may have been written for no one other than the author. "From," on the other hand, suggests the passage of something from one individual or group to another—a gift or a message, one welcome or not.

Shame, thus, was advertised as an authorless film, despite the fact that it had been written, produced, and directed by one of the paramount film auteurs of its era. Furthermore, it was presented as something exceeding the status of art, something posited, instead, as a transmission. As understandings of shame posited by queer theory suggest, this most intimate of affects is also the one most contingent upon a transfer from a person or persons to another, and yet it is a transfer that occurs as part of a denial of the shaming person's role. Put simply, no one admits to creating shame. One only passes it along.

A Brief History of Shame

Since the publication in 1993 of "Queer Performativity: Henry James's *The Art of the Novel,*" a startling and fecund essay by the late Eve Kosofsky Sedgwick, the affect of shame has assumed a central role in both queer studies and queer political activism. It has yet to receive sustained attention in film-studies discourses grappling with cinematic spectatorship, however, queer or otherwise.[18] This inattention might be due, at least in part, to the fact that Freud's original psychoanalytic texts, upon which the formative theories of spectatorship are founded, offer few and often inconsistent remarks on shame. In the original *Three Essays on the Theory of Sexuality,* Freud considers the affect to be organically determined. Shame, along with "disgust" and "the claims of aesthetic and moral ideals," is, he wrote, "organically determined and fixed by heredity, and it can occasionally occur without any help at all from education."[19] By the third edition of the *Three Essays* (1915), however, Freud was compelled to add a footnote that modifies his original position by suggesting the influence of ideological pressures of shame as he was coming to understand it:

> [The] forces which act like dams upon sexual development—disgust, shame and morality—must also be regarded as historical precipitates of the external inhibitions to which the sexual instinct has been subjected during the psychogenesis of the human race. We can observe the way in which, in the development of individuals, they arise at the appropriate moment, as though spontaneously, when upbringing and external influence give the signal.[20]

In other words, the "socially constructed" (to use a contemporary, somewhat hackneyed term) instincts triggering shame, disgust, and a "moral" sensibility have been hardwired into the psyche by historical determinants and are now inseparable from—although often hostile to—the basic animal instincts, which, in their current forms, both create and regulate libidinal drives. Elsewhere in his study, Freud mentions something that would eventually be seen as one of the most important factors in later theories of shame. "The force which opposes scopophilia," he writes, "but which may be overridden by it . . . is *shame.*"[21] From this point onward, looking and being looked at were considered fundamental components of the affect.

Freud did not make another significant statement about shame until

Civilization and Its Discontents (1930). Again, however, he connected the affect with issues of visuality and looking. Describing one of the key moments in the process of evolution, when "man" raised "himself from the ground" and assumed "an upright gait," Freud posits that the event, which might have been considered a moment of triumph for the species, actually "provoked feelings of shame in [early man]" because "his genitals, which were previously concealed," were now made "visible and in need of protection."[22] Francis J. Broucek would later remark that, "this idea clearly conflicts with [Freud's] earlier view of shame as the precipitate of external inhibitions against instinctual gratification."[23] The shift does, however, offer a clue to the rationale behind Freud's remarks about the struggle between the sexual compulsion to look (scopophilia) and the response of shame that it triggers. In the essay "Femininity" (1933), Freud further posits that shame should more directly be seen as an ally in the concealment of genital deficiency. With what has been taken to be a regrettable intimation of misogyny, he suggests that shame must therefore be considered "a feminine characteristic *par excellence.*"[24] In later years, these brief and, at times, seemingly incompatible references to the affect have led a number of theorists to conclude, as Broucek puts it, that Freud "had no consistent theory of shame."[25]

The fact remains, however, that in Freud's work, shame is always connected with images defining and marking biological sex. And when Freud's comment about "deficient" female genitalia is considered alongside his previous assertion that shame was felt specifically by males with external genitals, it seems as if he was struggling for a way to argue that the revelation of a more general kind of sexual shortcoming connected with gender difference (or gender division) is at the heart of the affect. Shame can thus be conceptualized as an affect provoked by a dawning, or triggered, understanding of an incompleteness within the self—what Broucek describes as a shocking moment of "objective self-awareness"—that is finally incompatible with the ideological underpinnings of a historically determined social order founded on sexual division and heterocentrism.[26] Pointing to the myth of Adam and Eve and the shame the first man and woman felt after gaining knowledge of their "nakedness," Broucek reads the book of Genesis as suggesting that this self-awareness and its accompanying shame marks the beginning of history itself, the beginning of "the suddenly altered perception of the world associated with that shame."[27]

From a decidedly nonpsychoanalytic perspective, the American affect theorist Silvan Tomkins studied shame in the 1960s and came to intriguingly compatible conclusions. His celebrated two-volume study charts nine primary affects, which, like shame as defined by Freud, might all be thought of as organic precipitations from historical determinants, and which ultimately find themselves attached to the instincts.[28] Developing these concepts further, Ann Cvetkovich argues for a "politics of affect that does not rest on an essentialist conception of affect," suggesting that, "like sexuality, affect should be understood as discursively constructed."[29] In Tomkins's own work, however, theories of the "linguistic turn" in modern thought—upon which concepts of discursive constructs rest—remain largely unaddressed. Nonetheless, Tomkins's work, particularly his analysis of shame—or what, in his conjoined term, becomes "shame-humiliation"—suggests a rhetoric of affective responses between a self and another, one that functions as a complex system of signs.

Tomkins offers an example of this form of shameful communication:

> The eyes not only can witness any affect in the face of the other but also express one's own affect to the other, and since this can be a shared experience, interocular intimacy becomes the occasion, for the adult, of experiencing shame . . .
>
> Since the face and particularly the eyes are the primary communicators and receivers of all affects, the linkage of shame to the whole spectrum of affect expression may result in an exaggerated self-consciousness, because the self is then made ashamed of all its feelings and must therefore hide the eyes lest the eyes meet.[30]

If there is a common thread throughout both the psychoanalytic and affect-theory literature on shame beyond the importance both grant to the realm of the visible, it is the sudden and distressful sense of self-consciousness Tompkins refers to in this passage. Unlike other affects, however, which may be triggered for a solitary person by anything from an unexpected loud sound (the affect of "surprise-startle") to an unpleasant smell ("dissmell"), shame seems to always be triggered by the contempt one feels is coming from one or more other persons. Although the other or others do not have to be present for a person to feel shame, it is, as Sedgwick puts it, unique among the affects in that it "both derives from and aims toward sociability."[31] With this in mind, Sedgwick is able to show how shame can be considered to be performatively (and thus discursively) constructed. In doing so, she put shame on queer theory's agenda in a bold way, leading to important new understandings of historical figures such as Henry James and Andy Warhol.[32] And although Sedgwick's initial investigations of the topic began in dialogue with Judith Butler and her concept of gender performativity, Sedgwick's insights point far beyond the fashionable use of Butler's ideas in the late 1980s and early 1990s in analyses of female impersonation. Rather, Sedgwick focused on the other aspect of the concept, which originated with the linguist J. L. Austin's theory of performative speech acts.

According to Austin's *How to Do Things With Words*, a performative speech act is one in which a person does something or brings something into being by saying something: "I promise," "I dare you," "I apologize," "I accuse." With this in mind, Sedgwick wondered how performative speech acts might work in a homosexual economy, arguing that the pejorative statement "shame on you" should be considered a "useful utterance from which to begin imagining *queer* performativity."[33] "Shame on you" (or in Douglas Crimp's provocative formulation, "for shame") seems central to the performative nature of queer subjectivity because, as Sedgwick puts it, the "gender-dissonant or otherwise stigmatized childhood" of the homosexual subject, the "childhood scene of shame," remains an undeniable formative force for the queer subject.[34] But like the shame-filled, waking dreamer imagined by Eva in Bergman's infernal war film, one who never reveals himself within the narrative, and like the "Ingmar Bergman" who would not confirm that *Shame* was, in fact, created by his hand, the performative enunciator conferring shame, both in this particular film's spectatorial matrix and everywhere else, is necessarily a disavowed presence.

As Sedgwick explains:

> The absence of an explicit verb from [the phrase] "Shame on you" records the place in which an I, in conferring shame, has effaced itself and its own agency. Of course the desire for self-effacement is the defining trait of—what else?—shame. So the very grammatical truncation of "Shame on you" marks it as the product of a history out of which an I, now withdrawn, is *projecting* shame—towards another I, an I deferred, that has yet and with difficulty to come into being, if at all, in the place of the shamed second person.[35]

This rich passage raises important questions for theories of shame and spectatorship, particularly those that address moments in the cinema in which the author or implied author, one projecting his or her own shame onto the spectator, is made perceptible through strategies of self-reflexivity that allow the spectator to recognize and identify with said author.

Tomkins implicitly offered a theory of the cinema when he explained how shame could be identified in the moment when one's vulnerability noticeably disallows extended face-to-face communication. He recounted an experiment that exposed the challenge of achieving an interocular, or eye-to-eye, intimacy:

> When the individual is asked to stare into the eyes of another, he does so if at all only briefly and then looks away. He looks away, however, in a rather subtle way. He stares at the top of the nose or the tip of the nose, or at one eye, or at the forehead, or he fixates on the face as a whole . . .
>
> The expression of shame or shyness is quite as shameful as shameless looking. This is why, under the conditions of our experiment, we rarely encounter subjects who hide their face in their hands, or grossly look away from their partners. [They are] caught between the shame of looking and the shame of being ashamed to do so.[36]

Why, one must wonder, is the subject unable to hold the gaze, and why, subsequently, is the subject ashamed that this inability might be exposed? Answers to these questions are suggested by a remarkable series of images in several Bergman films in which characters, usually female or feminized characters, look directly into the camera in a face-to-face confrontation between an on-screen character and an offscreen spectator. It is a cinematic strategy that, as Bergman employs it, seems, in a formulation that is crucial to its efficacy, both self-reflexive and uncannily naturalistic.

Face to Face, Eye to Eye

Jean-Louis Baudry's formative work on spectatorship theory emphasizes the setting that gives the process its power as a psychic mirror: "Projection and reflection take place in a closed space, and those who remain there, whether they know it or not (but they do not), find themselves chained, captured, or captivated. . . . And the mirror, as a reflecting surface, is framed, limited, circumscribed."[37] This setting, the movie theater, is particularly important for any historically grounded approach to Bergman's 1950s and 1960s films.

Crucially, the kind of cinema Baudry implicitly assumes to be shown upon the reflecting surface of a darkened auditorium's screen is as specific, and as vast, as the sorts of venues in which it is shown: the "classical cinema" perfected in Hollywood's studio system. This form of filmmaking, which Laura Mulvey used as her model and which includes films as disparate as *The Gold Rush* (Charles Chaplin, 1925) and *The Hurt Locker* (Kathryn Bigelow, 2009), does not, however, simply offer a reflection of "the body [or the face] itself." Rather, as Baudry concludes, it reflects "a world already given meaning."[38] In other words, the classical cinema promises its spectator much more than simple reproduction by a looking glass, providing instead a reflection in which a face staring out at the self may or may not correspond to one's previously determined sense of self—happily, in the form of an attractive film star, or unhappily, in the form of a cinematic monster. Instead, it disingenuously offers itself as the reflection of an entire psychic universe, one Baudry identifies as taking the philosophical perspective of idealism. For Bergman's part, his use of the cinematic apparatus is simpler and blunter, although certainly no less ideologically engaged, than that employed within more mainstream forms of filmmaking.

In a recent study of the cinematic phenomenon in which a film character seems to make eye contact with the spectator, Wheeler Winston Dixon reminds us that the practice, more common in recent years, has never been particularly rare. It can be found in everything from the films of "the reflexively sophisticated [George] Landow to [those of] such commercially and/or artificially diverse filmmakers as Ernst Lubitsch, Wesley E. Barry, Andy Warhol, Robert Montgomery, Laurel and Hardy (as directed by James Parrott), Jean-Luc Godard, and many other artists—all of whom employ the reciprocal gaze of the screen to mesmerize or entrance their intended audiences."[39] But if such moments are now taken for granted in mainstream films (particularly comedy), as well as in formally or politically challenging avant-garde productions, their recurrence in Bergman's art cinema, which is surprisingly unacknowledged in Dixon's study, are often far less "entrancing" or "mesmerizing" than they are unsettling.[40]

Near the end of *Monika* (1953), which follows a sexually driven young woman as she seduces a naive young man only to abandon him, leaving him to raise the child born of their affair, the eponymous character (Harriet Andersson) goes into a bar to pick up a man while her husband is out of town. Seemingly noticing the spectator in the theater catching her in the act, she stares silently into the camera—and into the spectator's eyes—for a full, awkwardly long thirty seconds. This

Figure 4.1. Monika looks back in *Monika* (Ingmar Bergman, Sweden, 1953). Svensk Filmindustri.

spectator, who had been both condemning and erotically objectifying the young woman for the previous eighty minutes, can hardly avoid a jolt at this instance of what Dixon calls the cinematic "look back" (figure 4.1).

Godard wrote enthusiastically of the shot in 1958, contending that it created a "brusque conspiracy between the spectator and the actor," since Monika's "mocking eyes . . . made us bear witness to her disgust at choosing hell over heaven."[41] For his part, Bergman would ultimately claim that the moment occasions not mocking disgust, but rather a "shameless, direct contact with the viewer."[42] Robin Wood, whose then-repressed homosexuality made him an exemplar of the male-identified, queerly motivated (though not fully queered) spectator, combined Godard's and Bergman's perspectives in his 1969 monograph. In an intriguingly dialectical formulation, he states: "The shot is held, the eyes, at once ashamed and defiant . . . stare into ours. Gradually we find it difficult to face this terrible steadiness: Identified with Harry [Monika's husband], we would like to be able simply to condemn Monika, but we can't." Declining to tease out the most radical, as I will argue, gender-commingling implications of the spectator's "difficulty," Wood retreats to his Christian upbringing in the final sentence of his analysis: "The shot is the perfect cinematic equivalent of 'Let him who is without sin among you cast the first stone.'"[43]

Had he written about the film ten years later, as an openly gay man, Wood might have concluded that Monika's expression of shamefulness mixed with defiance suggests an incompletely projected affect. If so, the shame this scene elicits has only one place to emerge: within the spectator. And beyond the relatively simple and straightforward shame of a voyeur, shocked to find himself or herself caught in the act of looking and judging, the extended duration of the shot creates a specific, disturbing effect of degendering for the film's male-defined spectator.

Unlike a face-to-face encounter in the real world, in which one could momentarily look down at one's hands or over the other person's shoulder, or even its simulation on a relatively small television monitor in one's home, where one could survey the room or the coffee table, someone watching *Monika* in a darkened theater essentially has nowhere to avert his or her eyes once he or she becomes uncomfortable with the extended eye-to-eye contact. Far more directly than in any other form of audiovisual media, the film spectator is obliged to consider the cinematic spyglass to be a looking glass, since, in a profoundly uncanny sense, the image of Monika's face is implicitly presented as a literal reflection of the spectator in a shift marked by the darkening of the space behind Monika and by an eerie sonic segue from a jaunty song playing on a jukebox at the bar to a much more foreboding nondiegetic musical score. Suddenly, like a subject in the Tomkins experiment, *Monika's* spectator truly is caught between "the shame of looking" (at the objectified but seemingly autonomous face that catches the voyeur in the act) and the "shame of being ashamed to do so." For the male-identified spectator, the effect of this latter, deeper sense of shame is multiplied: he is made aware of his own gendered construction in contradistinction to what he sees in front of him, and of his own otherness and impossible but longed-for unity with this staring-back other on the screen. In Bergman's unique aesthetic, gender inevitably becomes a vexing part of the equation as this reflection of a specifically female alienated self challenges the male-constructed spectator's masculinity. In short, the opposite-gender mirror image exposes the male spectator's once-possible femininity, now necessarily abolished by the gender positioning that has defined him.

In the film's last scene, this sense of discomfiture is partly negated—perhaps because of a failure of nerve on the young director's part—when Monika's radical "look back" is supplanted by a similar but crucially amended shot. In it, Monika's abandoned husband Harry (Lars Ekborg) stands on a sidewalk and holds the couple's infant daughter in his hands, positioning the child's head next to his own in order to look at their reflection in a large mirror displayed in a storefront window. If the previously projected image of Monika staring at the camera can be said to feminize the male-identified spectator by never cutting back to any diegetic character who might be looking at her, this image sutures, albeit belatedly, the veritable wound of psychic castration that has resulted from Monika's unsettling look back.[44] Shooting slightly from the left of the actor, the camera zooms into a close-up of Harry's face and then shifts to the left just enough to make it a literal point-of-view shot

Figure 4.2. Harry looks at himself in *Monika*. Svensk Filmindustri.

Figure 4.3. Looking at himself, Harry ultimately sees his lost Monika in *Monika*. Svensk Filmindustri.

of him looking, like Monika before him, directly at the camera, again as the background fades to black (figure 4.2). Unlike the earlier shot of Monika's face, however, a lap dissolve transports the spectator to a flashback of an earlier sequence showcasing Monika's eroticized body on display for Harry. After vanishing momentarily, the close-up of Harry reappears, and this image is superimposed upon those of Monika from the prior summer for several seconds (figure 4.3). Thus, the specter of inchoate femininity always already within the male subject is reflected back into the mirror and reinscribed into the narrative of the film in the form of an erotic memory of the sexualized Other.

When these memory images finally dissolve back to the initial image of Harry and his child, one is reassured by the belief that the femininity within the man has another, more concrete displacement in his biological daughter, a displacement at the core of a heterosexist ideology framing and exalting procreation. Therefore, *Monika's* conclusion can be said to offer a clever example of an all-too-common development in ideologically concerned narratives in which radical possibilities are briefly raised, only to be deflected in the denouements.

Post–Mulvey psychoanalytic film theory suggests that a female-identified spectator might be encouraged to consider a number of very different questions while watching a film like *Monika*. This consideration has been somewhat obscured by the fact that once the universality of a male spectatorship position was challenged by theorists in the late 1970s and 1980s, innumerable subdivisions based on sexuality, race, nationality, and so forth began to complicate the equation further. More fundamentally, the "female spectator," to the extent that she conforms to the culturally constructed gender patterns assigned to Western women, has historically been allowed the (Pyrrhic) freedom to shift her identifications from male to female characters and back again fairly easily (without shame) as a filmgoer. For example, Laura Hübner's excellent essay on issues of spectatorship and identification surrounding *Monika* assumes a spectator who comfortably and critically shifts identification across genders. Rightly contending that Bergman's use of a literal mirror in the climactic scene "problematizes the cuing of the male gaze" exemplified in the erotic flashback images, Hübner points out how the mirror, acting "as a reflective device [foregrounds] the act of looking and male voyeurism, making clear links between Harry's gaze at the mirror surface and the spectator watching the film."[45]

Such an assessment presumes a level of dispassionate, analytical engagement on the part of the spectator that is more characteristic of today's feminist film scholars and students than Cold War–era male art-film viewers. But Hübner's analysis taps into the perceptions of the era when she describes the earlier shot of Harriet Andersson looking into the camera: "The gaze at the camera marks a moving out of and beyond the fiction. It also signifies a defiant female response to the heterosexual male gaze long before Mulvey's influential article on the subject."[46] Indeed, one does not have to be familiar with feminist film theory to feel, at some level, that this shot represents a significant ideological challenge. It is a challenge, however, that, as Hübner suggests, is best understood as being addressed to a spectator adopting a classically heterosexual male gaze. But in her analysis—based on both *Monika*'s narrative developments and its formal elements—Hübner also recognizes that "the representation of Monika remains ambivalent, making her appear both as a figure for identification and an object."[47] Hübner's analysis points toward unsettling queer energies (though it doesn't systematically explore them) made apparent in *Monika*'s reflection of the self as an alienated other, since—even with the film's conventional ending—one can be left only with the sense that the "Monika" that Henry desires is, in large part, nothing more than his own femininity reflected back at him through her (re)constructed image.[48]

Much less compromising than the resolution of *Monika*—with its disavowed male femininity taking the form of a vanished but remembered love and a materialized female descendant—are the films produced by Bergman in the decade following that film's release. With a rigorously structured narrative that condenses a single afternoon at the beginning of a bleak northern Swedish winter into eighty-one minutes of film, *Winter Light* (1963), an account of a country pastor (Gunnar Björnstrand) and his emotionally abused mistress Märta (Ingrid Thu-

Figure 4.4. Märta stares down the spectator in *Winter Light* (Ingmar Bergman, Sweden, 1963). Svensk Filmindustri.

lin), remains a remarkable example of the director's radical use of the dynamics of spectatorship to challenge a filmgoer's belief in stable gender identifications. Throughout a celebrated seven-minute sequence, Tomas, the bitter, victimizing pastor, reads a letter by Märta that Bergman presents in the form of an extended on-screen monologue. In this unprecedented sequence, Märta speaks while staring, much as Monika had done almost a decade before, directly into the camera (figure 4.4).

> I prayed for clarity of mind, and I got it. I've realized I love you. I prayed for a task to apply my strength to, and I got it, too. It's you. . . .
>
> Whether it's God or my biological functions which have brought about my love for you, anyway I'm burning with gratitude. Nor does it make any odds whether it's my inborn tendency to assume responsibility for others that tempts me to find in you my great task in life . . .
>
> But now I've written what I don't dare to say even when you're in my arms: I love you and I live for you. Take me and use me. Beneath all my false pride and independent airs I've only one wish: to be allowed to live for someone else. It will be terribly difficult.[49]

This sequence can seem startlingly misogynistic, with its spoken assertions of female biology as destiny and its suggestion that a woman's proper role is as a mother and (a man's) helpmate. And despite the shame-inducing verbal abuse the pastor inflicts upon Märta throughout the film, she offers to devote her life to the utterly unsympathetic, failed patriarch. In tension with her self-abnegating words, however, Märta's eyes burrow into the male-identified spectator with a strangely secure and powerful intensity.[50] Throughout the tour de force sequence, Thulin's eyes are riveted on the camera's lens for nearly unbearable lengths of time—once for just over a minute, then just under a minute, and then, one final time, for forty-five seconds. The simulta-

neously empowering and infantilizing attributes of the cinematic apparatus make Märta's face at first seem to be the spectator's devoted lover
or mother, looking directly at her lover or son. Eventually, however, her
visage transforms, like Monika's, into a regressive, uncanny mirror image, talking back to the spectator with an autonomy that speaks what
that spectator is finally obliged to process as his own thoughts.[51] Although Tomas is seen silently reading Märta's letter to himself—in a
profoundly private moment for the pastor that bonds us, as spectators,
to him—the psychic effect of the scene, once Bergman segues to the
image of Thulin speaking in her own voice into the camera, is force-
fully extended to the film's visual and sonic levels.

But since the woman's voice is disquietingly presented as emanating from within the pastor's own psyche—and thus from within the
male-identified spectator, who identifies with him in this scene—
the cross-gender identification is justified within, and reinforced by,
the narrative. As an ultimate effect, both pastor and spectator have
been positioned to identify with a female subjectivity. The fact that the
male-identified spectator finds himself identifying with a man identifying with a woman gives this sequence an extra, subtly vertiginous quality. As with Harry at the end of *Monika*, the male-identified spectator's
sense of self is palpably diminished, and a return of the repressed in female form looms large on the screen. This time, however, the wound
of a castration effected by the disconcerting long take is not sutured.
Here, Bergman's aesthetic directly attacks the very foundation of normative heterosexual subjectivity. Judith Butler has explained the psychic foundation that underlies this phenomenon: "[The developing
child] must choose not only between the two object choices [of the
mother or father], but the two sexual dispositions, masculine and feminine. That the boy usually chooses the heterosexual would, then, be
the result, not of the fear of castration by the father, but of the fear of
castration—that is, the fear of 'feminization' associated within heterosexual cultures with male homosexuality."[52]

Following on this analysis, Eve Sedgwick reminds us that the lost
possibilities of these necessarily disavowed desires, as well as the necessarily disavowed gender positions that accompany them, are in large
part responsible for a systemic melancholia. This melancholia, argues
Sedgwick, remains with the subject through its life.[53]

From this perspective, the famous close-ups of Bergman's female
actors—while often constituting a shaming emotional-psychical rape
for a more unambivalently feminine-identifying spectator, as Constance Penley asserts—means something more complicated for the

male-identified spectator unreconciled to his lost or inchoate femininity. For him, Bergman's "look back" close-ups can be seen as the melancholic male subject's obsessional fugue, in which he is gazing not merely at "the self" within the other, a self, as Penley implies, that the male is compelled to penetrate violently in order to reclaim. Rather, for this male-identified subject, these faces represent "the Other" dormant within "the self," one now supernaturally materialized on the screen, one that this spectator stares at longingly, as if it were nothing less than a lost reflection.

Tomkins also connects the emotional state of melancholy with the affect of shame. After contending that "another major source of shame in interpersonal relationships is the loss of the love object, through separation or death," Tomkins explains that such "shame may be experienced in different ways": "as an alienation, as a rejection, as a defeat, as intolerable loneliness, as a temporary distancing between the self and the other, as a poignant, bitter-sweet longing."[54] This description perfectly describes the effect of Bergman's cinema on the male-identified spectator.

Deconstructing Cinema, Deconstructing Gender

In *Persona* and *Hour of the Wolf*, Bergman's most discomfortingly self-reflexive films, the male-identified spectator again is confronted with faces gazing outward from the screen. In *Persona* (1966), the famed actress Elisabeth Vogler (Liv Ullmann) suddenly and unaccountably stops speaking, and after a period in a hospital, where it is feared she has suffered a nervous breakdown, the woman is sent to recuperate at a seaside cottage in the care of a shallow and starstruck young nurse, Alma (Bibi Andersson). Once there, Sister Alma finds herself constantly under the gaze of the older woman, who silently studies her inexperienced and immature caretaker. Before long, the nurse senses in her patient a strong sexual and emotional desire that may (or may not) be little more than an act of projection on her own part. In short order, Alma dreams, hallucinates, or experiences (it is never made clear) a nighttime visit to her bedroom by Elisabeth, during which the two women quietly make love in the suddenly fog-shrouded cottage. Their image as a same-sex couple, seen in a mirror that is also Bergman's camera position, inaugurates the narrative's (female) homosexual passion, which finally results in a breakdown of both Alma and Elisabeth's demarcated identities (figure 4.5).

Figure 4.5. Alma and Elisabeth's mirrored merging in *Persona* (Ingmar Bergman, Sweden, 1966). Svensk Filmindustri.

Positing a basic female spectator's response to the film, B. Ruby Rich argues that "the loss of individual identity" functions as a "threat that haunts women's intimacy like a destructive specter."[55] For *Persona*'s male spectator, however, the development of an uncanny queerness, far from inducing fear (or shame), initially allows for a kind of comforting retreat. This spectator is encouraged to identify with the women on the screen in a way that, like a point-of-view mirror-image shot, merges primary and secondary forms of cinematic identification. Crucially, however, a male-defined spectator's sexual desire, elicited in *Persona* through lesbian-coded images, still represents, at the most basic level, an opposite-gender object choice, since a "lesbian man"—a term Bergman used to describe himself in his journal—can consider himself to be, essentially, a heterosexual man.[56] As a result, this celebrated image indirectly reasserts the heterosexuality of the male cinematic gaze. With *Persona*'s thick layer of cinematic self-reflexivity (jump cuts, lens flares, and even a celebrated moment in which the celluloid itself seems to burn and break in the projector), however, the film's construction and deconstruction of a female-desiring spectatorial position also serves to distance the spectator from any sense of secure gender-based subjectivity. *Persona*'s narrative, with the psychotic breakdown of Elisabeth and Alma in the final scenes, thus implies that (gendered) subjectivity—like the metacinematic, autocritical, and palpably self-destructive film itself—is a construct. And ultimately, if gender is a construct, all forms of sexuality—heterosexuality, homosexuality, male lesbianism, female male homosexuality—all find themselves under a productive cloud of ontological suspicion.

Watching *Hour of the Wolf* (1968), on the other hand, the spectator is made to identify directly with a paranoid man: the artist Johan Borg (Max von Sydow), who is constantly linked up with a series of phantom characters in a very male configuration of perverse, often explicitly homoerotic desire. Virtually alone on a small Baltic island with a naive young wife named, like the nurse in *Persona*, Alma (Liv Ullmann), Johan is erotically pursued by both a leering pubescent boy and a fawning middle-aged man in deranged hallucinations expressed through the conventions of cinematic horror. Referring to Harry M. Benshoff's study of the connections between the horror film and expressions of repressed homosexuality, Laura Hubner allows that Bergman's allusions to that particular genre might be intended to signal "the shifting of homosexual desire."[57] And yet, complicating what might otherwise be a simple film examining repressed male homosexuality, Johan is also shown to be obsessed to the point of delirium with a former female lover, Veronica Vogler (Ingrid Thulin), who is rumored to be living in a gothic castle on the other side of the island. In a surreal climax, Johan ventures to the castle for an assignation with Vogler, who, it should be remembered, shares a last name with both Elisabeth in *Persona* and the uncannily androgynous character von Sydow himself played in *The Magician*, thus, linking her with both female and male queer desire. In preparation for the tryst, the castle's demonic archivist decorates Johan's face with heavy powder and sloppily applied lipstick and mascara. Then, just like Monika, Märta, and Anna and Elisabeth before him, Johan stares directly into the camera and into the spectator's eyes. Once again, the Bergman spectator is caught between the shame of looking—here at a pathetically failed attempt by a man to feminize himself (too little, too late)—and the shame of being ashamed to do so (figure 4.6).

Looked at from the perspective of an urban homosexual, Johan, at the very least, comes across in this moment as a failed drag queen. With his haunted eyes and hesitant expression, he simply cannot learn to stop worrying and love not being a "real man." If Johan, unlike a successful drag queen, is unable to break free and perform a different

Figure 4.6. Johan is feminized by a queer demon in *Hour of the Wolf* (Ingmar Bergman, Sweden, 1968). Svensk Filmindustri.

gender differently, the stylish filmmaking itself seems all too eager to expose its own status as a performative construct. Just as a performing drag queen's "true" biological sex often pokes through in the form of a telltale Adam's apple or thick wrists, the illusion of the cinema as an unmediated window onto reality is, as it had been in *Persona*, constantly undermined in what is arguably Bergman's queerest work: by lens flares (on-screen at a time when many cinematographers still would have considered them an optical flaw), by the sounds of the crew building the film's sets during the opening credits, and, more subtly, by that whole catalogue of horror- and art-film clichés that finally push the film's pastiche style into the realm of delirium. As a result, *Hour of the Wolf*'s subtext of gender and sexual deconstruction is mirrored in the film's own deconstructed state.

Unlike the contemporaneous work of Godard, however, which seems to have influenced Bergman during this period, *Hour of the Wolf*, like *Persona* before it, is caught between a metacinematic, autocritical authenticity elicited through a cinema verité style and something that registers as an unwillingness to face up to what that newfound authenticity seems to be pointing to: a transcendence beyond the artificiality of gender roles.[58] In large part, this results from a related tension between the estrangement effects Bergman finds himself employing (effects that pull one out of the film) and the compelling, three-dimensional characterizations of Bergman's always-impressive actors. Unlike the self-aware performances characterizing Godard's films at that time, by hip young actors including Juliet Berto, Jean-Pierre Léaud, and Anne Wiazemsky, Bergman's performers hardly function as Brechtian spokesmen in the service of a Marxist revolution. They represent such a startling sense of painful sincerity that the self-reflective filmmaking presenting their plights effectively loses a great deal of the ideological reflexivity it might otherwise have offered. Both *Persona* and *Hour of the Wolf* seem to say: the world around these characters, and the identities they assume, may be insubstantial, but the pain they feel is not.[59]

Shame, on the other hand, is, finally, unlike *Persona* and *Hour of the Wolf*; it is almost entirely devoid of modernist or postmodernist self-reflexivity. Eva's statement about the shame of someone who has dreamed up the horrifying war-torn world initially seems self-reflexive, but it still functions as an observation plausibly made by a psychologically convincing character within the narrative. And yet the Pirandellian quality of the statement ("What do you think will happen when the person who has dreamed us wakes up and is ashamed of his dream?") functions as an authorial confession that is, again, simultaneously acknowledged and disavowed by its cinematic enunciator. Considering the well-worn theological concerns that characterized many earlier Bergman films, Eva seems to be saying, "God is ashamed of humanity"—and, by implication, that humanity should be ashamed of itself. As Tomkins and Sedgwick have pointed out, however, in the final analysis, the subject's shame always seems to be self-inflicted. "In contrast to all other affects," Tomkins asserts,

> shame is an experience of the self by the self. At that moment when the self feels ashamed, it is felt as a sickness within the self. Shame is the most reflexive of affects in that the phenomenological distinction between the subject and the object of shame is lost. Why is shame so close to the experienced self? It is because the self lives in the face . . . Shame turns the attention of the self and others away from other objects to this most visible residence of self, increases its visibility and thereby generates the torment of self-consciousness.[60]

What is finally so remarkable in Bergman films of this period is that although the spectator (and in this case, I would posit any spectator) is engendered with a profound sense of shame, the self-reflexive presence of the enunciator's shame—Bergman's own shame as the dreamer-creator of so many dysfunctional fictional worlds—works dialectically to expose its origins in gendered cinema, authorship, and the viewing subject.

Gender Shame, or the War between the Sexes

Although critics at the time of its release saw it as a rare political film for its director, alluding to the then-current Vietnam conflict as well as to Sweden's role as an ethically questionable neutral nation during World War II, *Shame* now seems to be the kind of film that critics often applaud as "universal."[61] The invitation for the New York press screening that Pauline Kael quotes in her review describes it simply as a "vision of war and its effects on two people," and this statement is accurate on at least three levels.[62] First, one is obliged to witness the increasingly ferocious civil war raging around Eva and Jan. Second, one observes the domestic war between Jan and Eva, a long-married couple who bicker repeatedly throughout the film and thus enact, at a microcosmic level, the larger conflict. (Psychically, one might feel just the opposite, that the civil war is a fierce macrocosm of the couple's personal battles.) Beyond this, however, a third level of conflict persists: the psychic wars within Jan and Eva individually as they attempt to function as separated halves of a gendered, heterosexual couple in the physical world. Time and time again, from early work like *Thirst*, *Secrets of Women* (1952), and *Dreams* (1955) through later, infernal dramas such as *Scenes from a Marriage* (1973), *From the Life of the Marionettes* (1980), and *Faithless* (2001), Bergman chronicled a seemingly endless war of the sexes, one (or sometimes two) heterosexual couples at a time.[63] Inevitable comparisons have been made between these films and the plays of August Strindberg, many of which were staged by Bergman on the Stockholm stage. But if the gender wars in the nineteenth-century playwright's work were regularly blamed on a series of hellish women born of the dramatist's misogyny, the fault in Bergman's dramas can always be traced back to characters of both genders acting destructively in typically "gender-appropriate" ways.

Persona and *Hour of the Wolf*, unique in Bergman's filmography for their twinned metacinematic and homosexually resonant qualities, chart trajectories in which the psyches of their protagonists seemed to merge in supernatural fusion. In *Persona*, Alma and Elisabeth appear to become emotionally and mentally connected in some vexed and painful way, and in *Hour of the Wolf* the consciousnesses of Johan and his meek wife similarly fuse together, even as Johan is drawn toward both adulterous and pederastic assignations. Problematically enough, the price paid for both the homoerotic and cross-gendered identifications in those films seems to be surreally conveyed forms of madness.

In *Shame*, however, set more drastically within a real world of bread and bullets, the ultimate transformation of the two characters' identities is of a more mundanely tragic sort. Eva wakes with the alarm clock in its first scene, strongly and forthrightly arising to begin her day. Jan, in contrast, sits on the side of his twin bed, recounting a wistful dream and then worrying about an aching wisdom tooth. Both wear men's pajamas, but against gender stereotype; it is Eva's top that, as Hubert I. Cohen puts it, "is unbuttoned male-style."[64] Jan, more modestly or self-protectively (or effeminately), has his pajama shirt completely buttoned, and beneath it one sees the additional layer of a T-shirt. In Cohen's assessment, Jan's "passivity and ineffectuality force Eva, who tries not to nag and would rather not usurp his authority, literally to wear the pants in the family."[65] From a heterocentric position—from which, of course, most Bergman scholarship has emerged—the fact that Eva "always wears men's clothing" might lead one to conclude, as has Cohen, that Eva "has lost the image of herself as a sexual object," and that she wishes only to return to traditional femininity by being dominated by a strong husband.[66] Of course, such a projection into Eva's mind tells us more about a male scholar's uncritical perspective on female sexual objectification than it does about this particular characters's own likely desires. One also might protest that as a woman working with her husband on a small farm in a war zone, Eva would be hard-pressed to wear traditional "women's clothing," regardless of her husband's patriarchal authority.

Cohen is right, however, to suggest that both Eva and Jan are utterly imprisoned within a structural logic of gender in which only one half of a couple can be strong at any given time, and that when one's partner "wears the pants" (or the unbuttoned shirt), one inevitably feels obliged to assume a concurring role of passivity. In his self-pity, Jan does not give a moment's thought to the notion that he ought to shave his face in the morning; Eva has to implore him to do so. But just as either shaving one's face or sporting beard stubble can connote manhood (just one example of how men often have more freedom to perform their gender in different, sometimes contradictory ways than do women), Eva's request that Jan groom himself can be queerly interpreted not simply as a desire that he "act like a man," but that he simply pull himself together and, by removing his facial hair, feminize his face a bit in a way that will equalize their relationship and ultimately bring him up to Eva's level of self-sufficiency.

Throughout *Shame*'s first third, the spectator identifies almost simultaneously with both this purposeful and strong (and a bit harshly critical) woman, on the one hand, and her almost pathetic (though not unsympathetic) husband on the other. But thirty minutes into the film, an incident occurs that presages an eventual role reversal, after which Eva will show a formerly repressed (and finally paralyzing) depth of feeling as Jan assumes a newfound (and increasingly monstrous) form of masculinity. Following a coerced on-camera interview conducted by the invading army that ends with Jan fainting, Eva and her husband take refuge inside their farmhouse. As the war now portends the bleakest of futures, the couple lies together on Eva's bed.[67] Now, although huddled on the same bed, their fundamental separateness is emphasized by the way the camera is situated in relation to the two. Eva is seen lying on her side and facing forward, with only the right side of her face visible; the left side is blocked by Jan's profile as he lies on his back. As an effect of this composition, one that defines another recurrent signature

Figure 4.7. Jan and Eva are seen as split halves in *Shame* (Ingmar Bergman, Sweden, 1968). Svensk Filmindustri.

shot for the director, the spectator sees only half of each of two different faces, one positioned frontally and one in silhouette: two incomplete human beings representing a single split subjectivity (figure 4.7).

As they rest together, Eva—referring to the ugly experience with the camera crew—quietly says, "I was thinking the whole time, what a good thing we haven't any children." Almost perfunctorily, Jan responds: "When peace comes, we'll have children." Immediately thereafter, Eva bursts into tears and blurts out: "No, we'll never have children."[68] Before the shot fades to black, the formerly ineffectual Jan displays uncharacteristic strength as he tries to comfort his wife, suggesting a new-found strength built, predictably enough, on her suddenly manifested vulnerability. As the scene develops, with Eva's shame-filled realization that she will likely not fulfill her gender's culturally assigned role by bearing a child, she, in another sense, effectively capitulates to that role by assuming her place as the "weaker" partner in this heterosexual couple. Jan, on the other hand, will, after a brief return to passivity and cowardice, again assert his strength. With a tragic sense of inevitability, however, this "strength" will manifest itself as a murderous, survival-at-all-costs form of masculinity. More ironically still, Jan's shame-induced masculinity results only in increasingly shameful behavior.

The remainder of the film constitutes a harrowing descent. With each development in the noxious civil war, and each resultant decision by Jan or Eva, their prospects become increasingly dire. First, Eva begins a halfhearted affair with Jacobi (Gunnar Björnstrand), a powerful local official, at least partly in an attempt to gain some security for Jan and herself—a decision that backfires once Jacobi's fortunes fall and he (and therefore Eva and Jan) becomes a target of the suddenly dominant partisans on the conflict's other side. Learning of his wife's affair with Jacobi, the cuckolded Jan fails to intercede in events when doing so could save Jacobi's life; thus he consigns his rival to an execution that, in a horrifying instance of poetic justice, the partisans coerce the formerly violence-averse Jan into carrying out. (That Jacobi's death is justified militarily suggests the extent to which all this war's appalling violence has roots in traditionally gendered struggles.) Although there may be an obvious dramatic logic in Jan playing a role in Jacobi's death, far less is apparent later when he kills a frightened deserter, Johan (Björn Thambert), perhaps meant to be the same Johan we were introduced to in *The Silence*, now a few years older. After finding Johan hiding in a greenhouse, Jan kills him in cold blood in order to steal, and thus literally step into, the young man's military boots and flee the island with his boat passage.

From Eva's perspective, the killing of the boyish soldier, to whom she had instantly shown maternal concern, may have been another, more definitive moment marking the death of her dreams of motherhood, as well as an instance of Oedipal logic on Jan's part: he killed once to avoid losing his wife to another lover, and he killed again to avoid losing her affections to a child substitute. For the queer spectator, however, the deserter's pronounced sense of traditionally understood attractiveness—harking back to the presentations of Alf Kjellin and Birger Malmsten in Bergman's earlier films—also seems related to a finally hinted-at homosexual repression on Jan's part, particularly since Jan goes to considerable effort to separate Johan from Eva so that he can shoot the young man in private, in marked distinction from his killing of Jacobi, which took place in the masculine environment of a military maneuver and, more painfully, in Eva's presence.[69] Having thus asserted a lethal form of masculinity (killing Eva's lover) and a correlated heterosexuality (by privately destroying the homoerotically enticing Johan), the now utterly decisive Jan is able to claim a space for Eva and himself—assuming Eva wants accompany him—on a small refugee boat. Although Eva initially reacts to Johan's murder by refusing to continue on, she quickly relents. The fact that Jan responded to her initial decision by coldly stating, "It'll be simpler if you stay," can be taken as appalling proof that once a man has proved to himself that he is sufficiently masculine and heterosexual, it doesn't matter whether he has a woman in his life.

With the logic of a nightmare, the couple's desperate, final attempt to escape the war ends in failure. Jan and Eva become stranded with a handful of other refugees far from land in still, briny waters. There they face death from dehydration, starvation, exposure, or drowning after their small craft's engine fails. In an echo of the film's first scene that also alludes to the Pirandellian moment of self-reflection half-

way through the film, *Shame* concludes with Eva waking from another dream. Jan lies beside his shattered wife, stone-faced, with his
eyes closed as she recounts it to him. The first of this sequence's two
shots is almost an exact replica of the shot in their farmhouse bedroom
in which Eva realized that she would never have children, although it
is reversed (mirrored), with the couple now facing the spectator's right.
Ultimately, a jump cut moves the spectator closer to Eva's face, so the
film's last image is of her alone. Her concluding monologue merits quotation in full:

> I had a strange dream, it was absolutely real. I was walking along
> a very beautiful street. On one side were white, open houses, with
> arches and pillars. On the other side was a lovely park. Under the big
> trees by the street ran cold dark-green water. I came to a high wall,
> that was over grown with roses. Then an aircraft came, roaring down
> and set fire to the roses. They burned with a clear flame and there
> was nothing particularly terrible about it because it was so beautiful. I
> stood with my face against the green-water and I could see the burn-
> ing roses. I had a baby in my arms. It was our daughter, she was only
> about six months old, and she was clutching my necklace and pressing
> her face to mine. I could feel her wet open mouth against my cheek.
> I knew the whole time that I ought to understand something impor-
> tant that someone had said, but I had forgotten what it was. I pressed
> the baby close to me and I could feel that she was heavy and wet and
> smelled good, as if she had just had her bath. And then you came on
> the other side of the street and I thought that you would be able to tell
> me about the important thing that I had forgotten.[70]

Enigmatic passages such as this, a staple in the European art cinema of
the era, inevitably elicit highly subjective readings, when not simply ex-
asperating their less committed viewers.[71] They thus tend to annoy critics hoping for a specific or dominant meaning. One wonders: Why do
the houses in Eva's dream have arches and pillars? Why roses? What
significance should one find in the greenness of the "cold," "deep"
water?[72]

With the second half of the passage focusing on the child Eva once
wanted, one might feel on firmer interpretive ground, but even here
one is left to guess. What is the important "thing" that Eva had forgotten? As with the scripted explanation of queer Oswald's arrest, *Shame's*
screenplay has one final dialogue exchange, one that seems to suggest
what it is that Eva and, by extension, everyone else in this dream text of

a film, has forgotten. Bergman, again perhaps shamefully, elected not to include these lines in the final film. Lying together and surely dying in the boat, Jan breaks his silence and speaks to Eva: "I was wondering what it said in those letters we wrote to each other during the summer tour. Whether it said 'My hand in yours' or 'Your hand in mine.'" Eva simply responds with the script's final line: "It said 'My hand in yours.'"[73]

Surely, before the wars between two sides of a once-unified whole (the civil war and the war within the gendered human being) reached such an appalling state, Jan and Eva had considered themselves to be in each other's hands. Through a simple metonymic association, one could say they were even more profoundly joined. Jan knew that Eva represented something in him, and Eva knew that Jan's characteristics were inside her as well. After a violent split, this essential fact was forgotten. Now, at the toxic, bitter end, the child that Eva once dreamed of having will not be able to be born.[74] *Shame* denies a redemptive offspring to a couple whose genders have functioned not to unify them, but to destroy them.

In a short essay analyzing Bergman's film as a "failed tragedy," Tarja Laine connects Thomas Elsaesser's concept of a "traumatic mode of spectatorship" with theories of shame to posit what she considers to be an ethical mandate implicit in the film. Defining shame as "the association *par excellence* of a (moral) failure with the self that brings about a traumatic configuration of indicative (what is) and conditional (what could have been) [understandings] for the person," Laine, except for one observation, avoids issues of gender and sexuality to read the film in existentialist terms.[75] Suggesting that the transformational energies Sedgwick ascribes to shame cannot counter the "failure of love" exemplified in Jan and Eva's joint disintegration, Laine argues instead that:

> *Shame* contains the possibility for the circulation of shame as a cinematic experience linked to ethics. The ethical dimension of *Shame* is the individual responsibility for the self and for the other, which rests upon a principle other than that of citizenship, the state, or the nation; namely, it depends upon [what Jean-Luc Nancy defines as] "an ontology of being-with-one-another . . . an ontology for the world."[76]

Thus Laine, evoking the more explicit mirror-image shots in Bergman's previous films, writes that "we see that at the heart of Bergman's film there is the hope that shame will be acknowledged in the mode of self-reflection, as a question of moral agency and a willingness to live up to one's chosen ideals."[77] Without, however, an understanding of how shame is associated with a conception of the two primary gender roles that ultimately function as a curse—in other words, without a queer perspective that includes a larger sample of Bergman's work—I would argue that such self-reflection will remain opaque at best.

And if one might be tempted to regard *Persona* and *Hour of the Wolf* simply as a pair of films displaying decadent and homophobic sentiments in an otherwise progressively modernist aesthetic, *Shame* offers a final, appalling (one is tempted to say "heterophobic") apotheosis. The film turns what might have been a homophobic diptych into a trilogy reflecting and expressing the melancholy and the shame of the dehumanizing results of gender itself. With *Shame*, the male-identified spectator (queer or not) feels this most debilitating of affects not because he is too close for comfort to a female subjectivity, too close to his own homosexual desires, but because he realizes, or at least suspects at some level, that he is not close enough. Like Jan and Eva, this spectator is adrift and isolated: in physical proximity to the other, but an eternity away psychically.

Rightly contending that "*Shame* can be seen as a mirror held in front of the spectators," Laine stops short of discussing the film's literal mirror-image shots—or those in which its characters, by looking into the camera, invoke those instances of the "look back" seen in Bergman's previous films.[78] Unlike *Monika, Winter Light, Persona*, and *Hour of the Wolf, Shame* uses the film screen as a mirror only fleetingly: accusatory without being revelatory, and thus symptomatic of the film's titular affect. As Jan and Eva get into the refugee boat in the film's final moments, they do, in fact, finally look directly into the camera in two separate shots (figures 4.8 and 4.9). But "caught between the shame of looking and the shame of being ashamed to do so," the eye contact they make with us is aborted almost instantly through cuts to subsequent shots. Similarly truncated is the film's single example in which the spectator is put in the position of a character looking at his reflection in a literal mirror. Unlike those more courageous characters in Bergman's earlier films (Harry, Tomas, Alma, Johan Borg, and the rest), a soldier in the process of destroying Jan and Eva's home catches sight of himself in the couple's dressing mirror. We momentarily share his view, but the soldier quickly finds this "look back" intolerable. Rather than seeing himself for what he is, he quickly destroys his reflection by shooting the looking glass.

Figure 4.8. The half-hidden Jan looks at the spectator in *Shame*. Svensk Filmindustri.

Figure 4.9. The defeated Eva looks at the spectator in *Shame*. Svensk Filmindustri.

Conclusion

Bergman's films up to and including *Shame* articulate the existence of a spectator with no sexuality, no gender configuration stable enough to compensate for the lack of unity within the fully formed human subject. Even if the shaming of gender and sexuality elicited by this painful film cannot be claimed by its director, the shame and the melancholy from which it emanates serves a valuable purpose. They help construct a demasculinized male spectator deeply critical of his own functioning within a heteronormative and sexually divided ideological order. With the era of gay liberation unfolding all around him at the time of this film's American release, *Shame*'s spectator could also find a disheartening compromise in the comfortable images of a fully formed and fully defined homosexuality seen in mainstream queer film characters, ones who stayed on their own side of the screen and acted in predictable ways, part of a countermove in a sexual revolution that, for better or worse, was built upon strongly essentialized foundations. These were unambiguously gay, though also unqueerly queer, characters, ones the spectator might come to relate to, but never fully identify with. Bergman's corpus, on the other hand, although it could hardly be described as politically correct, provided a radical, shameful epiphany of disengendering power. It pointed the way to a potentially transformational energy and a self-awareness that would finally be embraced in a number of more self-evidently queer films produced in the 1970s, 1980s, and 1990s, from the work of Rainer Werner Fassbinder to the early films of Todd Haynes and others.

To get to that point, queer spectators, filmmakers, and the critics and scholars accompanying them and describing their journey would be obliged to navigate a tortuous, frustrating, but unavoidable path. Surely, part of the difficulty stemmed from the fact that while the gender shame Bergman identified is most closely associated with male subjectivity, a shamed or ashamed man in Western culture is far less likely to acknowledge his feelings of insecurity than a woman. Bergman alluded to this in the television interview that gives this chapter its epigraph. It deserves to be quoted more fully: "If a man stands in front of a mirror and looks at himself," Bergman told Dick Cavett on American television in 1971, "he can perhaps feel a little bit ashamed of it. You know he looks at his clothes, at his hair and his face. A woman, by education, is not ashamed of looking at herself."[79] The most obvious interpretation of this statement assumes that Bergman is speaking simply of a woman's culturally constructed willingness to see herself as an object, to take narcissistic pleasure in the self-regard that a mirror, or any congruent performance of self, occasions. (One is glad that Bergman, in using the phrase "by education," acknowledges that this willingness he has noted on the part of women, rather than men, is a social construct.) But as I argue in this chapter, Bergman's perspective might well be far more radical. His work, queerly regarded, suggests that homophobic and misogynistic criticisms of "feminine narcissism" obfuscate a much more powerful reality, one in which a man, culturally constructed and even only partially self-aware, always risks the epiphany, when looking at his reflection in a mirror, of seeing what he is and what he is not, and thereby of being ashamed.[80]

Real adolescent, you know, fashionable pessimism
. . . Okay, okay, okay, I mean, I loved it when I was
at Radcliffe, but I mean, all right, you outgrow it,
you absolutely outgrow it.

Mary Wilke (Diane Keaton),
Manhattan **(Woody Allen, 1979)**

Conclusion

In the years following the release *Shame,* the
most recent film addressed in this study, American culture, particularly
culture as it regarded and was regarded within the queer American experience, began to change with increasing rapidity. Indeed, at the time
of *Shame*'s U.S. debut, queer moviegoers had a number of other film
options offering queer auras of one kind or another to consider. In 1968,
The Killing of Sister George, Flesh, The Queen, and *Secret Ceremony*
were all advertised in the same issue of the *New York Times* that announced *Shame*'s American premiere.[1] (Two days later, *The Sergeant*
would appear as well.) As problematic, in their individual ways, as each
of those films are, the culture of openness about homosexuality, as well
as the sex and gender deconstruction reflected by the presence of those
films, was in sharp distinction to August 27, 1949, when *Frustration*'s
only immediate competition in those regards was Howard Hawks's *I
Was a Male War Bride* (1949).

By the time *Cries and Whispers,* Bergman's first post-Stonewall critical and commercial success, appeared in the United States, in December 1972, the culture had changed so much that the belief that a Bergman film could offer a challenging critique of patriarchal culture and heteronormativity might well have seemed like a joke. In one telling remark captured on film and edited into a theatrical trailer for John Waters's *Pink Flamingos* (1972), a seemingly queer filmgoer exiting a screening of that particular film endorses it to an off-camera interviewer, puckishly lauding it as "better than *Cries and Whispers!*"[2] Despite the playful tone of the young man's voice, he is obviously being sincere about his preferences. But it was not simply the environment around Bergman that had changed. The new films bearing Bergman's name in the 1970s were decidedly different from the ones leading up to and including *Shame.* As the director began to focus almost exclusively on female protagonists, almost always ones portrayed by a single actor who was, by then, that man's ex-lover, Liv Ullmann, a disturbing element seemed to be present in the films, something beyond the scope of this project.

Molly Haskell, in her pioneering early study on women in film, *From Reverence to Rape,* finds a great deal of value in Bergman's pre-1970 films, including many of those discussed in this study:

> Any criticism of Bergman must be prefaced with the understanding that he, more than any other director and in movies that were a revelation for their time, took women seriously, looked with curiosity and respect at every facet of their lives . . . never thought of them as "second class citizens" (the reverse, if anything), and, by not fastening on one single woman as his Galatea, watched over the film-birth and blossoming and development of one extraordinary woman after another. He has provided us with an array of women characters as rich and complex as those of any novelist, male or female.[3]

Haskell was not, however, disposed to defend *Cries and Whispers* (the last Bergman film released before the publication of her book), which featured the fifth of what would be ten performances by the director's increasingly afflicted Galatea. Using language that does, insightfully enough, suggestively allude to a particularly queer form of woman hatred, she characterized that film as reflecting "a misogyny [which] is furtive, a hatred that dares not speak its name."[4] Pauline Kael, Constance Penley, Ann Morissett Davidson, and Joan Mellen would concur.[5] Even those feminist critics who have positively assessed much of the director's previous output, including Maria Bergom-Larsson and Marilyn Johns Blackwell, have not defended the film.[6] And as subsequent Bergman films were released throughout that decade, including *Scenes from a Marriage*, *Face to Face*, and *Autumn Sonata*, little would emerge on the screen to discourage the now-routine, strongly critical reading of "late-period Bergman" by those progressives concerned with issues of women and gender in motion pictures.

Saraband (2003), Bergman's final work (a made-for-television "chamber play") is of great interest as a film that can be read as something of an apology on the part of its director, an apology to feminists in general and to Liv Ullmann in particular for the way in which the filmmaker used women on screen, none more so than Ullmann, in much of his later work. In *Saraband*, Ullmann's character, Marianne, is allowed to smile and laugh and show a lightness and independence that the director rarely allowed her to display in her earlier performances for him; she is completely unlike the largely joyless victims she played in *Hour of the Wolf*, *Shame*, *The Passion of Anna*, *Cries and Whispers*, *Scenes from a Marriage*, *Face to Face*, *The Serpent's Egg*, and *Autumn Sonata*, something all the more remarkable because she is playing the same character she first played in *Scenes from a Marriage*, in a film that stands as something of a sequel to that production.

As if returning to his practice of the 1950s and 1960s, Bergman, in *Saraband*, presents a neurotic male character, Henrik (Börje Ahlstedt), directly, and the film trenchantly shows the ways in which he tries to control a female performer under his power: his cellist daughter Karin (Julia Dufvenius). Remarkably, in the film's final minutes, the spectator sees something utterly unprecedented in a Bergman production. After presenting many images of women, as Penley among others suggested, obsessively exposed and brutally unmasked throughout the years, Bergman concludes *Saraband* with something that represents a stark reversal of that practice.

In a scene in which Marianne is awakened in the middle of the night by her ex-husband, Johan (Erland Josephson), with whom she is staying, it is the man who is obliged by Bergman's script to fully expose his body, literally, and his long-hidden "inner self," metaphorically, to both the spectator and the female character's vision. Johan, who in this film can be thought of as Bergman's alter ego, strips to crawl into bed with his ex-wife after suffering from a night terror. Rather apologetically, it seems, he exposes his naked and now completely aged body, including his genitals, both to her and to the spectator before he does. It is a moment that communicates both a strong sense of male vulnerability and the implicit admission that this man—and by extension, Bergman—is doing something now that he should have done long before.

Bergman's post-*Shame*—pre-*Saraband* work would, of course, continue to feature gay men and lesbian characters—a lesbian and a gay man have central roles in *Face to Face* (1976), and *From the Life of the Marionettes* (1980) features one openly gay man and one potentially repressed one—and while none of these characters can simply be dismissed as homophobic images of queer individuals (although two mincing gay men seen briefly in a party scene in *Face to Face* come close), their appearances hardly seem to represent radical interventions in the sexual revolution, either, particularly since unambiguously radical queer films like *El diputado* (Eloy de la Iglesia, 1978) and *Taxi zum Klo* (Frank Ripploh, 1980) were playing at the art houses at the same time.[7] In some ways, the most interesting of Bergman's post-Stonewall-rebellion films, at least until *Fanny and Alexander*, is *From the Life of the Marionettes*. Arguably Bergman's darkest work, it offers a solution to the central mystery it posits—why does the protagonist, Peter Egermann (Robert Atzorn), suffer an emotional breakdown and kill a female prostitute?—an answer that can be taken as a criticism of the heteronormative social order: the repression of Peter's deeply buried homosexuality was finally untenable, and he attacked a woman who resembled his wife and shared her first name. Of course, the history of narratives in which repressed homosexuality leads one to murder has a much more ignoble tradition of perpetuating homophobia, from *Phantom Lady* (Robert Siodmak, 1944) to *The Silence of the Lambs* (Jonathan Demme, 1991). And yet, as the first Bergman theatrical film since *Shame* to be shot largely in black-and-white, and one that makes subtle allusions to both *Shame* and its immediate predecessor, *Hour of the Wolf*, *From the Life of the Marionettes* almost seems to be a direct continuation of those films' queer concerns, suggesting a metaphorical form (one would hope) of murderous madness as a result of homosexual repression and gender bifurcation.[8] And yet, after a decade of gay-rights advances and with the AIDS pandemic still several years away, the "fashionable pessimism" that a character in Woody Allen's *Manhattan* criticizes in Bergman's films (and by implication, in his spectators) was likely to be no more appealing to queer spectators than it was to those in the mainstream.

But the appearance of *Fanny and Alexander*, Bergman's final theatrical feature-length film, in 1982 also invites a return to a more positive queer perspective.[9] Perhaps related to this film—ultimately, a refreshingly clear and affirmative vision of sexual possibilities and alternative gender configurations—the ever-expanding queer discourses of the 1980s and 1990s began to make references and allusions to Bergman's earlier work, and in less derogatory terms than those used by Woody Allen's on-screen Bergman hater.[10]

Desert Hearts (Donna Deitch, 1985), the first female-directed U.S. feature film to chronicle a lesbian romance, begins with a scene in which a repressed lesbian steps off of a train in an outfit nearly identical to that worn by Ingrid Thulin in *The Silence*'s first scene, itself set on a train. The fact that Helen Shaver bears a strong facial resemblance to Thulin, and that *Desert Hearts*, like *The Silence*, is set in the Cold War era, allows one to consider Deitch's film, which ends happily for its newly unrepressed lesbian protagonist, something of an optimistic, respectful rejoinder to Bergman's finally tragic story, one offering its Ester a second chance at life.

Even more obviously a response to *The Silence*, Chris Munch's *The Hours and Times* (1991) premiered at the Sundance Film Festival in 1992 as part of a cresting tide of new queer cinema that included the Fassbinder- and Pasolini-influenced *Poison* (Todd Haynes, 1991) and the Godardian *The Living End* (Gregg Araki, 1992). Clearly a consciously intended queer remake of Bergman's film, *The Hours and Times* substitutes fictionalized versions of John Lennon and his manager, Brian Epstein, for Anna and Ester, but places them in a similarly labyrinthine Continental hotel, one also shot in bleak monochrome. As the gay Epstein silently desires his hopelessly straight traveling companion, resentments simmer beneath the surfaces of both men's façades. To make the comparison clear, the two men attend a screening of *The Silence* in a local theater.[11] While standing as a nice, though obvious, allusion, the scene also reminds us that Bergman's were the kind of films many of our queer forebears were inclined to watch, and for reasons that still resonate on-screen, and in life, today.

Like something of a better-humored continuation of *The Silence* almost twenty years later, *Fanny and Alexander* focuses upon an adolescent male, approximately twelve years old, coming of age in a period—the early twentieth century—when the patriarchy was revealing itself as bereft of any sense of legitimate authority; its remaining intransigence would be revealed as more and more perniciously unjust as the century unfolded. The young protagonist, Alexander (Bertil Guve), like Johan in *The Silence*, seems to have no real father. His mother Emilie (Ewa Fröling), we are told, has had so many lovers over the years that Oscar Ekdahl (Allan Edwall), the man credited as the boy's father, may be so in name only. (In an example of brilliant casting, the child actors playing Alexander and his sister, Fanny [Pernilla Allwin], bear a strong resemblance to the actor playing their mother, but almost none to the performer cast as their assumed father.) After Oscar dies and Emilie marries an authoritarian bishop (Jan Malmsjö), the young man finds himself in direct conflict with a new, and equally "illegitimate," patriarchal figure, one shown to be as insecure as he is fascistic. (The bishop's surname is Vergerus, a name that seemed to haunt Bergman, since it appears also in *The Magician* and *The Serpent's Egg*.) Even after Emilie realizes her mistake in marrying this abusive man of God and asks him for a divorce, the family remains under the bishop's charge, since he refuses his young wife's request. Claiming, accurately we are later told, that the law is on his side and that if Emilie leaves him, he will maintain custody of the two children, the bishop effectively keeps the family imprisoned in his home.

No one, to my knowledge, has yet fully accounted for the radical way in which the young man, along with his mother and sister, are freed from their imprisonment. Put briefly, Alexander's grandmother Helena (Gunn Wållgren) sends her lifelong sometime lover, Isak (Erland Josephson), surreptitiously to retrieve the boy and his sister. Isak, it must be noted, is doubly illegitimate as a patriarchal figure in the Ekdahl family, since he is both not married to Helena and a Jew, and thus, his conspiring with Helena to free the children takes on a distinct quality of outsiders attempting to free a family from a paradigmatic figure of official authority. Taking them to his vast home filled with Jewish cultural artifacts and exotic antiques—one, in other words, characterized by its utter (but delightful) foreignness to the children—this elderly and, in a positively portrayed sense, mystical Jew puts the children to bed. When Alexander wakes late in the night to urinate, he finds himself having an experience of queer uncanniness that will forever change his subjectivity and will lead to the film's happy ending.

Encountering Isak's nephew Aron (Mats Bergman), whom he has already met, Alexander is taken to a locked room to meet another of the old man's nephews, Ismael, who is considered mad and has been locked away in the house for many years. According to Aron: "Human beings are more than [Ismael] can bear. Sometimes he gets violent and then he's dangerous. . . . The doctors say that his intelligence is far above the normal. He never stops reading. He's incredibly learned and knows everything by heart."[12] As Aron unlocks the bolts to Ismael's door, one expects something out of a horror film, and the spectator can have only something of a confused response, at least initially, when the occulted

Figure 5.1. Ismael looks at the spectator in *Fanny and Alexander* (Ingmar Bergman, Sweden, 1982). Cinematograph/Svenska Filminstitutet.

nephew is revealed to be a beautiful androgyne (Stina Ekblad)—one seen at first, like so many of the characters discussed in the previous chapter, staring directly into the camera and the spectator's eyes (figure 5.1). Unlike the androgyny of Aman in *The Magician*, however, the discrepancy between Ismael's male name, clothing, and haircut, on the one hand, and his otherwise completely female appearance and voice goes unexplained.[13]

Ismael represents the most explicit connection between queerness and foreignness in Bergman's films. S/he is an androgyne whose name refers to the Old Testament figure that was both Abraham's "illegitimate" son and the ancestor of the Arabs, considered a paradigmatic race of Others by both Jews and Christians. Still this seemingly utter foreigner presents him/herself as Alexander's uncanny self. He tells the boy to write his own name down, but after Alexander does, he looks down and sees that the name on the paper reads "Ismael Retzinsky." "Perhaps we are the same person," Ismael suggests. "Perhaps we have no limits; perhaps we flow into each other, stream through each other, boundlessly and magnificently." Then, in a conclusion to the scene that is so intimate and erotically charged that criticisms of pedophilia might have resulted,[14] Ismael wraps his arms around Alexander and continues to read the boy's thoughts (figure 5.2).

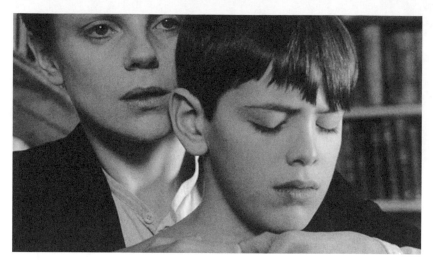

Figure 5.2. Ismael and Alexander merge their psyches in *Fanny and Alexander*. Cinematograph/Svenska Filminstitutet.

Referring to the bishop, Ismael says:

> You have in mind a man's death, . . . [a] tall man with fair graying hair and a beard. . . . He is asleep and dreaming that he is kneeling at the altar. Above the altar hangs the Crucified Prophet. In his dream he gets up and cries out through the huge cathedral: "Holy, holy, holy is the Lord of Hosts" . . . No one answers him, not even a laugh.[15]

Alexander begs him, "Please don't talk like that," but the androgyne replies:

> It is not I talking. It is yourself. I am saying your mental pictures aloud. I am repeating your thoughts. . . .
>
> You have only one way to go and I am coming with you. I obliterate myself; I merge into you, my little child. Don't be afraid. I am with you; I am your guardian angel.[16]

Intercut with this scene, the spectator sees an accident (or in the supernatural logic of the film, a miracle), in which the bishop is killed in a house fire. As a result, Alexander, his mother, and his sister are now free to return to the extended family of Emilie's original in-laws, one justly overseen by a matriarchal grandmother.

Perhaps it is the utterly conventional, classical cinema aesthetic of

Queer Bergman

Fanny and Alexander, used in the service of a narrative that is the film equivalent of a Dickens novel, that has discouraged critics from addressing the film's rather radical denouement. Surely, however, a queer spectator, seeing a young boy liberated by an encounter with a character as queer and as foreign as Ismael, is invited to read the film's ultimate developments as an affirmation of an antipatriarchal, antiessentialist spirit. As a personification of the foreign, ungendered depths within, Ismael has provided Alexander with the insight to challenge a patriarchal oppressor and to come to a new and more ethically queer sense of subjective relationality. It seems to be an ending Julia Kristeva might applaud. Talking about the discovery and theorization of the unconscious, she writes: "With Freud indeed, foreignness, an uncanny one, creeps into the tranquility of reason itself, and without being restricted to madness, beauty, or faith anymore than to ethnicity or race, irrigates our very speaking-being, estranged by other logics, including the heterogeneity of biology . . . Henceforth, we know that we are foreigners to ourselves, and it is with the help of that sole support that we can attempt to live with others."[17]

It almost goes without saying, of course, that many of the filmmakers associated with the European art-cinema tradition were ideologically "with Freud." Certainly, Bergman's work has been. Thus, with his and others' "foreign films," generations of queer spectators have come to the same understanding Kristeva has, and perhaps they are therefore better prepared to attempt to live most harmoniously with others and with the foreignness within themselves. In an increasingly globalized world, dynamics such as this will surely be replaced by others that bear only structural resemblances to it. Perhaps, however, foreignness will then be able to operate as a more obviously psychic component in the work of developing human subjectivity. Perhaps then, having learned the formative lessons taught by a briefly popular body of work associated with an equally short historical period, as well as lessons still to come, we will all be able to see ourselves as foreign, see ourselves as queer.

Notes

Introduction

1. The reader may feel I am being inconsistent in my terminology, as I sometimes use the term "GLBT studies" or "GLBT theory," and "GLBTQ studies" or "GLBTQ theory" at other times. There is a conscious method behind this, however. The Q of the last two abbreviations refers to "queer," and "queer theory" or "queer studies" names a distinct discourse first defined as such in the late 1980s, although many of the specific insights associated with queer theory were articulated much earlier—in the work of Michel Foucault and Guy Hocquenghem—and, arguably, before that in the work of Sigmund Freud, even if only indirectly. (Teresa de Lauretis is credited with coining the term "queer theory" at a conference in 1990; see de Lauretis, "Queer Theory.") Therefore, I will use the abbreviation "GLBTQ" adjectivally (as in "GLBTQ studies") only to refer to post-1980s discourse. On the other hand, I agree with many scholars who posit the existence of queer forms of subjectivity in general across time, and so I will use "queer" to refer to such forms much more broadly.

2. As of this writing, the only other English-language example I have found is Gwendolyn Audrey Foster, "Feminist Theory and the Performance of Lesbian Desire." Although not without its problems (for instance, it conflates theories of performativity developed by J. L. Austin, Judith Butler, and Eve Sedgwick—which I discuss in Chapter Four—with performance theory, which is a very different academic discourse), Foster's is a valuable case study that demonstrates how one can read an ostensibly non-queer text from a queer perspective, and so bears some similarity to my own work here. But I will attempt to chart how Bergman's films could have been read queerly at the time of their original appearances in American art theaters, while Foster, for her part, articulates a queer reading as one would make it today, by looking back at one specific Bergman film.

3. Penley, "*Cries and Whispers*," 205.

4. Wood, "Responsibilities of a Gay Film Critic," 400.

5. Ibid.

6. See Bergman, *Images*, 243–244; Björkman, Manns, and Sima, *Bergman on Bergman*, 167–168.

7. Bergom-Larsson, *Ingmar Bergman and Society*, 116.

8. For instance, see B. Ruby Rich, who characterizes Bergman's evocation of lesbianism in a famous lap dissolve (in *Persona*) as "pernicious" ("From Repressive Tolerance to Erotic Liberation," 186), and Raymond Murray, who claims Bergman's *The Silence* juxtaposes a "life-affirming" image of heterosexuality against an image of lesbianism used as a "symbol of neuroses" (*Images in the Dark*, 366).

9. Blackwell, *Gender and Representation in Bergman*. In addition to Penley's essay, she cites, among others, Bergom-Larsson's *Ingmar Bergman and Society*; Ann

Morrisett Davidson, "A Great Man Who Humiliates Women"; and Joan Mellen, "*Cries and Whispers.*"

10. Koskinen, *Ingmar Bergman's "The Silence,"* 56.

11. Modleski, *Women Who Knew Too Much.*

12. Benshoff, *Monsters in the Closet.*

13. I thank Maaret Koskinen for reminding me of this crucial point.

14. Corber, *Homosexuality in Cold War America*, 18.

15. Ibid., 19.

16. Ibid.

17. Wood, "Responsibilities of a Gay Film Critic," 389–390.

18. T. Waugh, review of *Sebastiane*, 19. When the review was reprinted in a recent anthology of Waugh's early criticism, the author expressed regret for his original condemnation of the film: "Of all the pieces in [this volume], this is perhaps the one I am most ashamed of, the one where I was most wrong, wrong, wrong. . . . [This was a] film I didn't get. . . . I'm sorry, Derek" ("Derek Jarman's *Sebastiane*," in *The Fruit Machine*, 69). (The suspension points before "I'm sorry" are in the original.) Robin Wood, more tentatively and with more reservations, reclaimed Bergman as a filmmaker of value, both in his writing (see Wood, "*Persona* Revisited") and in his work as an editor for the progressive film journal *CineAction*, where he published Tony French's "Suffering into Ideology" (on *Through a Glass Darkly*) and Göran Persson's "*Persona* Psychoanalyzed."

19. Quoted in Corrigan, *New German Film*, 68–69.

20. Haynes, introduction to *"Far from Heaven," "Safe," and, "Superstar,"* xii.

21. A fecund new essay has recently appeared, albeit one focused largely on films more recent than those I am concerned with here: San Filippo, "Unthinking Heterocentrism."

22. Corber, *Homosexuality in Cold War America*, 19.

23. J. Baldwin, "Northern Protestant," 246.

24. Bergman, "*The Communicants (Winter Light)*" (1963), in *A Film Trilogy*, 94. Since a number of different English-subtitled versions of the films this book addresses are in general circulation, I have opted to attribute the dialogue I quote to the translations found in the English-language versions of the published screenplays (in cases in which the screenplays have been published), unless I have reason to do otherwise—for instance, when the published dialogue differs significantly from the dialogue used in the film itself.

25. Bergman, "*The Communicants*," 94.

26. One can only wonder how conscious Bergman was of his film's theme of gender difference. Considering how unlikely it is that such a small school would, in fact, have separate bathrooms for boys and girls, the unavoidable image of the keys hanging next to the doorway seems to suggest some conscious emphasis on the filmmaker's part.

27. Modleski, *Women Who Knew Too Much*, 77.

28. Discussing a gay character in Bergman's 1980 German-language film *From the Life of the Marionettes*, Peter Cowie writes: "Once again, then, Bergman has

the courage to confront and discuss his own deepest feelings of sexual ambivalence. Not for nothing does he admire Fassbinder for using the cinema to flirt with his own proclivities. In every artist there exists to some degree that exquisite sensitivity habitually associated with the homosexual temperament. The need for nearness to another human being; conversely, the need also for infidelity" (Cowie, *Ingmar Bergman*, 334). While one can hardly endorse Cowie's pat association of "exquisite sensitivity" with a purported "homosexual temperament," the acknowledgment of Bergman's queer side by the preeminent English-language Bergman scholar is noteworthy, to say the least.

29. Bergman, *Images*, 28–29.

30. Ibid., 109.

31. Quoted in Björkman, Manns, and Sima, *Bergman on Bergman*, 6–7.

32. Ibid.

33. Staiger, "Self-Fashioning in Authoring and Reception," 89.

34. Bergman, "Why I Make Movies," 295; quoted in Staiger, "Self-Fashioning in Authoring and Reception," 94.

35. Staiger, "Self-Fashioning in Authoring and Reception," 94.

36. Benshoff, *Monsters in the Closet*, 15; Doty, *Making Things Perfectly Queer*, 15.

37. Hansen, "Pleasure, Ambivalence, Identification," 9. Hansen paraphrases terms used in a debate that emerged between E. Ann Kaplan and Linda Williams a few years earlier, which can be followed in Kaplan, "Case of the Missing Mother"; Williams, "'Something Else Besides a Mother'"; and Kaplan, "Dialogue: Kaplan Responds to Williams." Read in sequence, these three essays offer a fascinating case study of the debates that would form subsequent understandings of spectatorship.

38. See White, *Uninvited*; Farmer, *Spectacular Passions*; and Robert J. Corber, "Resisting the Lure of the Commodity: *Laura* and the Spectacle of the Gay Male Body," in *Homosexuality in Cold War America*, 55–78.

39. See Abelove, "Freud, Male Homosexuality, and the Americans."

40. Allen, "How Paranoid are Homosexuals?"; Robertiello, "A Psychoanalyst Replies." Despite the title of the latter article, and its placement directly after Allen's article, the two are unconnected. For the assessment of Huston's biopic, see Layne, review of *Freud*.

Chapter One

1. "Home Away from Homer," *The Simpsons*, season 16, episode 20, aired May 15, 2005, Fox.

2. Bech, *When Men Meet*, 148.

3. Ibid., 149.

4. Ibid.

5. Ibid., 150.

6. Ibid.

7. Bergman, *Images*, 109; Koskinen, *Bergman's "The Silence,"* 91–92.

8. See D'Emilio, *Sexual Politics, Sexual Communities* and "Capitalism and Gay Identity."

9. See Chauncey, *Gay New York*; Gray, *Out in the Country*.

10. Ibid., 38.

11. http://www.williamejones.com/collections/about/14.

12. The scene, including the Pachelbel music, comes from *Delivery Boys* (William Higgins, 1985). The subtitled French sound track is taken from the film *La Bouche de Jean-Pierre* (Lucile Hadzihalilovic, 1996).

13. The latter establishment, located on Santa Monica Boulevard in an unincorporated part of Los Angeles County, had been a heterosexual porn theater until it changed its programming in 1972 to become one of the higher-profile "all male" venues in the Greater Los Angeles area. Thereafter, according to William E. Jones, it was considered to be a particularly "sleazy" establishment, even for a gay porn theater (personal correspondence, June 27, 2009), although it used virtually the same sophisticated, calligraphy-style font to spell out its name in newspaper advertisements as did its more prestigious Manhattan counterpart.

14. The queer-themed films *The Ostrich Has Two Eggs* (1957), *La Fuga* (1964), and *This Special Friendship* (Jean Delannoy, 1964) all had their first New York City engagements at The Paris.

15. Charles Stinson, "One of *Ostrich Eggs* Hatches Strange Bird," review of *The Ostrich Has Two Eggs*, *Los Angeles Times*, November 9, 1960; reprinted in the *Mattachine Review* 6, no. 11 (November 1960): 19.

16. Untitled announcements in the *New York Mattachine Newsletter* 5, no. 10 (October 1960): 4; and *New York Mattachine Newsletter* 5, no. 9 (September 1960): 3.

17. Untitled announcement, *New York Mattachine Newsletter* 5, no. 10: 4.

18. See my essay on *The Time of Desire*, "One Summer of Heterosexuality."

19. Bruce, review of *Zazie dans le metro*.

20. "The Woman's Viewpoint," *New York Mattachine Newsletter*, issue 16 (September 1957): 5.

21. R.H., review of *The Confessions of Felix Krull*.

22. Dal McIntire, "Tangents: News & Views," *One* 6, no. 5 (May 1958): 22; *One* 10, no. 11 (November 1962): 16; *One* 9, no. 7 (July 1961): 18.

23. I might not otherwise have mentioned a scene many viewers have found so innocent and asexual, assuming Bergman's comedy was mentioned in *One* merely as an example of a film censored for representing (hetero)sexuality on the screen. When I recently showed *Smiles of a Summer Night* to a class of advanced undergraduates, however, the majority of my students felt the scene gives off a distinct lesbian vibe, some admitting it made them uncomfortable in that regard. Admittedly, this reaction from 2010 may not have been a common one in the mid-1950s. Nevertheless, after that classroom experience, I find it difficult to imagine female homosexuals, at the very least, in the Cold War era not finding that scene remarkable.

24. "Readers Respond," *Ladder* 4, no. 8 (May 1960): 24–25.

25. Ermayne, "Sapphic Cinema."

26. As one might expect in what was, in some ways, not much more than a community newsletter, the references are often inaccurate: *The Broadway Melody* is listed as "Broadway Melodies"; both versions of *Mädchen in Uniform* are discussed, but they are counted as one film; a single film focusing exclusively on male homosexuality—*Compulsion*—gets added, seemingly based on an incomplete description a reader came across in the press while the film was competing at the Cannes Film Festival, etc. For the record, a corrected version of what may well have been the first attempt to create a lesbian filmography, which combines three queer cinephiles' efforts published across the two issues of *The Ladder*, gives us:

The Adventures of King Pausole [*Die Abenteuer des Königs Pausole/Les aventures du roi Pausole*] (Alexis Granowsky, France, 1933)

Avventura a Capri (Giuseppe Lipartiti, Italy, 1959)

The Broadway Melody (Harry Beaumont, United States, 1929)

Children of Loneliness [*The Third Sex*] (Richard C. Kahn, United States, 1934)

The Children's Hour (William Wyler, United States, 1961)

Club des Femmes (Jacques Deval, France, 1936)

Compulsion (Richard Fleischer, United States, 1959)

Escape From Yesterday [*La bandera*] (Julien Duvivier, France, 1935)

The Girl of Berlin (This is listed and described as a German production, but I have been unable to identify a film with this title. One feature that [partially] matches the description—Nadia Tiller as star, a nightclub setting—seems the likely reference: *Du rififi chez les femmes* [Alex Joffé, France, 1959], featuring Tiller as a character called "Vicky de Berlin.")

Hands across the Table (Mitchell Leisen, United States, 1935)

Mädchen in Uniform (Leontine Sagen, Germany, 1931)

Mädchen in Uniform (Géza von Radványi, West Germany, 1958)

No Exit [*Huis clos*] (Jacqueline Audry, France, 1954)

Open City [*Roma, città aperta*] (Roberto Rossellini, Italy, 1945)

Pandora's Box [*Die Büchse der Pandora*] (Georg Wilhelm Pabst, Germany, 1929)

Prisons without Bars [*Prisons sans barreaux*] (Léonide Moguy, France, 1938)

The Pit of Loneliness [*Olivia*] (Jacqueline Audry, France, 1951)

Three Strange Loves [*Törst*] (Ingmar Bergman, Sweden, 1949)

Time of Desire [*Hästhandlarens flickor*] (Egil Holmsen, Sweden, 1954)

Turnabout (Hal Roach, United States, 1940)

Two Thousand Women (Frank Launder, UK, 1944)

It should be emphasized that these were not mentioned as films primarily focused on queer characters or homosexuality. They were merely described as films with queer content in "varying degrees." Several were mentioned sight unseen and were included based on secondhand information.

27. McIntire, "Tangents," *One* 9, no. 7: 18; Richards, review of *The Silence*.

28. Bruce, review of *The Silence*.

29. Corber, *Homosexuality in Cold War America*, 114.

30. Untitled announcement, *New York Mattachine Newsletter* 9, no. 6 (June 1964): 3.

31. Peter Sereel, "Films," *Eastern Mattachine Magazine* 10, no. 7 (August 1965): 15–16.

32. Ibid., 15.

33. Ibid.

34. Ibid., 16.

35. Richards, review of *The Silence*, 8–9.

36. Ibid., 9.

37. On the other hand, it would not be fair to suggest that the review (or the film) was met with complete indifference by *Ladder* readers. Issues of space in later issues may have kept temperate reactions from getting published.

38. Mulvey, "Visual Pleasure and Narrative Cinema."

39. Blackwell, *Gender and Representation in Bergman*, 19.

40. Citron et al., "Women and Film," 87.

41. In discussions of male homosexuality, the terms "top" and "bottom" usually refer to the penetrator and penetrated in anal sex, but the terms can also be used to signify the dominant or active partner and the submissive or passive partner, particularly in sadomasochistic and heterosexual contexts.

42. Marcella Althaus-Reid discusses this idea at length but somewhat implicitly in her *Indecent Theology*, 160–164. She subsequently reiterates the idea more directly, although just in passing, when she mentions "the placing of Jesus-bottom in a dialectic of tops and bottoms which come[s] from sadomasochism" (Althaus-Reid, *The Queer God*, 37–38).

43. See Bech, *When Men Meet*; Glick, *Materializing Queer Desire*.

44. Cory, *The Homosexual in America*, 105.

45. Lucey, *Gide's Bent*, 173.

46. Pauline Kael, review of *Amici per la Pelle*, in *5001 Nights at the Movies*, 24.

47. Leo Sullivan, "An Italian Tale—But So Very Nice," review of *The Woman in the Painting*, *Washington Post and Times Herald*, July 11, 1958.

48. See Edelman, *Homographesis*, 192–241; Corber, *Homosexuality in Cold War America*, 55–78; and Dyer, "Queer Noir."

49. *Washington Post and Times Herald*, display ad for *The Woman in the Painting*, July 10, 1958.

50. Sullivan, review of *The Woman in the Painting*.

51. Howard Thompson, "Italian Childhood Studied in *The Woman in the Painting*," review of *The Woman in the Painting*, *New York Times*, January 15, 1959.

52. Olson, *Queer Movie Poster Book*, 8.

53. Gerstner, *Manly Arts*, 5, 6 (emphasis added).

54. Ibid., 6.

55. Ibid., 49–50 (emphasis added).

56. Martin, "'Enviable Isles'," 69.

57. Martin, "American Literature," 28.

58. Warner, "Homo-Narcissism."

59. As Beauvoir puts it, "For the male it is always another male who is the fellow being, the other who is also the same, with whom reciprocal relations are established" (*The Second Sex*, 70).

60. Kristeva, *Strangers to Ourselves*, 13.

61. Ibid., 102, 103 (emphasis in the original).

62. Edith Oliver, review of *My Name Is Ivan*, *New Yorker*, July 6, 1963, 42; quoted in "Notes and Quotes," *New York Mattachine Newsletter* 8, no. 7–8 (July–August 1963): 13.

63. There have been a number of dramatic or melodramatic American films about homosexual tensions in the United States military, including *The Strange One* (Jack Garfein, 1957), *Reflections in a Golden Eye* (John Huston, 1967), *The Sergeant* (John Flynn, 1968), and *Streamers* (Robert Altman, 1983). While they have their merits, particularly the Huston and Altman films, a strong sense of homoerotic pleasure for the spectator cannot be considered one of them. An Australian production later released in the United States by Paramount Pictures, *Gallipoli* (Peter Weir, 1981) might be the best English-language equivalent to *Ivan's Childhood* or *Father and Son*.

64. Hoberman, "Roads to Perdition," 122.

65. Ibid.

66. Alton, *Painting with Light*, 95–96.

67. Ibid., 171.

68. Mulvey, "Visual Pleasure and Narrative Cinema," 203, 204, 205–206.

69. Billed as Kent Douglass in this film and four others made in 1930–1931, the actor would have his screen name permanently changed to Douglass Montgomery (his real middle and last name) two years later.

70. Richard Maltby, "*It Happened One Night*," 229.

71. Ibid. The embedded quotation can be found in its original context in Faith Baldwin, "Why All the Mystery about Gable's Appeal," 46.

72. Nikolay Burlyaev, the actor portraying Ivan, was, in fact, fourteen at the time of the film's production.

73. Bordwell, *Narration in the Fiction Film*, 206, 207.

74. Ibid., 206, 209.

75. Ibid., 212–213.

76. Le Fanu, *Andrei Tarkovsky*, 22.

77. Ibid.

78. Not to be too coy myself here, but I mean to allude to possible feelings one might have about the relative propriety of a father figure acting in ways that can seem erotically driven—perhaps excused by a cursory acknowledgment of generally accepted Oedipal drives—as opposed to an older "brother figure" acting in the same way, which does not have basic psychoanalytic tenets to serve to make it seem legitimate, if only as an underlying tension.

79. Le Fanu, *Andrei Tarkovsky*, 23–24 (emphasis added).

80. Bersani, "Is the Rectum a Grave?"

81. Le Fanu, *Andrei Tarkovsky*, 25.

82. Edelman, *Homographesis*, 7.

83. Humphrey, "One Summer of Heterosexuality," 35.

84. Elsaesser, "Putting on a Show," 27; Gervais, *Bergman: Magician and Prophet*, 28. *Törst* is also noted as having "done better" financially (in Sweden), "than any of Bergman's films" previously produced (Long, *Bergman: Film and Stage*, 36).

85. That date was, in fact, for the belated U.S. debut of Bergman's 1952 feature *Secrets of Women*. Steene may have conflated the two films when compiling her release dates; see Steene, *Bergman: Reference Guide*, 183.

86. *Washington Post*, display ad for *Thirst*, August 30, 1956.

87. Although there may have been showings in small towns or various noncommercial venues (film festivals, film societies, etc.), my research has found only a single other screening of the film in the United States before its title was changed, one sponsored by the Roosevelt University Film Society (in Chicago) on March 27, 1957.

88. It is titled *Thirst* on the *Early Bergman* DVD boxed set released in 2007 by Criterion Eclipse. On the other hand, Singer's *Ingmar Bergman: Cinematic Philosopher*, published also in 2007, refers to it as *Three Strange Loves*. Previous home-video releases in both the United States and the UK carry the three-word title.

89. *Boston Globe*, display ad for *Three Strange Loves*, March 9, 1958.

90. *Baltimore Sun*, display ad for *Three Strange Loves*, August 2, 1959 (emphasis in the original).

91. Ermayne, "Sapphic Cinema," 7.

92. *Los Angeles Times*, display ad for *Three Strange Loves* and *Sins of Casanova* (a double feature), October 17, 1958.

93. "2 Women Film Censors Ousted: Spats Revealed," *Chicago Daily Tribune*, October 16, 1959. It should be remembered that, as pointed out in an earlier note, the film had played at a film-society screening two years previously and that by 1960, the film, perhaps in a cut version, was playing in a number of Chicago-area theaters.

94. Steene, *Bergman: Reference Guide*, 183, 184.

95. *The Swedish Film Database* entry for the film reports that the national censor board cut less than two meters of film (i.e., less than five seconds) from the finished film and that some of the deleted material involved an unacceptably revealing shot of a woman's upper thigh from an unrelated scene. Obviously, then, the remaining cuts could hardly have been enough to obscure the lesbianism inherent in a seduction scene that runs longer than five minutes (*Törst, The Swedish Film Database*, http://www.sfi.se/en-GB/Swedish-film-database/, accessed July 12, 2011).

96. Janus Films catalogue (New York: Janus Films, 1973), n.p.

97. Tengroth, *Törst*. A number of studies of Bergman's work seem to have been confused by the film's second English-language title, reporting that the screenplay was based on only three of Tengroth's stories. But the Swedish scholar Jörn

Donner accurately connects the film's narrative to four: "Journey with Arethusa," "Thirst," "The Faith Healer," and "Avant de Mourir"; see Donner, *Films of Ingmar Bergman*, 67.

98. I refer to that period in Rut's life as "pre-heterosexual" because in an earlier flashback—one that chronologically takes place between Rut's friendship with Valborg (and whatever that entailed) and her marriage to Bertil—Rut was involved in a disastrous affair with a married man, ending in a botched abortion that leaves her unable to have children; at one point the man refers to the fact that she had been a virgin before meeting him.

99. Singer, *Bergman: Cinematic Philosopher*, 166.

Chapter Two

1. Gross, "Five Ways to Think about Bergman."

2. Quoted in "Overheard," *Time*, March 30, 1992, 23. For a more recent attack on Bergman from the political right, see John Podhoretz, "Death and the Director," *New York Post*, July 30, 2007, http://www.nypost.com/seven/07312007/post opinion/opedcolumnists/death__the_director_opedcolumnists_john_podhoretz .htm?page=0.

3. Perhaps the most characteristic look at Bergman as a specifically Swedish director is Vernon Young's deeply critical *Cinema Borealis: Ingmar Bergman and the Swedish Ethos*. As the Swedish-born Bergman scholar Birgitta Steene puts it: "[The book] is highly opinionated and full of factual errors. Not reliable but might be read for its wittily acerbic views of a society and a filmmaker that the author obviously dislikes" (Steene, *Bergman: Guide to References*, 235).

4. "'I Am a Conjurer,'" *Time*, March 14, 1960, 60.

5. Corber, *Homosexuality in Cold War America*.

6. According to Steene, it earned "Honorable Mention" at Cannes (*Bergman: Reference Guide*, 170).

7. Steene has suggested the idiomatic "Ship to Never-Never Land" (*Bergman: Reference Guide*, 168), whereas the Ingmar Bergman Foundation lists the English title as *A Ship to India* in its online filmography: http://www.ingmarbergman.se/page .asp?guid=69972D24-BB65-4E2E-BC96-4275C47D7C4F. Most recently, Artificial Eye, in a Blu-ray set (*Classic Bergman: 5 Films by the Master of Cinema*) released in the UK in 2012, labels it *A Ship Bound for India*.

8. Bergman, *Images*, 137, 139.

9. Wanda Hale, "Dull Swedish Film at Rialto," review of *Frustration*, *New York Daily News*, August 27, 1949; review of *Frustration*, *New York Herald Tribune*, August 27, 1949; review of *Frustration*, *New York Times*, August 27, 1949; and review of *Frustration*, *New York Sun*, August 27, 1949.

10. Shearer, "Crime Certainly Pays on the Screen," *New York Times*, August 5, 1945.

11. Silverman, *Male Subjectivity at the Margins*, 64.

12. Ibid., 64–65.

13. Ibid., 2 (emphasis added).

14. Ibid., 8.

15. Ibid.

16. Silverman also focuses extensively on *The Guilt of Janet Ames* (Henry Levin, 1947), while mentioning, in passing, *Pride of the Marines* (Delmer Daves, 1945), *Hail the Conquering Hero* (Preston Sturges, 1944), *State Fair* (Walter Lang, 1945), *Those Enduring Young Charms* (Lewis Allen, 1945), *The Lost Weekend* (Billy Wilder, 1945), *Spellbound* (Alfred Hitchcock, 1945), and *Gilda* (Charles Vidor, 1946).

17. Wilinsky, *Sure Seaters*, 102–103.

18. Steene, *Bergman: Guide to References*, 32.

19. Bosley Crowther, "A Study from Sweden," review of *Torment*, *New York Times*, April 22, 1947. Although *Hets* was released in Sweden uncensored, it was cut, like many other foreign imports, by the U.S. distributor, or perhaps by the New York state censorship board before being presented commercially in Manhattan.

20. Steene, *Bergman: Guide to References*, 32.

21. Crowther, "A Study from Sweden."

22. All quotations are taken from the English subtitles of the videocassette (*Torment*, directed by Alf Sjöberg, written by Ingmar Bergman [1944; Chicago: Home Vision Cinema, 2000]).

23. For an exemplary reading of the film that argues this thesis, see B. Ruby Rich, "Repressive Tolerance to Erotic Liberation."

24. Bergom-Larsson, *Ingmar Bergman and Society*, 17–18.

25. Russo, *Celluloid Closet*; White, *Uninvited*; Wood, "Responsibilities of a Gay Film Critic."

26. Bosley Crowther, "RKO Mystery Starring Robert Mitchum, New Feature at Palace," review of *Out of the Past*, *New York Times*, November 26, 1947; Crowther, "Exercise in Suspense Directed by Alfred Hitchcock is New Bill at the Globe," review of *Rope*, *New York Times*, August 27, 1948.

27. Tyler, *Classics of the Foreign Film*, 134.

28. See review of *Torment*, *Time*, April 28, 1947, 100–101; Donner, *Films of Ingmar Bergman*, 31–36; Young, *Cinema Borealis*, 38–42; Ulrichsen, "The Early Films"; Bergom-Larsson, *Ingmar Bergman and Society*, 15–20; and Cowie, *Bergman: A Critical Biography*, 28.

29. Gado, *Passion of Ingmar Bergman*, 60. A more recent study that summarizes the film in Oedipal terms is Macnab, *Bergman: The Life and Films*, 45.

30. Wood, *Ingmar Bergman*, 27.

31. Wood, *Hitchcock's Films Revisited*, 235n.

32. See, for example, Russo, *Celluloid Closet*; and Hepworth, "Hitchcock's Homophobia."

33. Sigmund Freud, "A Child Is Being Beaten," in *Standard Edition* 17:180.

34. Laplanche and Pontalis, "Fantasy and the Origins of Sexuality," 22–23 (emphasis in the original).

35. See Barton, "'Crisscross.'"

36. Gado, *Passion of Ingmar Bergman*, 60.

37. See Mulvey, "Visual Pleasure and Narrative Cinema." Much as in *Vertigo* (Alfred Hitchcock, 1958), it is not until very late in the film that one is able to identify with the female lead.

38. It would be pressing the point to bring up Flynn's rumored bisexuality and Nazi sympathies, not to mention the image of Santa and three elves positioned beside the photos of the American star.

39. Barton, "'Crisscross.'"

40. Sigmund Freud, *"The Ego and the Id,"* in *Standard Edition* 19:33.

41. Bergom-Larsson, *Ingmar Bergman and Society*, 17.

42. Making the film's Oedipal subtext utterly clear, a shot cut from the film's original US prints reveals Jan-Erik's mother and father sitting in his bedroom, just as Jan-Erik is falling asleep, occupying the same positions Bertha and Caligula occupy in the dream. This then is one of the almost thematically redundant images Crowther nonetheless seemed grateful he was "spared."

43. Bersani, "Is the Rectum a Grave?," 212, 222.

44. Gado, *Passion of Ingmar Bergman*, 61.

45. Ibid.

46. Ibid.

47. Wood, *Ingmar Bergman*, 27.

48. Silverman, *Male Subjectivity at the Margins*, 40.

49. Review of *Skepp till India land*, *Variety*, October 22, 1947, 13.

50. Film Classics distributed, among others, *Sangue sul sagrato* (as *Rapture*; Goffredo Alessandrini, 1950), *Lost Boundaries* (Alfred L. Werker, 1949), *Blonde Ice* (Jack Bernhard, 1948), and the 1948 rerelease of *Bride of Frankenstein* (James Whale, 1935).

51. Mayer, *Merely Colossal*, 170.

52. Ibid., 175–177.

53. "Rialto, Broadway Horror Showcase, May Switch to Class Lingos," *Variety*, October 29, 1947, 5.

54. Wilinsky, *Sure Seaters*, 70.

55. "Rialto, Broadway Horror Showcase," 5.

56. Review of *Frustration*, *New York Times*.

57. Review of *Frustration*, *Variety*, August 25, 1949, 8.

58. A scene of the runaway Birgitta-Carolina (Doris Svedlund) spending a night safely hidden away in an attic with her boyfriend, Tomas (Birger Malmsten), in *The Devil's Wanton*; one of the knights, Antonius Block (Max von Sydow), sharing a meal of strawberries and milk with his followers in *The Seventh Seal*; and the final flashback of the three sisters serenely walking through the park in *Cries and Whispers* are perhaps the most celebrated of these privileged moments of happiness in Bergman's filmography.

59. Cut by seventeen minutes, the American-release version ran approximately seventy-five minutes.

60. All quotations are from the subtitles of the Film Classics version. A 16 mm

copy can be found at the Library of Congress, and a 35 mm print has been preserved at George Eastman House. The subtitles are credited to Walter Ruckersberg.

61. Gado, *Passion of Ingmar Bergman*, 352 (emphasis in the original).

62. More obviously, it offers a textbook example of the failure of a filmmaker-focused auteurist project that completely ignores the visual aspect of the films. Gado's analysis is devoted exclusively to Bergman's written output, analyzing his film work only through the screenplays.

63. Malmsten appeared in ten Bergman directed or written films before 1953, but only two thereafter, and then only in very small roles.

64. Display ad for *The Naked Night*, *New York Times*, April 9, 1956.

65. Quoted in Steene, *Bergman: Guide to References*, 74.

66. Display ad for *The Naked Night*, *New York Times*. The film is now known in the U.S. as *Sawdust and Tinsel*.

67. "Splash in Sweden," review of *The Naked Night*, *Newsweek*, April 23, 1956, 53.

68. Desmond Fennell, "Goodbye to Summer," *Spectator* (London), February 9, 1962, 163, 164.

69. Ibid., 165.

70. Ibid., 164.

71. In an article written to dispel many of these myths, a young woman is reported to have "rejoiced to discover that Stockholm shops sell bathing suits": "She had been worried over whether she would have the courage to appear in the nude at a public beach, as she thought Swedes always did" (Werner Wiskari, "Rejoinder to Sweden's Critics" *New York Times*, October 23, 1960). On the other hand, *Look* reminded its readers that not all outdoor swimming is public, claiming that in Sweden, "nude bathing is enjoyed by all in private" (Edward M. Korry, "Sex Education in Sweden," *Look*, September 3, 1956, 35).

72. Fennell, "Goodbye to Summer," 164.

73. Desmond Fennell, "What Shall It Profit Fat-Cat, Joyless Sweden?," *Washington Post*, February 25, 1962. Suggesting an impulse to follow the political imperative to criticize what could otherwise have been called Sweden's socialist miracle, the article was published at least one more time in the United States, under its original title, in the *National Review*, April 9, 1963, 273–278.

74. Nott, *A Clean, Well-Lighted Place*, 37.

75. "Lobsters for Tourists, Herring for Swedes," *U.S. News and World Report*, April 23, 1948, 61–62.

76. Evelyn Waugh, "Scandinavia Horrifies an Eminent British Novelist," *Washington Post*, January 25, 1948.

77. Quoted in Frank Eleazer, "Ike Urges GOP to Shun 'Political Gutters,'" *Washington Post*, July 28, 1960.

78. Philip and Kersti French point out that Swedish officials were simply more honest in listing suicide as a cause of death on death certificates in the 1950s, which gave the country a higher *recorded* number of suicides than other nations (French and French, *Wild Strawberries*, 59).

79. Two years later, as an ex-president visiting the country, Eisenhower confirmed that Sweden was the nation to which he had referred, and he apologized for what he called "my error" ("Eisenhower and the Swedes," *Christian Science Monitor*, August 2, 1962).

80. Display ad for *The Devil's Wanton*, *New York Times*, July 2, 1962.

81. Quoted in Klinger, "Film History Terminable and Interminable," 109. The useful term "discursive surround" comes from Dana Polan.

82. Foucault, *History of Sexuality*, 27.

83. Embassy Home Video quietly released a dubbed version on home video along with several other Bergman films to complement the video debut of *Fanny and Alexander* (1982) in 1984. In 2007, Criterion/Eclipse released it on DVD in the United States as part of a set of films under the title *Early Bergman*.

84. The film remains quite unknown in the United States. It has not yet been released on videotape or DVD through an American distributor. For the Swedish award, see Steene, *Bergman: Reference Guide*, 166; for the *Variety* review, dated January 8, 1947, see *Variety Film Reviews*, vol. 7.

85. The quotations are from Steene, *Bergman: Reference Guide*, 165; and Cowie, *Bergman: A Critical Biography*, 50.

86. Hubner, *Films of Ingmar Bergman*, 12.

87. Urquhart, *Hammarskjold*, 27.

88. Ibid. A recent book claiming Hammarskjöld as a gay icon, although possibly a celibate one, is Vargo, *Noble Lives*.

89. Kelen, *Hammarskjöld*, 156; "Like a Mirror," *New Yorker*, April 18, 1953, 26.

90. Chesly Manly, "Swede OK'd as Head of U.N.," *Chicago Daily Tribune*, April 1, 1953.

91. Quoted in McIntire, "Tangents: News and Views," *One* 4, no. 8 (December 1956): 21–22.

92. Review of *The Third Sex*, *One* 7, no. 9 (October 1959): 18–19. Harlan, who is best known as the director of the anti-Semitic Nazi propaganda film *Jud Süß* (1940), stood trial in the 1950s for war crimes related to its production. *The Third Sex*, also released in the United States as *Bewildered Youth*—in West Germany, it appeared as *Anders als du und ich* (*Different from You and Me*)—demonstrates nearly as much homophobia as *Jud Süß* demonstrates anti-Semitism; see Guenther-Pal, "Sexual Reorientations."

93. Display ad for *Monika*, *New York Times*, January 27, 1960. The film is now known in the U.S. as *Summer with Monika*.

94. Bosley Crowther, "Film from Sweden Opens," review of *Illicit Interlude*, *New York Times*, October 27, 1954.

95. See *Los Angeles Times*, display ad for *Illicit Interlude*, December 25, 1954. As this note suggests, the film was originally released in the U.S. as *Illicit Interlude*.

96. Jay Jacobs, "Afterthoughts," review of *Brink of Life*, *New York Reporter*, December 24, 1959.

97. McCarten, "Bergman on Birth."

98. Gill, "Cuckolds and Cooks."

99. In her fine essay on Bergman, Janet Staiger focuses on Bergman's work and how the filmmaker created and perpetuated an image of himself as a cinematic author "by duplicating recipes and exercises of authorship within a cultural and institutional context that understands such acts as agency and repetition of such acts as signs of individuality" ("Self-Fashioning in Authoring and Reception," 89, 91). Although I focus on external political and ideological forces that molded Bergman's image as author (what Roland Barthes would call Bergman's "author effect"), I consider our approaches to be complementary rather than contradictory. I appreciate Staiger stressing that while "real people act as authors," one still must acknowledge "the social, cultural and discursive restraints on an individual subject" (91). For my part, I readily acknowledge that Bergman's "citational practice[s]"—employed as part of a process of "self-fashioning" (to use Staiger's Foucauldian terminology)—have indeed registered within the cultural field to affect significantly Bergman's image as author. I differ in approach from Staiger, however, by being more concerned with those citational instances that have not registered within public consciousness, and by focusing on those elements outside of Bergman's self-fashioning, which were employed often against the director's own efforts.

100. Steene, "'Manhattan Surrounded by Bergman,'" 142.

Chapter Three

1. "Tangents: News and Views," *One* 13, no. 8 (August 1965): 9. The column's claim that the Reuters article appeared in the *Los Angeles Times* on July 18 seems to be erroneous. The archived "final edition" of that date's *Times* contains no such story. It does exist, however; I found it in the *Montreal Gazette*, June 10, 1965.

2. Childs, *Sweden*.

3. Childs, *Sweden*, rev. ed.; the quotation is from Felix Belair, Jr., "Trend in Sweden Runs to Left," *New York Times*, January 2, 1956.

4. Belair, "Trend in Sweden Runs to Left."

5. Cixous, "Fiction and Its Phantoms," 530.

6. Werner Wiskari, "Another Bergman Gains Renown," *New York Times*, December 20, 1959. A ProQuest database search showed this sentence to be the first instance in which the words "uncanny" or "uncanniness" are found in the same article as the name "Ingmar Bergman" in the following U.S. papers: the *Chicago Tribune*, *Christian Science Monitor*, *Los Angeles Times*, *New York Times*, *Wall Street Journal*, and *Washington Post*.

7. Sigmund Freud, "Das Unheimliche."

8. Freud, "The 'Uncanny,'" in *Standard Edition* 17:222.

9. Ibid., 223.

10. Ibid., 224 (emphasis in original).

11. Freud, "Notes upon a Case of Obsessional Neurosis," in *Standard Edition* 10:162, 163, 165.

12. Freud, "*Leonardo Da Vinci and a Memory of His Childhood*," in *Standard Edition* 10:127.

13. Ibid., 82.

14. Ibid., 87.

15. Freud, *Three Essays on the Theory of Sexuality*, in *Standard Edition* 7:141.

16. In 1920, Freud distinguished between three characteristics of what he called homosexuality: "Physical sexual characters (physical hermaphroditism), Mental sexual characters (masculine or feminine attitude), [and] Kind of object-choice" ("The Psychogenesis of a Case of Homosexuality in a Woman," in *Standard Edition* 18:170). For early influential writings that assert the independence of object choices from gender positions, see Hocquenghem, *Homosexual Desire*; and Wittig, "The Straight Mind."

17. Freud, *Interpretation of Dreams*, in *Standard Edition* 5:358–359.

18. Freud, *Three Essays on the Theory of Sexuality*, in *Standard Edition* 7:179–181, 185–187.

19. Ibid., 191.

20. Ibid., 231.

21. Here, I depart from other, more traditional interpretations of Freudian thought. While it is generally felt that homosexual men are arrested at an anal stage of development, one could instead consider that a homosexual object choice, coupled with the reality of the male body, obliges or encourages men to return to anal eroticism. In other words, one reclaims one's anal eroticism by becoming a homosexually driven man; one is not simply homosexual because one was arrested at that stage. Indeed, many gay men do not make this return and eschew anal intercourse throughout their lives as fully formed sexual beings. This distinction is important for my argument when I posit that homosexuality and heterosexuality represent "forks in the road" that one is obliged to choose between at the moment of engendering.

22. Freud, *Three Essays on the Theory of Sexuality*, in *Standard Edition* 7:176.

23. Freud, "The 'Uncanny,'" in *Standard Edition* 17:219, 241 (emphases in original).

24. Ibid., 249.

25. Freud, "Analysis Terminable and Interminable," in *Standard Edition* 23:251.

26. Freud, *Interpretation of Dreams*, in *Standard Edition* 5:358–359 (emphasis in the original).

27. Freud, "The Infantile Genital Organization (An Interpolation into the Theory of Sexuality)," in *Standard Edition* 19:143–144 (emphasis in the original).

28. Wood, "Brian de Palma," 135.

29. See, for example, Freud, *Interpretation of Dreams*, in *Standard Edition* 5:256, 260–264.

30. Freud's insistence that castration be seen as a complex specifically relating to the penis, and not to other forms of loss (like the loss of the mother's breast or the loss of intrauterine existence), as his fellow psychoanalysts often argued, lends support to the theory that the shock of sexual difference and the subsequent gen-

dering of the child are at the core of this anxiety, at least according to Freud. See Laplanche and Pontalis, *Language of Psycho-Analysis*, 58, for a brief discussion of this debate in Freud's time.

31. Freud, "The 'Uncanny,'" in *Standard Edition* 17:248.

32. Ibid., 247–248.

33. "'I Am a Conjurer,'" *Time*, March 14, 1960, 60–66.

34. Display ad for *The Magician*, *New York Times*, August 27, 1959.

35. Charles Stinson, "Bergman's *Magician* Continues Brilliance," review of *The Magician*, *Los Angeles Times*, February 9, 1960.

36. Kevin Heffernan discusses the U.S. distributor's framing of *The Magician* as a horror film briefly but informatively in *Ghouls, Gimmicks, and Gold*, 119–120.

37. Display ad for *The Magician*, *New York Times*.

38. The similarities between the first scene of *The Naked Night* and the beginning of *The Magician* have been routinely noted by Bergman scholars; see Bergom-Larsson, *Ingmar Bergman and Society*, 59; Mosley, *Bergman: Cinema as Mistress*, 88; Livingston, *Bergman and the Rituals of Art*, 70; and Gervais, *Bergman: Magician and Prophet*, 63. But a larger number of spectators would have seen *The Seventh Seal* and made connections between that film and *The Magician*.

39. Blackwell, *Gender and Representation in Bergman*, 31.

40. Ibid., 30–34.

41. Ibid., 31.

42. In fact, Thulin, fluent in English and known to American filmgoers for her role opposite Robert Mitchum in *Foreign Intrigue* (1956), was a visible part of the publicity campaign for *The Magician* in the United States upon its premiere in North America. She was advertised as making a personal appearance at the Fifth Avenue Cinema in Manhattan on opening night (display ad for *The Magician*, *New York Times*).

43. Butler, *Gender Trouble*.

44. Bergman, *The Magician*, in *Four Screenplays*, 303, 304.

45. Ibid., 304.

46. Ibid., 304–305.

47. Intriguingly, Kael reports that on the print of the film she saw, surely an original release print of the American subtitled version, the dialogue was translated into English as "I always longed for a knife to cut away my tongue and my *sex*" (emphasis added); see Kael, review of *The Magician*, in *5001 Nights at the Movies*, 451.

48. Bergman, *The Magician*, in *Four Screenplays*, 311.

49. Kael, review of *The Magician*.

50. Bergman, *The Magician*, in *Four Screenplays*, 350.

51. Freud devotes considerable space in "The 'Uncanny'" to the relationship between intellectual uncertainty and the effect of the uncanny, which comes from a definition by Ernst Jentsch in a 1906 essay (Jentsch, "On the Psychology of the Uncanny"). Freud considers Jentsch's definition to be "incomplete," and declares his own essay an attempt to "proceed beyond [that] equation" ("The 'Uncanny,'" *Standard Edition* 17:221). Still, it is important to note that Freud does not at all attempt to

negate Jentsch's connection between uncanniness and the kind of intellectual uncertainty that vexes Vergérus in *The Magician*.

52. Bergman, "*The Magician*," in *Four Screenplays*, 316.

53. Blackwell, *Gender and Representation in Bergman*, 31.

54. Bergman, "*The Magician*," in *Four Screenplays*, 351.

55. Although we never see Manda put the wig on, and one might be tempted to think of her heretofore-unseen blond hair as her real hair, there is simply no way those voluminous, cascading locks, which extend below her shoulders when finally seen, could fit under the short crop of black hair that tops her head in her public appearances.

56. Blackwell, *Gender and Representation in Bergman*, 32.

57. While Freud allows that death and reanimation "have been represented" as "uncanny themes," he takes issue with their being thought of as universally uncanny in and of themselves, citing literary examples where such things can be seen to be beautifully miraculous (i.e., the fairy tale about Snow White) or even comic in effect ("The 'Uncanny,'" *Standard Edition* 17:246; emphasis added).

58. Ibid., 244.

59. Ibid., 231.

60. Ibid., 244.

61. See Wood, *Ingmar Bergman*, 92–95; and Gervais, 63–64.

62. Blackwell, *Gender and Representation in Bergman*, 34.

63. John Beufort, "Swedish Film from Bergman's Camera," review of *The Magician*, *Christian Science Monitor*, March 1, 1960.

64. Blackwell, *Gender and Representation in Bergman*, 30, 33–34.

65. Stinson, "Bergman's *Magician* Continues Brilliance."

66. Cowie, *Bergman: A Critical Biography*, 211. The other examples of this subset include *Persona* and *Fanny and Alexander*.

67. Sontag, *Illness as Metaphor*.

68. Bosley Crowther, "Brooding and Grim Bergman," review of *The Silence*, *New York Times*, February 4, 1964.

69. Bosley Crowther, "Bergman's Trilogy: *The Silence* Caps His Series of Grim Films," *New York Times*, February 9, 1964.

70. Richards, review of *The Silence*.

71. Freud, "The 'Uncanny,'" in *Standard Edition* 17:246.

72. Nykvist, "Photographing the Films of Bergman," 627, 628.

73. Kael, "A Sign of Life," 218.

74. Freud, "The 'Uncanny,'" 237.

75. Wood, *Ingmar Bergman*, 123 (emphasis in the original).

76. Tyler, *Screening the Sexes*, 239.

77. Blackwell, *Gender and Representation in Bergman*, 36.

78. Blackwell suggests that Bergman seems to have made a point of using the term "little people" rather than "dwarfs" in *The Silence*'s screenplay (Bergman, *The Silence*, in *A Film Trilogy*, 115–116) because of the strongly negative connotations of the latter in European culture at the time, connotations Bergman did not want to

encourage (*Gender and Representation in Bergman*, 35). In the sequence in which Johan interacts with the performers in the script, they are in fact called "little people." Later, however, when Ester sees them, they are referred to, for the first time, as "dwarfs" (Bergman, *The Silence*, 137). This change in terminology seems to suggest the lack of judgment Johan might feel regarding the performers as opposed to the more culturally corrupt reaction to which Ester might be inclined.

79. Perhaps wanting to create a link with his early, palpably homoerotic films like *Skepp till India land* and *Night Is My Future* (1948), Bergman cast his original leading man, Birger Malmsten, for the first time in more than ten years in this small role. He would appear one more time for the director, in what would barely constitute a cameo, as a man who holds down a female victim for his adolescent friend to rape in *Face to Face* (1976)—a scene which has its own obvious and disconcerting homoerotic energies.

80. Perhaps the most controversial examples from the twentieth century are, in literature, Pär Lagerkvist, *The Dwarf*, and in film, *Freaks* (Tod Browning, 1932).

81. Blackwell, *Gender and Representation in Bergman*, 35.

82. Wood, *Hitchcock's Films Revisited*, 337.

83. Wood, *Ingmar Bergman*, 133–134.

Chapter Four

1. If anything can be said to threaten the relevance of spectatorship theory, it is the decline of the theatrical experience—an immobile, passive spectator in a large, darkened auditorium—since much of this discourse's origins in apparatus theory presupposes the sense of oneiric infantilization occasioned in that setting. Simply put, a film does not seem as though it is an overpowering dreamscape when watched on a laptop computer.

2. Baudry, "Effects of the Basic Apparatus."

3. Mulvey, "Visual Pleasure and Narrative Cinema," 199, 208.

4. Williams, "When the Woman Looks."

5. Studlar, *In the Realm of Pleasure*, 192.

6. Penley, "*Cries and Whispers*," 205; quoted in "Overheard," *Time*, March 30, 1992, 23.

7. Bergman subsequently shot his television film *The Ritual* (1968) in black-and-white and filmed his German-language theatrical film *From the Life of the Marionettes* partly in black-and-white.

8. Although they went into production almost simultaneously in the fall of 1967, it is tempting to think of *Shame*, which followed *Weekend* onto the screen after an interval of several months, as a rebuke to Godard's film. The two have a great deal in common at the level of plot and structure: both follow a quarreling heterosexual couple of roughly the same age as they journey across an increasingly savage countryside while facing an all-too-mundane apocalypse. Furthermore, both films contain a number of (functionally) near-identical scenes. For instance, *Weekend*'s "ac-

tion musicale" sequence, in which the carnage stops long enough for a pianist to play Mozart for a group of farmers, is comparable to *Shame*'s brief moment of quietude in a richly adorned antique shop where the proprietor (Sigge Fürst) plays a tune for Jan and Eva on an old porcelain music box; both function as final nods to European civilization on the brink of collapse. Ultimately, however, Bergman's elegiac and humanistic vision of humanity's self-destruction stands in sharp contrast to Godard's seemingly flippant, often savage, black comedy.

9. Examples include Pier Paolo Pasolini's *Salò, or the 120 Days of Sodom* (1975), Dennis O'Rourke's *The Good Woman of Bangkok* (1991), and Michael Haneke's two versions of *Funny Games* (1997, 2007).

10. Blackwell, *Gender and Representation in Bergman*, 4.

11. I risk criticism for making claims based on only portions of these films, with the exception *Shame*, rather than their entirety. I hope it becomes clear by the end of this chapter that by showing the links between the effects of a distinctive kind of shot found in multiple Bergman films, I am not dismissing other meanings to be found in each film as it functions as a stand-alone work.

12. Two noteworthy exceptions occur when dialogue that we see being spoken and would normally expect to hear, considering the proximity of the actors from the position of the spectator, is puzzlingly absent from the sound track. Since the film functions as a dream text, the absence of these diegetic utterances, rather than functioning as an estrangement device, is most easily understood as indicating psychic censorship on the part of the film's characters.

13. Bergman, *Shame*, 144.

14. Ibid.

15. Two months before *Shame*'s American release, the German anti-Nazi activist Martin Niemöller spoke before the United States Congress, offering a statement that distills one of the most resonant arguments regarding human rights: "When Hitler attacked the Jews I was not a Jew, therefore I was not concerned. And when Hitler attacked the Catholics, I was not a Catholic, and therefore, I was not concerned. And when Hitler attacked the unions and the industrialists, I was not a member of the unions and I was not concerned. Then Hitler attacked me and the Protestant church—and there was nobody left to be concerned" (114 Cong. Rec. 31,636 [1968]). Since this kind of cultural soul-searching was commonplace in the late 1960s, it is plausible that the Oswald episode in *Shame* was meant to take part in that kind of political argument.

16. Certainly, some totalitarian regimes have been disinclined to punish same-sex erotic behavior, even thriving (generally right-wing) homosexual subcultures, when doing so could be seen as counterproductive to their goals (or simply more trouble than it was worth).

17. Bergman, *Shame*, 145–146.

18. A recent exception is Tarja Laine, *Shame and Desire*.

19. Freud, *Three Essays on the Theory of Sexuality*, in *Standard Edition* 7: 177–178.

20. Ibid., 162n.

21. Ibid., 157 (emphasis in the original).

22. Freud, *Civilization and Its Discontents*, in *Standard Edition*, 21:99n.

23. Broucek, *Shame and the Self*, 12.

24. Freud, "Femininity," in *Standard Edition* 22:134 (emphasis in the original).

25. Broucek, *Shame and the Self*, 12.

26. Ibid., 3.

27. Ibid., 4.

28. Tomkins, *Affect, Imagery, Consciousness*.

29. Cvetkovich, *Mixed Feelings*, 18, 30.

30. Tomkins, *Affect, Imagery, Consciousness*, 385, 386.

31. Sedgwick, "Queer Performativity: James," 5.

32. See Sedgwick's follow-up essay on queer performativity: "Queer Performativity: Warhol"; and Douglas Crimp's "Mario Montez, For Shame." The latter essay does, in fact, use spectatorship theory to indirectly assess shame.

33. As Sedgwick suggests, Austin's central example of "I do [marry you]" is an unlikely speech act for queer appropriation ("Queer Performativity: James," 3).

34. Ibid., 4.

35. Ibid. (emphasis in the original).

36. Tomkins, *Affect, Imagery, Consciousness*, 380.

37. Baudry, "Effects of the Basic Apparatus," 294.

38. Ibid., 295.

39. Dixon, *It Looks at You*, 3.

40. Woody Allen, perhaps inspired by Bergman, effectively introduced the technique to the American cinema in *Annie Hall* (1977). Subsequently, it was used in *Ferris Bueller's Day Off* (1986) to such successful effect that it has become a regular trope in American character-based comedies. Regarding Bergman's films, I find their omission from Dixon's work surprising not simply because I consider them so remarkable, but also because Dixon has expressed an enthusiastic engagement with the director's films elsewhere; see Dixon, "*Persona* and Art Cinema," 44–61. And although Bergman was fond of the technique, it should be noted that not every instance in which a character in a Bergman film looks into the camera creates the effect I discuss here. The dinner-party scene in *Smiles of a Summer Night* features brief shots in which four of the main characters look into the camera to express a wish just as they are about to take a sip of a supposedly spell-inducing wine. Since these shots are relatively brief and set in the context of a self-consciously theatrical sex comedy, their function is much more conventional. It is telling, however, that of the seven main characters in this sequence, it is only the four women who look into the camera, while the three men, who also sip the wine and make wishes, look just off to the side of the camera's lens in their close-up shots.

41. Godard, "Bergmanorama," 59–60.

42. Bergman, *Images*, 296. (The sentence has been translated from the original Swedish edition—"*skamlös direktkontakt med åskådaren*"—accurately.)

43. Wood, *Ingmar Bergman*, 43.

44. For an extended discussion of the ways in which shot-countershot editing (or

lack thereof) works in such a dynamic, see the account of suture in Kaja Silverman's *The Subject of Semiotics*. Briefly, the concept of film editing and psychic suture can be traced back to Jacques-Alain Miller's essay "Suture" (1966; English trans., 1977/78). Although Miller's formulation does not specifically deal with the cinema, it had been applied to film studies by the end of the 1960s. According to the theory, in one psychological and ideological practice of classical Hollywood cinema, a master shot of actors A and B cuts to a close-up of A, then to a close-up of B, and back to a shot of A. Through it, the spectator is "stitched," in a sense, into the text of the film. In the process, which remedies any anxiety the spectator has about the offscreen space by cutting to a new angle before any anxiety can arise, the spectator trades whatever sovereignty he or she might have for a subjectivity structured by the filmic apparatus. Silverman, paraphrasing Jean-Pierre Oudart, explains: "Cinematic signification depends entirely upon the moment of unpleasure in which the viewing subject perceives that it is lacking something, i.e., that there is an absent field. Only then, with the disruption of imaginary plenitude, does the shot become a signifier, speaking first and foremost of that thing about which the Lacanian signifier never stops speaking: castration. A complex signifying chain is introduced in place of the lack . . . suturing over the wound of castration with narrative" (*Subject of Semiotics*, 204).

45. Laura Hübner, "Her Defiant Stare," 104.

46. Ibid., 111.

47. Ibid., 109.

48. For her part, Hübner considers the ending to be far less conclusive than I argue it to be here. Not without merit she writes: "Alongside the suggestion that Harry has matured from his summer illusions is the possible alternative suggestion that he has not moved on at all. After all, there can be little consolation in the final shot of Harry walking off round the drab street corner passing Monika's father with his drunken colleagues" ("Her Defiant Stare," 108).

49. Bergman, "*The Communicants*," in *A Film Trilogy*, 82. *The Communicants* is an alternate title for *Winter Light*.

50. As Marian Eide has pointed out to me, Märta's endeavors can also be seen as an attempt at self-empowerment within the Christian context of the film. In her ostensible self-sacrifice, Märta takes both the moral high ground (above her pastor lover) and the power position of a human god by claiming the role of martyr exemplified by Jesus Christ as he sacrificed himself for a sinful mankind.

51. Since I am considering a male-identified spectator in this chapter, I will use the masculine pronoun in order to keep that crucial consideration clear, unless, in a given instance, I specifically have a different spectator in mind.

52. Butler, *Gender Trouble*, 59.

53. Sedgwick, "Queer Performativity: James," 1.

54. Tomkins, *Affect, Memory, Consciousness*, 391–392.

55. Rich, "Repressive Tolerance to Erotic Liberation," 191.

56. Quoted in Koskinen, *Bergman's "The Silence*," 56.

57. Between publishing her short essay about *Monika* and publishing her mono-

graph on Bergman, Hübner dropped the umlaut above the *u* in her last name. I will note her name in reference to the latter work just as she does. For the quotation, see Hubner, *Films of Ingmar Bergman*, 104–105.

58. Blackwell addresses this concern in detail throughout *Gender and Representation in Bergman*.

59. This discrepancy, which I find to be one of the most interesting aspects of these films, may, in fact, explain their critical neglect within the canons of political modernism. Unlike Godard's films, they are not simplistically "all of a piece." The "classical acting" is in dizzying contrast to that used in modernist filmmaking. One has to consider what Jeffrey Weeks alludes to when he writes: "Sexuality may be an historical invention but we are ensnared in its circle of meaning. We cannot escape it by act of will" (Weeks, "Uses and Abuses of Michel Foucault," in *Against Nature*, 166). In other words, sexuality and gender are constructed, but they are also (painfully) real.

60. Tomkins, *Affect, Memory, Consciousness*, 359.

61. For the Vietnam connection, see Kael, "A Sign of Life"; for the link with Sweden's neutrality during World War II, see Alpert, "Vision and Resign."

62. Kael, "A Sign of Life," 214.

63. *Faithless* was written by Bergman and directed by Liv Ullmann after he had retired from feature-film directing (not counting films for television) in 1982.

64. Of course, the unbuttoned pajama top simultaneously masculinizes and feminizes Eva, since such an image might serve to indicate the character's decision to exercise a male's prerogative while she rewards the heterosexual male gaze with the erotic pleasure of her bare breasts; see Cohen, *Bergman: Art of Confession*, 282.

65. Ibid.

66. Ibid.

67. Obviously the two beds can be seen as a subtle indication of a fundamental split.

68. Bergman, *Shame*, 134.

69. Those spectators who still had *Hour of the Wolf* fresh in their minds from its release eight months earlier would also have been able to compare this killing to the more obviously homoerotic murder in that film, in which von Sydow's character kills a pubescent boy (Mikael Rundquist), perhaps only in a dream or a fantasy, who had been arousing him sexually on a secluded rocky shoreline.

70. Bergman, *Shame*, 188–190.

71. *Shame's* conclusion is remarkably similar to that of *No Country for Old Men* (Joel and Ethan Coen, 2007), which also ends abruptly after its aging protagonist recounts a similar and equally puzzling dream to his wife, one in which he encounters his long-deceased father who appears to him as a still-young man who passes him on a dark trail in order to light the way ahead. In fact, *Shame* and *No Country for Old Men's* comparable endings encourage us to consider a number of other intriguing similarities between the films. Both trouble their spectators with an elegiac rumination on the malice that operates in ostensibly civilized societies, both focus on traditional forms of masculinity presented as crippling afflictions, both suggest

repressed homosexuality as factors in the erupting violence, both allude to the psychic cost of the Vietnam War (*Shame* as a concurrent event, *No Country for Old Men* as a historical one—in the latter, it is clear that a number of the male characters are Vietnam veterans), and both are remarkable for their ability to create tension and suspense with a complete lack of diegetic music.

72. Going against the logic that the French filmmaker Eric Rohmer, for one, insisted upon when he shot in black-and-white, Bergman here refers to color in a colorless world. According to the cinematographer Nestor Almendros, "Rohmer's guiding principle was that in a black-and-white film there must be no reference to colors. For example, if the characters say they are drinking a *crème de menthe*, the spectator will feel frustrated, because he wants it to look green" (Almendros, *Man with a Camera*, 77). Eva's reference to a way of seeing beyond what the characters and the spectator have privy to does elicit a sense of frustration, but not that of a spectator noticing a mistake. In political terms, it works as a form of distancing that gives the film's ideological critique additional nuance. Referring to color in a black-and-white world suggests the limits of our ways of seeing, limits that, through our yearning for something more, point to a world beyond the one we inhabit. This strategy would be put to more obvious use throughout Sally Potter's *The Gold Diggers* (1983), in which the colors red, blue, ruby, and gold are repeatedly referred to on the sound track, even though the spectator is consigned to look at the film's monochrome images.

73. Bergman, *Shame*, 191.

74. A far more conservative reading is possible, one in which Jan and Eva's descent into incivility is seen as a direct result of their childlessness. Considering how monstrously the parent characters in Bergman's films act toward their children, however, the series of Bergman films climaxing with *Shame*—if taken as a body of work—can hardly be considered to seriously endorse child rearing as a character-building enterprise.

75. Laine, "Failed Tragedy and Traumatic Love," 61; Laine's references to "tragic failure" and certain connections between trauma and melodrama are credited to Thomas Elsaesser, *Melodrama and Trauma*. Defining the change in Jan's behavior as a result of trauma, Laine writes: "Unable to control or comprehend the situation, Jan undergoes a transformation from a useless, annoying coward to a brutal killer . . . thereby epitomizing the prototype of the traumatized male who communicates his symptoms through violence and rage" (61).

76. Ibid., 66, 67. The embedded quotation comes from Jean-Luc Nancy, *Being Singular Plural*, 53.

77. Laine, "Failed Tragedy and Traumatic Love," 67.

78. Ibid. I hasten to add that I do not see the omission of gender considerations in Laine's essay to represent a failure or misreading of the film. Indeed, it might well represent an example of academic "fair play" on Laine's part, who knew of my work analyzing Bergman's film along these lines after we appeared together on a panel I organized for the Society for Cinema and Media Studies conference in 2003. At the time, Laine presented work on issues of shame and spectatorship that have now ap-

peared in her *Shame and Desire* (2007), while I offered an early version of the analysis I present here. The fact that Laine subsequently developed her own reading of Bergman's film as she continues her work on shame—in a stand-alone essay that made it to press before my work could—without appropriating aspects of my central argument, is appreciated.

79. *The Dick Cavett Show*, August 2, 1971.

80. For a discussion of homophobic and sexist deployments of narcissism in somewhat different, although not antagonistic, terms, see Lee Edelman, "The Mirror and the Tank," in *Homographesis*.

Conclusion

1. *New York Times*, December 23, 1968.

2. *Pink Flamingos* preview, in *Pink Flamingos* 25th Anniversary Edition, directed by John Waters (New Line Home Entertainment, 2001), DVD.

3. Haskell, *From Reverence to Rape*, 315.

4. Ibid., 38.

5. Kael, "Flesh"; Penley, "*Cries and Whispers*"; Davidson, "Great Man Who Humiliates Women"; and Mellen, "*Cries and Whispers*."

6. Blackwell's analysis is particularly comprehensive and persuasive; see "*Cries and Whispers*: The Repression of the Sexual Body and the Reification of the Maternal," in *Gender and Representation in Bergman*, 165–196.

7. A typical critical response to the sexual content in Bergman's work of the period was offered by David Denby regarding a gay character's monologue in the latter film: "[It's] a wheeze—a heterosexual's clichéd notion of homosexual despair" ("A Dream of Murder").

8. The brief prologue and epilogue of *From the Life of the Marionettes* are presented in garish color, while the rest of the film is offered in high-contrast black-and-white. Both *Hour of the Wolf* and *From the Life of the Marionettes* feature nearly identical lines of dialogue regarding their repressed, potentially homo- or bisexual characters: "The glass is shattered, but what do the splinters reflect?" The very title of the latter film alludes to Eva's statement in *Shame* about life being controlled by outside forces: "Sometimes everything seems like a long strange dream . . . someone else's, that I'm forced to take part in."

9. While many critics would point out that Bergman continued producing films sporadically up through *Saraband*, each of the post–*Fanny and Alexander* productions was envisioned and crafted as a television project.

10. Occasionally I have heard people who dislike Bergman quote Allen's dialogue from *Manhattan* as if it were, somehow, an irrefutable, self-evident statement of fact, without pausing to consider that a character that is hardly presented as having an authoritative voice speaks it. A pseudo-intellectual who projects her own pretences onto others, Mary (in Diane Keaton's sly performance) repeatedly betrays her shallow understanding of the cultural touchstones she constantly invokes. For in-

stance, in one scene she mispronounces Diane Arbus's first name, something that would surely have earned her contemptuous smirks in the social circles to which she aspires.

11. This would have been impossible. *The Hours and Times* is speculative fiction based upon historical fact, a trip that Epstein and Lennon actually took together to Barcelona in April 1963, and Munch sets his film at that precise time. *The Silence*, in fact, premiered in Sweden in September 1963 and had no international engagements until the following year.

12. Bergman, *Fanny and Alexander*, 193.

13. As her name suggests, Stina Ekblad is a female performer.

14. I say "might have" because I have not come across any such criticisms in print.

15. Bergman, *Fanny and Alexander*, 199–200.

16. Ibid., 200.

17. Kristeva, *Strangers to Ourselves*, 170.

Bibliography

Abelove, Henry. "Freud, Male Homosexuality, and the Americans." In Abelove, Barale, and Halperin, *Lesbian and Gay Studies Reader,* 381–393.

Abelove, Henry, Michèle Aina Barale, and David M. Halperin, eds. *The Lesbian and Gay Studies Reader.* New York: Routledge, 1993.

Allen, Luther. "Just How Paranoid Are Homosexuals?" *Mattachine Review* 6, no. 10 (October 1960): 10–17.

Almendros, Nestor. *A Man with a Camera.* New York: Farrar, Straus and Giroux, 1984.

Alpert, Hollis. "Vision and Resign." Review of *Shame. Saturday Review,* January 25, 1969, 22.

Althaus-Reid, Marcella. *Indecent Theology: Theological Perversions in Sex, Gender and Politics.* London: Routledge, 2000.

———. *The Queer God.* London: Routledge, 2003.

Alton, John. *Painting with Light.* New York: MacMillan, 1949.

Austin, J. L. *How to Do Things with Words.* Edited by J. O. Urmson and Marina Sbisa. Oxford: Clarendon Press, 1962. Reprint, Cambridge, Mass.: Harvard Univ. Press, 1975.

Baldwin, Faith. "Why All the Mystery about Gable's Appeal." In *The Best of Modern Screen,* edited by Mark Bego, 46–48. London: Columbus, 1986.

Baldwin, James. "The Northern Protestant" (1960). In *Collected Essays,* 236–246. New York: Library of America, 1998.

Barton, Sabrina. "'Crisscross': Paranoia and Projection in *Strangers on a Train.*" In *Male Trouble,* edited by Constance Penley and Sharon Willis, 235–262. Minneapolis: Univ. of Minnesota Press, 1993.

Baudry, Jean-Louis. "Ideological Effects of the Basic Apparatus" (1970). In *Narrative, Apparatus, Ideology,* edited by Philip Rosen, 286–299. New York: Columbia Univ. Press, 1986.

Beauvoir, Simone de. *The Second Sex.* New York: Vintage, 1989. First published in 1949 by Gallimard (Paris).

Bech, Henning. *When Men Meet: Homosexuality and Modernity.* Chicago: Univ. of Chicago Press, 1997.

Benshoff, Harry M. *Monsters in the Closet: Homosexuality and the Horror Film.* Manchester, UK: Manchester Univ. Press, 1997.

Bergman, Ingmar. *Fanny and Alexander.* Translated by Alan Blair. New York: Pantheon, 1982.

———. *A Film Trilogy.* Translated by Paul Britten Austin. London: Boyars, 1978.

———. *Four Screenplays of Ingmar Bergman.* Translated by Lars Malmstrom and David Kushner. New York: Simon and Schuster, 1960.

———. *Images: My Life in Film.* Translated by Marianne Ruuth. New York: Arcade, 1994.

———. *"Persona" and "Shame": The Screenplays of Ingmar Bergman*. Translated by Keith Bradfield. London: Calder, 1972.

———. "Why I Make Movies" (1960). In *The Emergence of Film Art*, edited by Lewis Jacobs, 294–302. New York: Hopkinson and Blake, 1969.

Bergom-Larsson, Maria. *Ingmar Bergman and Society*. Translated by Barrie Selman. London: Tantivy, 1978.

Bersani, Leo. "Is the Rectum a Grave?" In *AIDS: Cultural Analysis/Cultural Activism*, edited by Douglas Crimp, 197–222. Cambridge, Mass.: MIT Press, 1988.

Björkman, Stig, Torsten Manns, Jonas Sima, eds. *Bergman on Bergman: Interviews with Ingmar Bergman*. Translated by Paul Britten Austin. New York: Simon and Schuster, 1973.

Blackwell, Marilyn Johns. *Gender and Representation in the Films of Ingmar Bergman*. Rochester, N.Y.: Camden House, 1997.

Bordwell, David. *Narration in the Fiction Film*. Madison: Univ. of Wisconsin Press, 1985.

Broucek, Francis J. *Shame and the Self*. New York: Guilford, 1991.

Bruce, E. Review of *The Silence*. *New York Mattachine Newsletter* 9, no. 5 (May 1964): 11–12.

———. Review of *Zazie dans le metro*. *New York Mattachine Newsletter* 9, no. 2 (February 1964): 9.

Butler, Judith. *Gender Trouble: Feminism and the Subversion of Identity*. New York: Routledge, 1990.

Citron, Michelle, Julia Lesage, Judith Mayne, B. Ruby Rich, Anna Marie Taylor, Helen Fehervary, and Nancy Vedder-Shults. "Women and Film: A Discussion of Feminist Aesthetics." *New German Critique* 13 (Winter 1978): 82–107.

Chauncey, George. *Gay New York: Gender, Urban Culture, and the Making of the Gay Male World, 1890–1940*. New York: Basic Books, 1994.

Childs, Marquis W. *Sweden: The Middle Way*. New Haven, Conn.: Yale Univ. Press, 1936; rev. ed., 1947.

Cixous, Hélène. "Fiction and Its Phantoms: A Reading of Freud's *Das Unheimliche* (The 'Uncanny')." Translated by Robert Dennomé. *New Literary History* 7, no. 3 (Spring 1976): 525–645.

Cohen, Hurbert I. *Ingmar Bergman: The Art of Confession*. New York: Twayne, 1993.

Corber, Robert J. *Homosexuality in Cold War America: Resistance and the Crisis of Masculinity*. Durham, N.C.: Duke Univ. Press, 1997.

Corrigan, Timothy. *New German Film: The Displaced Image*. Bloomington: Indiana Univ. Press, 1994.

Cory, Donald Webster [Edward Sagarin]. *The Homosexual in America: A Subjective Approach*. New York: Greenberg, 1951.

Cowie, Peter. *Ingmar Bergman: A Critical Biography*. New York: Scribner's, 1982.

Creekmur, Corey K., and Alexander Doty, eds. *Out in Culture: Gay, Lesbian, and Queer Essays on Popular Culture*. Durham, N.C.: Duke Univ. Press, 1995.

Crimp, Douglas. "Mario Montez, For Shame." In *Regarding Sedgwick: Essays on*

Queer Culture and Critical Theory, edited by Stephen M. Barber and David L. Clark, 57–69. New York: Routledge, 2002.

Cvetkovich, Ann. *Mixed Feelings: Feminism, Mass Culture, and Victorian Sensationalism*. New Brunswick, N.J.: Rutgers Univ. Press, 1992.

Davis, Francis. *Afterglow: A Last Conversation with Pauline Kael*. Cambridge, Mass.: Da Capo, 2002.

de Lauretis, Teresa. "Queer Theory: Lesbian and Gay Sexualities—An Introduction." In *differences: A Journal of Feminist Cultural Studies* 3, no. 2 (1991): iii–xviii.

D'Emilio, John. "Capitalism and Gay Identity." In Abelove, Barale, and Halperin, *Lesbian and Gay Studies Reader*, 467–476.

———. *Sexual Politics, Sexual Communities: The Making of a Homosexual Minority in the United States, 1940–1970*. Chicago: Univ. of Chicago Press, 1983.

Denby, David. "A Dream of Murder." Review of *From the Life of the Marionettes*. *New York Magazine*, November 17, 1980, 81.

Dixon, Wheeler Winston. *It Looks at You: The Returned Gaze of Cinema*. Albany, N.Y.: SUNY Press, 1995.

———. "*Persona* and the 1960s Art Cinema." In Michaels, *Ingmar Bergman's "Persona*," 44–61.

Donner, Jörn. *The Films of Ingmar Bergman: From "Torment" to "All These Women."* New York: Dover, 1972.

Doty, Alexander. *Making Things Perfectly Queer*. Minneapolis: Univ. of Minnesota Press, 1993.

Dyer, Richard. "Queer Noir." In *The Culture of Queers*, 90–115. New York: Routledge, 2002.

Edelman, Lee. *Homographesis: Essays in Gay Literary and Cultural Theory*. New York: Routledge, 1994.

Elsaesser, Thomas. "Melodrama and Trauma: Modes of Cultural Memory in the American Cinema." Amsterdam University

———. "Putting on a Show: The European Art Film." *Sight and Sound*, April 1994, 22–27.

Ermayne, Laurajean. "The Sapphic Cinema." *Ladder* 4, no. 7 (April 1960): 5–7.

Farmer, Brett. *Spectacular Passions: Cinema, Fantasy, Gay Male Spectatorships*. Durham, N.C.: Duke Univ. Press, 2000.

Fennell, Desmond. "Goodbye to Summer." *Spectator*, February 9, 1962, 163–166; subsequently published in *National Review*, April 9, 1963, 273–278.

Foster, Gwendolyn Audrey. "Feminist Theory and the Performance of Lesbian Desire in *Persona*." In Michaels, *Ingmar Bergman's "Persona*," 110–129.

Foucault, Michel. *The History of Sexuality*. Vol. 1, *An Introduction*. Translated by Robert Hurley. New York: Vintage, 1978.

French, Philip, and Kersti French. "*Wild Strawberries*." London: British Film Institute, 1995.

French, Tony. "Suffering into Ideology: Bergman's *Såsom I en Spegel*." *CineAction* 34 (1994): 68–72.

Freud, Sigmund. *The Standard Edition of the Complete Psychological Works of Sigmund Freud.* 24 vols. Edited by James Strachey. London: Hogarth, 1962–1974.

———. "Das Unheimliche." *Imago* 5–6 (1919): 297–324.

Gado, Frank. *The Passion of Ingmar Bergman.* Durham, N.C.: Duke Univ. Press, 1986.

Gerstner, David A. *Manly Arts: Masculinity and Nation in Early American Cinema.* Durham, N.C.: Duke Univ. Press, 2006.

Gervais, Marc. *Ingmar Bergman: Magician and Prophet.* Montreal: McGill-Queen's Univ. Press, 1999.

Gill, Brendan. "Cuckolds and Cooks." Review of *The Devil's Eye. New Yorker,* November 4, 1961, 207.

Glick, Elisa. *Materializing Queer Desire: Oscar Wilde to Andy Warhol.* Albany, N.Y.: SUNY Press, 2009.

Godard, Jean-Luc. "Bergmanorama." *Cahiers du Cinema in English* 1 (January 1966): 56–62.

Grant, Barry Keith, ed. *The Dread of Difference: Gender and the Horror Film.* Austin: Univ. of Texas Press, 1996.

Gray, Mary L. *Out in the Country: Youth, Media, and Queer Visibility in Rural America.* New York: New York Univ. Press, 2009.

Gross, Larry. "Five Ways to Think about Bergman as a Genius." *Movie City News,* July 7, 2007. http://www.moviecitynews.com/voices/2007/070730_gross_bergman .html.

Guenther-Pal, Alison. "Sexual Reorientations: Homosexuality versus the Postwar German Man in Veit Harlan's *Different from You and Me* (1957)." In *Light Motives: German Popular Film in Perspective,* edited by Randall Halle and Margaret McCarthy, 148–170. Detroit: Wayne State Univ. Press, 2003.

Hansen, Miriam. "Pleasure, Ambivalence, Identification: Valentino and Female Spectatorship." *Cinema Journal* 25, no. 4 (Summer 1986): 6–32.

Haskell, Molly. *From Reverence to Rape: The Treatment of Women in the Movies.* New York: Holt Reinhart, 1973.

Haynes, Todd. *"Far from Heaven," "Safe," and, "Superstar": Three Screenplays.* New York: Grove, 2003.

Heffernan, Kevin. *Ghouls, Gimmicks, and Gold.* Durham, N.C.: Duke Univ. Press, 2004.

Hepworth, John. "Hitchcock's Homophobia." In *Out in Culture,* edited by Corey K. Creekmur and Alexander Doty, 186–196. Durham, N.C.: Duke Univ. Press, 1995.

Hocquenghem, Guy. *Homosexual Desire.* Translated by Danielle Dangoor. London: Allison and Busby, 1978.

Hubner, Laura. *The Films of Ingmar Bergman: Illusions of Light and Darkness.* New York: Palgrave, 2007.

Hübner, Laura. "Her Defiant Stare: Dreams of Another World in *Summer with Monika.*" *Studies in European Cinema* 2, no. 2 (2005): 103–113.

Humphrey, Daniel. "'Blame the Swedish Guy': The Cultural Construction of a Cold War Auteur." *Post Script: Essays in Film and the Humanities* 28, no. 4 (Fall 2008): 22–44.

———. "One Summer of Heterosexuality: Lost and Found Lesbianism in a Forgotten Swedish Film." *GLQ: A Journal of Lesbian and Gay Studies* 13, no. 1 (2006): 33–61.

Jentsch, Ernst. "On the Psychology of the Uncanny." Translated by Roy Sellars. *Angelaki* 2, no. 1 (1996): 7–16.

Kael, Pauline. *5001 Nights at the Movies.* Rev. ed. New York: Holt, 1991.

———. "Flesh." Review of *Cries and Whispers.* In *Reeling,* 89–94. Boston: Little, Brown, 1976.

———. "A Sign of Life." Review of *Shame.* In *Going Steady: Film Writings, 1968–1969,* 214–221. New York: Boyars, 1994.

Kaminsky, Stuart M., ed. *Ingmar Bergman: Essays in Criticism.* Oxford: Oxford Univ. Press, 1975.

Kaplan, E. Ann. "The Case of the Missing Mother: Maternal Issues in Vidor's *Stella Dallas.*" *Heresies* 16 (1983): 81–85.

———. "Dialogue: 'Ann Kaplan Responds to Linda Williams's "'Something Else Besides a Mother': *Stella Dallas* and the Maternal Melodrama.""" *Cinema Journal* 24, no. 2 (Winter 1985): 40–43.

Kelen, Emery. *Hammarskjöld.* New York: Putnam's Sons, 1966.

Klinger, Barbara. "Film History Terminable and Interminable." *Screen* 38, no. 2 (Summer 1997): 107–128.

Korry, Edward M. "Sex Education in Sweden." *Look,* September 3, 1956, 34–39.

Koskinen, Maaret, ed. *Ingmar Bergman Revisited.* London: Wallflower, 2008.

———. *Ingmar Bergman's "The Silence": Pictures in the Typewriter, Writings on the Screen.* Seattle: Univ. of Washington Press, 2010.

Kristeva, Julia. *Nations without Nationalism.* Translated by Leon Roudiez. New York: Columbia Univ. Press, 1993.

———. *Strangers to Ourselves.* Translated by Leon Roudiez. New York: Columbia Univ. Press, 1991.

Lagerkvist, Pär. *The Dwarf.* Translated by Alexandra Dick. New York: Hill and Wang, 1945.

Laine, Tarja. "Failed Tragedy and Traumatic Love in Ingmar Bergman's *Shame.*" In *Mind the Screen: Media Concepts according to Thomas Elsaesser,* edited by Jaap Kooijman, Patricia Pisters, and Wanda Strauven, 60–70. Amsterdam: Amsterdam Univ. Press, 2008.

———. *Shame and Desire: Emotion, Intersubjectivity, Cinema.* Amsterdam: Amsterdam Univ. Press, 2007.

Laplanche, Jean, and Jean-Bertrand Pontalis. "Fantasy and the Origins of Sexuality." In *Formations of Fantasy,* edited by Victor Burgin, James Donald, and Cora Kaplan, 5–34. London: Methuen, 1986.

———. *The Language of Psycho-analysis.* Translated by Donald Nicholson-Smith. New York: Norton, 1973.

Layne, David. "Performing Arts." Review of *Freud. Mattachine Review* 9, no. 4 (April 1963): 22.

Le Fanu, Mark. *The Cinema of Andrei Tarkovsky*. London: British Film Institute, 1987.

Livingston, Paisley. *Ingmar Bergman and the Rituals of Art*. Ithaca, N.Y.: Cornell Univ. Press, 1982.

Long, Robert Emmet. *Ingmar Bergman: Film and Stage*. New York: Abrams, 1994.

Lucey, Michael. *Gide's Bent: Sexuality, Politics, Writing*. Oxford: Oxford Univ. Press, 1995.

Macnab, Geoffrey. *Ingmar Bergman: The Life and Films of the Last Great European Director*. London: Tauris, 2009.

Maltby, Richard. "*It Happened One Night*: Comedy and the Restoration of Order." In *Film Analysis: A Norton Reader*, edited by Jeffrey Geiger and R. L. Rutsky, 216–237. New York: Norton, 2005.

Martin, Robert K. "American Literature: Nineteenth Century." In *The Gay and Lesbian Literary Heritage*, edited by Claude J. Summers, 27–30. New York: Holt, 1995.

———. "'Enviable Isles': Melville's South Seas." *Modern Language Studies* 12, no. 1 (Winter 1982): 68–76.

Mayer, Arthur. *Merely Colossal: The Story of the Movies from the Long Chase to the Chaise Longue*. New York: Simon and Schuster, 1953.

McCarten, John. "Bergman on Birth." Review of *Brink of Life*. *New Yorker*, November 21, 1959, 172–173.

McIntire, Dal [Jim Kepner]. "Tangents: News & Views." *One* 4, no. 8 (December 1956): 21–22.

———. "Tangents: News & Views." *One* 6, no. 5 (May 1958): 22.

———. "Tangents: News & Views." *One* 9, no. 7 (July 1961): 18.

———. "Tangents: News & Views." *One* 10, no. 11 (November 1962): 16.

Mellen, Joan. "*Cries and Whispers*: Bergman and Women." In Kaminsky, *Ingmar Bergman: Essays in Criticism*, 297–312.

Michaels, Lloyd, ed. *Ingmar Bergman's "Persona."* Cambridge: Cambridge Univ. Press, 2000.

Miller, Jacques-Alan. "Suture (Elements of the Logic of the Signifier)" (1966). *Screen* 18, no. 4 (1977/78): 24–34.

Modleski, Tania. *The Women Who Knew Too Much: Hitchcock and Feminist Theory*. New York: Routledge, 1988.

Mosley, Philip. *Ingmar Bergman: The Cinema as Mistress*. London: Marion Boyars, 1981.

Mulvey, Laura. "Afterthoughts on 'Visual Pleasure and Narrative Cinema' Inspired by *Duel in the Sun*." *Framework* 15–17 (1981): 12–15.

———. "Visual Pleasure and Narrative Cinema" (1975). In *Narrative, Apparatus, Ideology: A Film Theory Reader*, edited by Philip Rosen, 198–209. New York: Columbia Univ. Press, 1986.

Murray, Raymond. *Images in the Dark: An Encyclopedia of Gay and Lesbian Film and Video*. Philadelphia: TLA Publications, 1994.

Nancy, Jean-Luc. *Being Singular Plural*. Palo Alto, Calif.: Stanford Univ. Press, 2000.

Newsweek. "Splash in Sweden." Review of *The Naked Night*. April 23, 1956, 53.

The New Yorker. "Like a Mirror." April 18, 1953, 26.

New York Mattachine Newsletter. Announcement. Vol. 5, no. 9 (September 1960): 3; vol. 5, no. 10 (October 1960): 4; vol. 9, no. 6 (June 1964): 3.

———. "Notes and Quotes." Vol. 8, nos. 7–8 (July–August 1963): 13.

———. "The Woman's Viewpoint." Issue 16 (September 1957): 5.

Nott, Kathleen. *A Clean, Well-Lighted Place: A Private View of Sweden*. London: Heinemann, 1961.

Nykvist, Sven. "Photographing the Films of Ingmar Bergman." *American Cinematographer* 43, no. 10 (October 1962): 613.

Oliver, Edith. Review of *My Name is Ivan*. *New Yorker*, July 6, 1963, 42.

Oliver, Robin G., ed. *Ingmar Bergman: An Artist's Journey*. New York: Little, Brown, 1995.

Olson, Jenni. *The Queer Movie Poster Book*, San Francisco: Chronicle, 2004.

One. Review of *The Third Sex*. Vol. 7, no. 9 (October 1959): 18–19.

———. "Tangents: News and Views." Vol. 13, no. 8 (August 1965): 9.

Penley, Constance. "*Cries and Whispers*" (1973). In *Movies and Methods*, edited by Bill Nichols, 204–208. Berkeley and Los Angeles: Univ. of California Press, 1976.

Persson, Göran. "*Persona* Psychoanalyzed: Bergman's *Persona*; Rites of Spring as Chamber Play." *CineAction* 40 (1996): 21–31.

H.R. Review of *The Confessions of Felix Krull*. *New York Mattachine Newsletter* 2, no. 12 (May 1958): 5.

Rich, B. Ruby. "From Repressive Tolerance to Erotic Liberation: *Maedchen in Uniform*." In *Chick Flicks: Theories and Memories of the Feminist Film Movement*, 179–206. Durham, N.C.: Duke Univ. Press, 1998.

Richards, Robin. Review of *The Silence*. *Ladder* 8, no. 9 (June 1964): 8–9.

Robertiello, Richard C. "A Psychoanalyst Replies." *Mattachine Review* 6, no. 10: 17–18.

Russo, Vito. *The Celluloid Closet*. Rev. ed. New York: Harper and Row, 1987.

San Filippo, Maria. "Unthinking Heterocentrism: Bisexual Representability in Art Cinema." In *Global Art Cinema: New Theories and Histories*, edited by Rosalind Galt and Karl Schoonover, 75–91. Oxford: Oxford Univ. Press, 2010.

Sedgwick, Eve Kosofsky. "Queer Performativity: Henry James's *The Art of the Novel*." *GLQ: A Journal of Lesbian and Gay Studies* 1, no. 1 (1993): 1–16.

———. "Queer Performativity: Warhol's Shyness, Warhol's Whiteness." In *Pop Out: Queer Warhol*, edited by Jennifer Doyle, Jonathan Flatley, and José Esteban Muñoz, 134–143. Durham, N.C.: Duke Univ. Press, 1996.

Sereel, Peter. "Films." *Eastern Mattachine Magazine* 10, no. 7 (August 1965): 15–16.

Shearer, Lloyd. "Crime Certainly Pays on the Screen: The Growing Crop of Homicidal Films Poses Questions for Psychologists and Producers," *New York Times*, August 5, 1945. Reprinted in *Film Noir Reader 2*, edited by Alain Silver and James Ursini, 9–13. New York: Limelight, 2004.

Silverman, Kaja. *Male Subjectivity at the Margins*. New York: Routledge, 1992.

———. *The Subject of Semiotics*. Oxford: Oxford Univ. Press, 1983.

Singer, Irving. *Ingmar Bergman: Cinematic Philosopher*. Cambridge, Mass.: MIT Press, 2007.

Sontag, Susan. *Illness as Metaphor*. New York: Farrar, Straus and Giroux, 1978.

Staiger, Janet. "Analyzing Self-Fashioning in Authoring and Reception." In Koskinen, *Ingmar Bergman Revisited*, 89–106.

Steene, Birgitta. *Ingmar Bergman: A Guide to References and Resources*. Boston: Hall, 1987.

———. *Ingmar Bergman: A Reference Guide*. Amsterdam: Amsterdam Univ. Press, 2005.

———. "'Manhattan Surrounded by Ingmar Bergman': The American Reception of a Swedish Filmmaker." In *Ingmar Bergman: An Artist's Journey—On Stage, On Screen, In Print*, edited by Roger W. Oliver, 137–154. New York: Arcade, 1995.

Studlar, Gaylyn. *In the Realm of Pleasure: Von Sternberg, Dietrich, and the Masochistic Aesthetic*. Urbana: Univ. of Illinois Press, 1988.

Tengroth, Birgit. *Törst*. Stockholm: Wahlström and Widstrand, 1948.

Time. "'I Am a Conjurer.'" March 14, 1960, 60–66.

———. "Overheard." March 30, 1992, 23.

———. Review of *Torment*. April 28, 1947, 100–101.

Tomkins, Silvan S. *Affect, Imagery, Consciousness: The Complete Edition*. New York: Springer, 2008.

Tyler, Parker. *Classics of the Foreign Film: A Pictorial Treasury*. New York: Bonanza, 1962.

———. *Screening the Sexes: Homosexuality in the Movies*. 1972. New ed., New York: Da Capo Press, 1993.

Ulrichsen, Erik. "The Early Films: Ingmar Bergman and the Devil." In Kaminsky, *Ingmar Bergman: Essays in Criticism*, 136–138.

Urquhart, Brian. *Hammarskjold*. New York: Knopf, 1972.

U.S. News and World Report. "Lobsters for Tourists, Herring for Swedes." April 23, 1948, 61–62.

Vargo, Marc E. *Noble Lives: Biographical Portraits of Three Remarkable Gay Men*. Binghamton, N.Y.: Harrington Park, 2005.

Variety. Review of *Frustration*. August 25, 1949, 8.

———. Review of *Skepp till India land*. October 22, 1947, 13.

———. "Rialto, Broadway Horror Showcase, May Switch to Class Lingos." October 29, 1947, 5.

Variety. *Variety Film Reviews*. Vol. 7: 1943–1948. New York: Garland, 1983.

Warner, Michael. "Homo-Narcissism; or, Heterosexuality." In *Engendering Men:*

The Question of Male Feminist Criticism, edited by Joseph A. Boone and Michael Cadden, 190–206. London: Routledge, 1990.

Waugh, Thomas. *The Fruit Machine: Twenty Years of Writing on Queer Cinema*. Durham, N.C.: Duke Univ. Press, 2000.

———. Review of *Sebastiane*. *Body Politic* 41 (March 1978): 19.

Weeks, Jeffrey. *Against Nature: Essays on History, Sexuality and Identity*. London: Rivers Oram, 1991.

White, Patricia. *Uninvited: Classical Hollywood Cinema and Lesbian Representability*. Bloomington: Indiana Univ. Press, 1999.

Wilinsky, Barbara. *Sure Seaters: The Emergence of Art House Cinema*. Minneapolis: Univ. of Minnesota Press, 2001.

Williams, Linda. "'Something Else Besides a Mother': *Stella Dallas* and the Maternal Melodrama." *Cinema Journal* 24, no. 1 (Fall 1984): 2–27.

———. "When the Woman Looks." In *The Dread of Difference: Gender and the Horror Film*, edited by Barry Keith Grant, 15–34. Austin: Univ. of Texas Press, 1996.

Wittig, Monique. "The Straight Mind." *Feminist Issues* 1 (Summer 1980): 103–111.

Wood, Robin. "Brian de Palma: The Politics of Castration." In *Hollywood from Vietnam to Reagan*, 135–161. New York: Columbia Univ. Press, 1986.

———. *Hitchcock's Films Revisited*. New York: Columbia Univ. Press, 1989.

———. *Ingmar Bergman*. New York: Praeger, 1969.

———. "*Persona* Revisited." In *Sexual Politics and Narrative Film: Hollywood and Beyond*, 248–261. New York: Columbia Univ. Press, 1998.

———. "Responsibilities of a Gay Film Critic" (1978). In *Personal Views: Explorations in Film*, 387–405. Rev. ed. Detroit: Wayne State Univ. Press, 2006.

Young, Vernon. *Cinema Borealis: Ingmar Bergman and the Swedish Ethos*. New York: Avon, 1972.

Index